Salvaging the Real Florida

UNIVERSITY PRESS OF FLORIDA

Florida A&M University, Tallahassee
Florida Atlantic University, Boca Raton
Florida Gulf Coast University, Ft. Myers
Florida International University, Miami
Florida State University, Tallahassee
New College of Florida, Sarasota
University of Central Florida, Orlando
University of Florida, Gainesville
University of North Florida, Jacksonville
University of South Florida, Tampa
University of West Florida, Pensacola

University Press of Florida

Gainesville · Tallahassee · Tampa · Boca Raton

Pensacola · Orlando · Miami · Jacksonville · Ft. Myers · Sarasota

Salvaging
the Real Florida

Lost and Found in the State of Dreams

Bill Belleville

16   15   14   13   12   11   6   5   4   3   2   1

Frontispiece, photograph by Robert Boswell. All photographs are by the
author unless otherwise credited.

LIBRARY OF CONGRESS CATALOGING-IN-PUBLICATION DATA
Belleville, Bill, 1945–
Salvaging the real Florida : lost and found in the state of dreams /
Bill Belleville.
p. cm.
Includes index.
ISBN 978-0-8130-3577-2 (alk. paper)
1. Florida—Description and travel. 2. Natural history—Florida.
3. Belleville, Bill, 1945–   —Travel. I. Title.
F311.5.B35   2011
975.9—dc22   2010040992

The University Press of Florida is the scholarly publishing agency for the
State University System of Florida, comprising Florida A&M Univer-
sity, Florida Atlantic University, Florida Gulf Coast University, Florida
International University, Florida State University, New College of Florida,
University of Central Florida, University of Florida, University of North
Florida, University of South Florida, and University of West Florida.

University Press of Florida
15 Northwest 15th Street
Gainesville, FL 32611-2079
http://www.upf.com

For Yvette

*we did not know what we wanted from the land . . . we were
entering, a land for which we had no description, without
knowing what kind of place it was, nor by what people it
was inhabited, nor in which part of it we were. . . .*
Conquistador Álvar Núñez Cabeza de Vaca, upon landing
in Florida in 1528 and promptly getting lost for eight years.

*I am inclined to believe that it can never be thickly peopled
& certainly not so until the vast quantity of vegetable
matter shall be cleared away.*
Master Edward C. Anderson, U.S. Navy, Florida Territory in 1844

Supercalifragilisticexpialidocious!
Headline in a central Florida newspaper after the opening
of Walt Disney World near Orlando in October 1971

Contents

Introduction

This collection of narrative essays is about natural places and what draws me to them. Although I've always been fascinated by the details of the landscape and how it plays out around us, it's less about nature as a rigid science than nature as a salve—a place where you might discover something about the place or about yourself, and then come away better for having done so. It's identifying the disparate pieces of our natural

Archival photo of Rock Springs near Apopka, Florida. With Wekiwa Springs, this is one of two major springs that feed the Wekiva River. There are another thirty or so of varying sizes that all contribute in some way to its flow. In this way, it is a typical Florida spring-fed river.

world and then trying to piece them together so we might better know the wholeness of it all. Since I've intentionally spent most of my life in Florida, nearly all of these pieces take place here—even though they sometimes encircle the larger world of memory just beyond.

Sometimes wild animals and plants play big, sometimes those people with wildness in their hearts. In many cases, there's a "secret" I'm hunting for somewhere. Often, it's revealed in a search or a quest—whether for a tiny snail, a ship under the sea, a spring, or some mythical place I imagine or that has been imagined by others. So, as you will see, this is also about having fun outdoors, maybe even having a bit of an adventure, just as the great Florida naturalist Archie Carr once promised we could all do, if we really wanted.

I've been careful to use the term "essays" to describe these pieces since they are much closer to that genre than they are to journalistic "articles." Certainly, they are told from the author's point of view, and in the best of worlds, they record personal observations and reflections. Essayist Aldous Huxley once defined the essay as an overlap between an article and a short story, calling it a "literary device for saying almost everything about anything," and I figure that just about covers it. Although you'll find real information gleaned from "journalistic" research, you won't find the self-conscious attempt to be objective that so often distinguishes articles in periodicals. More often than not, the pieces here are little stories, nonfiction vignettes that attempt to capture a slice of life.

I like to think what links these individual stories is an expressed caring about what happens in nature, and sometimes, what happens to the people whose lives are swayed by the experience of it. I'm guessing this begins at the most essential level, right at the transect between our senses, our feelings, our most primal thoughts. La Florida—the original Land of Flowers to Spanish explorers—is surely not the wilderness it once was. But nearly one-third of its land and water is protected as parks, preserves, refuges, and conservation areas. Treks to some of these places on land—or to many of them on or under the water—can take us beyond the domestic and the known.

But discovery doesn't always require a backpack or scuba tanks, or even a wild place. Sometimes, a stroll under a canopy of trees into an authentic small Florida town can give us new eyes; sometimes, the glint of the twilight on a backyard pond might do the same. That's when nature plays a secret chord, and we let loose of our intellect and allow our senses a go at it.

As Henry David Thoreau reported, the natural world can be the source of "vigor, inspiration and strength," and thus, can provide an antidote to the banality of civilization. To this end, the old transcendentalist used a superb term to characterize how he moved across the landscape. He called it *sauntering*, and explained it as a derivative of a word used to describe pilgrims in the Middle Ages who were traveling to la Sainte Terre, the Holy Land. Some travelers left behind jobs and asked for charity along the way. In doing so, he morphed into a sort of mystical hobo (a description Zen poet Gary Snyder would appreciate, surely.) The intrepid pilgrim became known as a *Sainte-Terrer*, which was later anglicized as "saunterer." Thoreau seemed to appreciate those who really had no homes to return to, as they were "at home everywhere" and this was the secret to successful sauntering. More to the point, they were unbound by materialism, and their spirits were thus unencumbered by the transience of human conceits. "Every walk is a sort of crusade," he wrote, "to go forth and reconquer this *Holy Land* from the hands of the Infidels."

Sauntering, then, becomes far more than a physical movement. It becomes a behavior that sets you squarely in the moment. In doing so, you retrieve the real Florida from those who would turn the Land of Flowers into one giant, giddy corporate amusement park, or a series of walled and gated communities wedged onto a fragile landscape that is simply not equipped to handle them.

In one essay, I yearn for the chance to "sink into gator time," and really, that yearning is far more earnest than not. To allow yourself to "sink" into a more atavistic state is simply an expression of appreciation for the long natural continuum that our wildlife—especially the ancient alligators—enjoyed, long before upright walking mammals arrived on the scene. It's not a feeling or condition one blunders onto while watching a kept gator leap out of the water to grab a dead chicken at a tourist attraction. Nor is it found in a theme park "wilderness" ride or in some godforsaken outlet mall, regardless of how many "green" things are being peddled. Instead, "sinking" is an act that requires the timeless patience of a reptile to be so deep inside nature that you become blissfully unaware of all else. One sinks slowly into such sublime moments, following the trail the senses have left to show us the way.

In this way, I've expanded the idea of sauntering to include nearly any outdoor behavior that allows new ways of seeing natural places—each of which I hold dear as a "Holy Land." Sometimes these essays devote energy to pondering an animal, a plant, or even an idea. In these cases, the movement is often one of reflection, of considering the possibilities. Sometimes it's authentic places that are worth a deeper look. Most often, these are places that have been shaped by something essential in the landscape—a river, a spring, a tropical swash of ocean water, a vast, rolling sea of scrub.

As Roderick Nash pointed out in the classic *Wilderness and the American Mind*, the benefits of sustaining such natural places are as necessary for ecological reasons as they are for the human soul. As for the morality of protecting nature, Nash explains that it predates the twentieth-century concerns of ethicists Aldo Leopold and Robert "Bob" Marshall—even the spirituality of the Transcendentalists and the Romanticists. It extends, in fact, all the way to the ancient Greek concept of cherishing "a great chain of being." Certainly, thoughtful leaders of religious congregations in the twenty-first century are revisiting their own doctrines to more fully consider earth stewardship on a finite planet with rapidly diminishing resources.

Our best educators are now learning the value of using nature as a giant classroom with no walls or windows. And, despite the obtuse political clamor to teach to a standardized test, elemental lessons remain tucked away in Florida's natural world—lessons that simply aren't negotiable. Or, as Henry David Thoreau once wrote: "When a traveler asked Wordsworth's servant to show him her master's study, she answered, 'Here is his library, but his study is out of doors . . .'"

But there's a sense of urgency about all of this, too. In a postindustrial, cubicle-driven world that emphasizes safety above all else, the need to seek meaning and enchantment in natural places is more essential than it's ever been. Since we've emerged as living beings from the jungles of the world, we suffer when isolated from it, as E. O. Wilson explains in

The Biophilia Hypothesis. The need to connect "subconsciously with the rest of life," says Wilson, is so deep that it's rooted in our biology. This deep affinity between humans and nature isn't limited to plants and trees; it also includes wildlife, the topography, and the weather.

Author Richard Louv in *Last Child in the Woods* draws a tighter bead on this notion by considering how newly developing children are also affected. Indeed, it is most often impressionistic children—robbed of the capacity to free-roam outdoors as children did a half century ago—who may even be afflicted with what Louv calls "nature deprivation disorder."

Despite the abundance of public land in Florida, intense sprawl-like development on private land continues at a rate that is predicted to "build out" the state in another half century or so. The recession of 2009–10 slowed this, allowing time to reconsider true sustainable development, but the future of natural Florida still hangs in the balance. If corrections aren't made, even protected and publicly owned land will suffer since it is either downhill or—thanks to our porous underground aquifer—downstream from everything that is topographically above it. So our sense of urgency is not just to tend to our immediate human need to "connect," but also to ensure enough healthy land and water exist to continue to sustain our human population.

Despite woefully outdated ideas that embrace squandering as a mark of American individualism, more realistic ways of living are finally being considered. When there were only two million people living in Florida, one could catch, cook, and eat a herd of gopher tortoises without worrying about the consequences. Now, the population of humans has boomed almost beyond belief, and that of the tortoise has diminished so that the species is threatened with extinction. If there is a monkey wrench that jeopardizes the intricate mechanism of thoughtful sustainability, it is a prideful refusal to use new and realistic information to dissolve paradigms that no longer work. In the same way, a new migrant to Florida isn't a bad thing—unless that migrant refuses to learn and honor the natural rules that bind our physical world together.

I so enjoy folks who unabashedly profess their caring for our wild places, especially those with courage in their hearts. As the great nature writer Ed Abbey once wrote: "Sentiment without action is the ruination of the soul." I deeply respect those who get off their butts and take a stand without worrying about how it affects their job security, their perceived social standing, or their public image. The pervasive corporate mentality can breed a dangerous sort of toadyness in human nature that will sooner or later dissolve all that is righteous and fair. Corporations are good at giving us places to hide, whether they're in the business of constructing computers or manufacturing newspapers. Imposing a "distance" between you and reality only delays the reality, insulates it for a moment, a year, a lifetime. It's the difference between trusting the wisdom of the senses, or succumbing to the compromising lock-step of socialization. I've worked hard to resist those compromises, not always with great success and with less finesse than I'd like to admit.

Despite my advocacy, I try to avoid becoming part of what poet and novelist Jim Harrison once described as the "burgeoning legion of eco-ninnies." The political correctness of it all can sometimes be a bit much. In too many cases, the quest to be politically correct is really a high profile act to "seem" or "appear" to be so. When that happens, the core message is often lost and the illusion of ethics takes its place.

Although this collection may be considered to be within the genre of "nature writing," it's certainly intended to appeal to anyone who has a steadfast curiosity for the world around us. In the same way, folks who enjoy categorizing things might also describe a few of these tales as "adventure travel," but it's certainly not the sort that's staged to evoke danger. Like a comfortable pair of hiking boots, a durable and light-weight paddle, or a reliable scuba regulator, the menagerie of behaviors reported here are simply tools to lead us to hidden places. And, when all's said and done, I seem far more vulnerable to danger and treachery back in our so-called civilized world than I do when immersed inside some wild geography.

I live at the edge of the historic district in the old riverboat town of Sanford, a place that came to be by its strategic location on an aquatic highway that led travelers into the heart of Florida. I've made my living as a nonfiction writer for a while now. Early on, I was enthralled with what was being called "new journalism," which was essentially using fiction techniques to tell a nonfiction story. Since this was not conventional reportage, writers could be part of the story, and not simply a disembodied persona. As a result, I tried to get as close to the core of a subject as I could.

Eventually, it struck me that the stories that made me feel good as a person were the ones in which I immersed myself in natural places. E. O. Wilson, of course, could have told me this right off the bat. Since I also grew up out in the country, surrounded by wildness, I also felt at home in such places as an adult. Once that notion settled in, I made the decision to learn as much as I could about Florida and its singular natural systems. As an itinerate writer, I traveled extensively overseas to rainforests and coral reefs and blue holes to report stories on assignment. But Florida was my home, and I felt a strong obligation to learn as much as I could about what made its natural heart beat as it does.

Not surprisingly, I also began to see trends in other tropical countries that reflected many of our issues here on the peninsula. Essential resources, like potable fresh water, were coming under siege nearly everywhere. And wetlands, which kept rivers, lakes, and lagoons clean and functioning, were disappearing at an alarming rate. Florida is not unlike an island in this way: Since it's mostly surrounded by water, it's easier to identify its natural gifts, as well as the threats to those gifts. And, as other writers have noted, Florida is also a sort of bellwether state, a place where people experiment with trends and concepts, picking and choosing from the ones that seem to work. Today, three out of four Floridians were not born in Florida. Certainly, it's easier to tinker around when newcomers arrive with little understanding of the unique theater that surrounds them.

I've done my own special brand of tinkering, although it's mostly been to figure out how stuff works. If mucking through wild places fascinated me, so too did the chance to actually go under the water whenever I could. In fact, the word "salvage" in the title has more than one meaning. On one level, it refers to a few essays in which the work of "salvers" is chronicled. But more importantly, it implies the larger definition of that word: Retrieving, recovering, or preserving something valuable from potential loss. This "something valuable" is Florida herself, and at this point in her existence, she surely needs all the help she can get to rescue her soul from irretrievable loss.

I admire the spiritual naturalist William "Billy" Bartram a lot and relish the symmetry between what he saw in La Florida in the eighteenth century and what can be identified in the landscape now. What I find particularly enchanting are our magical springs, our misunderstood and vital swamps, and our ever-blooming wildflowers—the tiny, seasonal icons that perhaps identify us as the "Land of Flowers" as much as anything. Bartram blazed the trail for early naturalists who would journey to Florida because the peninsula was warm and wet, and its plants and animals largely unknown. It was—and in many ways still is—a hotspot of biological diversity.

Isolated by the remote wilderness of the New World's South, Bartram did his best to fully communicate what he saw and felt to readers and naturalists thousands of miles away. This never fully occurred to me until Tom Hallock, a former colleague at USF when I was a Writer in Residence at its Florida Studies program there, explained the mechanics of this. He did so in a book that explores the unpublished letters to and from "Billy." As Tom wisely observes, the incandescent spirit that transported Bartram's sensibilities successfully over the Atlantic or back to the northern colonies is the same spirit that reaches us today—traveling not geographic distances, but across the great void of time. Bartram's words and art were a grand invitation to the real Florida, and I'm thankful they remain so.

❧

As recently as the end of World War II, Florida was the least densely settled state east of the Mississippi, and even then, most of that settlement was confined to its coasts. Although land promoters and chamber of commerce hypesters would not dare say so at the time, most of Florida was still a *frontier*. A frontier can be defined as the border where the "savage meets the civilized," according to scholar Nash. When the U.S. Bureau of Census declared the Western frontier "closed" in 1890, renegades and dreamers continued to slip down into Florida because they knew its soggy wilderness would be open for a while to come.

I hope that some of these little stories in this collection illustrate that relic chunks of our landscape still remain as "frontiers" today, places where you can still go and have a legitimate experience of discovery, perhaps even a revelation of sorts. I have been literally "lost" in this Florida at times, and I've always been gratified that there's still enough room for that. Perhaps in becoming lost, I've also had the chance to re-discover myself—a chance to be "found." And that has been enormously satisfying.

As for the specifics of my personal connection, it is this: I grew up on the then-rural Eastern Shore of Maryland, a smaller, more temper-ate version of the Florida peninsula. It was a flat terrain that, with all its tidal rivers and creeks, was nearly as wet. Before modern bridges changed the equation, population centers across the wide Chesapeake Bay to the west and the south were kept at arm's length for a long time by the slow moving ferries that serviced the Shore. As a kid, I grew up with a mom and dad with enough kindness in their hearts to encour-age me in all that I did. With my younger brother, we spent a lot of weekends fishing and crabbing together. We went to church together. When I played sports, they came to all of my games. During summer vacations on "The Shore," I sometimes worked in farm fields loading watermelons, and by winter, spent some weekends culling oysters on a small open work boat on the Tangier Sound of the lower Chesapeake Bay. It was bitter cold, but I can still see the sunrises with the sails of the old Skipjacks slicing into the red horizon. Caring for nature didn't begin as an intellectual experience. It came right out of my gut, because when you grow up in the country so much of what you do takes place outdoors. The "Shore," as we knew it, seemed apart from the rest of the world. Florida appeared likewise to me when I first traveled here as a little boy, and later, moved here as a young man.

These stories don't include logistics on getting anywhere, beyond an oblique reference to place names here and there. There are, thankfully, great guides—and excellent guide books—that will introduce you to the trails and the "blueways," that will help you identify plants and wildlife, even specific habitats. Some of our earlier naturalists and explorers, such as Bartram, have left behind detailed accounts of their own treks here, and these chronicles function as historic charts that help us key in on certain plants, animals, even places. Sooner or later, though, if we take this nature-exploring business seriously, we learn to trust the most essential guides of all—our own sensibilities. I'm figuring the most any of us can hope for is to have a chance to be surprised and refreshed by the natural world; setting up strict rules to do so is counterintuitive. If you go anywhere outside with an open heart, I believe this chance for discovery is unending. After all, any place is mythic if we really want it to be. And, the core geography of the human spirit—where the transcendent rush of the unexpected dwells—is a place unlikely to be found on any map.

In the subtitle, the phrase "State of Dreams" is a nifty steal of a title shard from Gary Mormino's enlightening nonfiction book about the history of Florida, *Land of Sunshine, State of Dreams*. And it's also a nod to the dizzying comic history epic by Diane Roberts, *Dream State: Eight Generations of Swamp Lawyers, Conquistadors, Confederate Daughters, Banana Republicans, and other Florida Wildlife*. Both writers have an insightful knack for seeing beyond the obvious slogans and bringing us stories of Florida that are far more revealing than nonfiction chronicles traditionally have been. Both understand the many ways in which Florida has been imagined, shaped, and constantly reinvented—yet still it remains, inextricably, the Land of Flowers.

I hope you'll consider this book as an invitation to saunter along with me, salvaging what is real in your own place, and getting lost and found in this state of dreams. If any of these stories leads you to a gratifying, even revelatory, experience in a dense hammock, a spring run, or on or under the water, you have my deepest congratulations. You will know for sure your saunter has been a righteous crusade, and you've scored one up on the Infidels by making it squarely to La Saint Terre.

1

Fire, Water, Friendship in the Night

We launch in a shallow Florida cove just before sunset, excited with the possibility of having fire rise from the water.

Clumps of turtle grass float at the surface, and black mangroves hug the shore, their characteristic air roots poking up under the bushes like black pencils. My friend Bobby is in a single canoe and the rest of us— Michelle, her daughter Alex, and a few more—are in kayaks. We scuttle about until everyone is ready, and then we paddle out into the Haulover,

Crab traps and buoys in the clear waters of the Mosquito Lagoon, which is rimmed with a healthy shoreline of native black mangroves. It's linked to the Indian River Lagoon via the old Haulover Canal, creating a wonderfully diverse estuary on the east coast of Florida.

an old canal that links the Mosquito Lagoon to the north with the Indian River to the south. Long-legged herons and egrets hunt near the black mangroves, each a study in precision.

The fire in the water we are hunting is bioluminescence, less of a burn than a dazzle of cold, blue-green light. Although this happens in the night seas worldwide, it's more realized in some places than others. In Puerto Rico, Phosphorescent Bay is named for the phenomenon. In the Galapagos, I've dived into Tagus Cove late at night and the bio-light there consumed me, exploding with each exhalation. On the beaches of the Outer Banks of North Carolina, I've seen puddles of it abandoned on the sand by the ebb of tide. I guess it's been taking place in this particular lagoon for thousands of years, but we've only recently caught on.

Guides will take people to such places, but I usually like to go it alone, or with a few good friends. The risks may be a bit greater, but the surprises always seem somehow more real. I paddle out into the deeper canal and the surface around me becomes suspiciously flat, as if something immense is moving just below. My little boat wobbles gently. Within seconds, the back of a manatee materializes a few feet away, its gray, barnacled body like a gigantic sausage.

A shaggy snout gently breaks the water, human-like eyes deeply set, each inside a starburst of wrinkles. It glances at me, inhales. From inside its massive body, the air resonates as if in a cave. Then it sinks back down. I look over at Michelle, smiling broadly, without guile. Despite its size, the coming and going of such an animal was incredibly delicate, almost like a disassembling of molecules. It could have flipped me in a heartbeat if it had wanted. I am exhilarated, and also deeply thankful I am still upright.

We paddle north where the canal meets the Mosquito Lagoon. It is twilight and the primitive landscape is golden. Men are fishing and drinking beer on the shore, many of them fried after hours of it. A really bad country music song celebrating the glories of "redneck women" blares from a pickup truck. There is a small mangrove island offshore and we paddle toward it, riding a gentle evening breeze. As we go, the gray dorsals of a pod of bottlenose dolphins slice through the water nearby.

The sun vanishes and a dark cloud bank on the horizon begins to shoot out jagged spires of lightning, soundlessly. I look back to the land, now a half mile away, and see most of the fishermen packing to leave. The music shuts off and what remains is the slosh of our hulls, the cry of wading birds, the muffled sighs of anticipation.

The lagoon is encircled by public land; like the manatee, it's a relic of what used to be. The landscape here was protected decades ago when the government bought a massive swatch of coastline to buffer its rocket launching at the Kennedy Space Center. In a strange twist, the ambitions of the future have preserved the past. Bobby, a cardiologist by day, sometimes brings his flats boat here to fish for the sea trout and reds that school over the sea grasses and sandy shoals of the shallow, clear lagoon.

The cold light remains hidden and I find myself wondering if it will actually turn on tonight at all. We have brought Cyclamen sticks and we individually snap the plastic tubes to make them glow and hang them around our necks to keep track of each other. This seems a simple task, but I botch it and, for the moment, the lanyard tightens on my forehead, the glow stick hanging against my nose, and I can't help but smile. A few of the others laugh good-naturedly at this. These are people who cherish the immediacy and enchantment of this moment, and I am glad to be here with them.

We float in the lagoon, letting the gentle evening breeze push us. It is almost completely dark now. We are all silhouettes with light sticks, finer details lost to the night. Suddenly I hear Alex's voice from somewhere nearby, as if announcing the arrival of a special guest, one syllable at a time: "It's hap-pen-ing."

I look over to where I know Michelle to be. As she moves her paddle through the water, it glows dim with turquoise and she lets out a long, low *woooow*. I turn in my seat, watching as my own blade draws up the cold light. I hear murmurs rise around me, voices slightly higher and full of wonder, and I realize everyone is doing a version of the same thing, creating light from water. The alchemy has taken time to cook, but now it has us in its grip.

We paddle back toward the canal, where marine life is more concentrated. The lagoon water under us is so clear we can see through it, can watch as the grasses on the bottom glow with the light. Small fish and then larger ones, down deep, are outlined in blue-green.

Once we are in the canal, sunken logs on the bottom effervesce with color. Suddenly, the form of a massive alligator swims under us, odd, tiny arms from its body swishing the blue. It's amazingly graceful, and, like the wading birds, its movements are precise.

Crabs drift along, glowing, sometimes bumping into my hull, hard calcium shells clanking oddly against plastic. Alex cups her hand in the water, and the liquid she holds sparkles as if electrified. In the distance, a dolphin arches out of the water, bringing a massive column of light with it.

I know, intellectually, that tiny, single-celled plankton called dinoflagellates do this, absorbing energy from the sun and releasing it to confuse predators at night, twisting and turning in the water. But that doesn't explain the full magic of it to my senses. Another cove splays from the canal and we paddle into it. It is shallow and populated with great schools of mullet. When Bobby and others move far ahead they spook the mullet and the fish begin to leap from the water in great explosions of energy, like low-level skyrockets. Sometimes, in their jumps they whack into our boats; sometimes, into us. I look down and see a blue-green stingray move next to my hull, its wings undulating as if it is flying in the water.

Above, stars have filled the void over the cloud banks, and now a meteor traces a line through them. A collective murmur rises at once from us, an exhalation of natural awe. It seems as if the sky has split in two, no distinction left any more between it and the water around us. And now we have stopped being writers and doctors and whatever else we are and have become kids, alive only for this moment, in this place.

I drift some more and it vaguely occurs to me that stardust started it all, showering this earth with its energy so long ago, and now, many molecules later, here we are in a dark Florida lagoon, watching it happen all over again. Like the dinoflagellates, we twist and turn in the night, glowing blue-green ourselves, a theater of creation in the mangroves.

We are all quiet now, and, soaked with the energy of the stars, as fully conversant as we will ever be.

2

The Apple Snail

The Ecology of Mollusk Zen

The tiny, pinkish eggs of the apple snail on the stem of an aquatic bulrush. The presence of these eggs is a good sign that the waters where they are found are healthy since the apple snails graze on an algae that grows on eel grass. Eel grass helps filter and clean the water and underpins a diverse food chain. When waters are clouded with sediment and polluted, eel grass does not do well.

I saw my first clutch of apple snail eggs on Juniper Creek Run in the Ocala National Forest years ago. They were clumped together on the green stem of a flowering pickerel weed, and each was the size of a fat BB. A friend insisted they were "lizard eggs." That seemed plausible at the time, although I had trouble picturing terrestrial reptiles skipping over the water to lay their eggs on an aquatic plant. But Florida was a peculiar place, so I figured most anything was possible.

Not long afterwards, I started paddling the Wekiva closer to home and found scads of similar eggs along that river. Some of the clutches were white while others were pink. I did some research this time and discovered the eggs belonged to an aquatic mollusk, the Florida apple snail (*Pomacea paludosa*). I also learned the eggs were laid on stems of plants just above the water for good reason: They were high enough up so the egg would not drown, but not so high that the newly hatched baby snails would have trouble finding the water. And the short crawl from the safety of the river to the egg site was just right for the mama. Like the massive sea turtles, the only time the snail left the water was to lay its eggs.

This was a key part of my information gathering—of learning the right name, and the right behavior.

I also found that *Pomacea* was the largest freshwater snail in the world, that there were over 100 species, and its range was almost entirely subtropical. The Florida version could grow to two inches in shell diameter; its South American cousins could grow twice that. Florida apple snails graze on algae mats attached to underwater plants like eel grass, a plant that needs clean, clear water to flourish. The grass does well in healthy lakes rimmed with wetlands and spring-fed rivers like the Wekiva, where eel grass still thrives.

Once when I was out paddling by myself in the scarlet glow of twilight, I saw a limpkin pecking at a live apple snail with her curved beak. Sweetgum sagged with moss overhead, and cypress knees lined the soggy river bank, creating a moment that was heartbreakingly timeless and rare. The limpkins, the wading birds with the plumage reminiscent of a deer fawn, were becoming scarce. Wildlife biologists had figured a mainstay of the bird's diet was the apple snail. But the snail's own fodder—the eel grass-algae—was declining because its habitat was in trouble. As the apple snail goes, so goes the limpkin. This lesson was about ecology.

I learned of a study in the spring-fed Wakulla River of north Florida. It revealed that nutrients from an upland spray field for wastewater from the city of Tallahassee were emerging from the deep, powerful head spring. Nutrients spike a growth in algae, just as they do in grass back on land. As a result of the accelerated algae growth, eelgrass died and apple snails virtually disappeared from the spring run. Consequently, the limpkin population took a dramatic nosedive. Back home, our once-pristine Wekiva was facing similar dilemmas with nutrients, and I wondered when the limpkins here would also be affected.

This part of my learning was the most disturbing: putting waste into the ground takes it out of sight, but it doesn't make it go away. This is especially true in Florida where the limestone under our earth is so porous. Protecting a spring extends far outside the basin of its run, deep into the labyrinthine limestone of the aquifer—miles upstream of where the spring emerges from the ground. Thus, the apple snail has meaning far beyond its own life and death, and it often extends down to the deep, hidden aquifer that feeds the springs of our landscape.

Once, I seined an apple snail from a wild stream. I put it into my office aquarium, which is populated with native plants and fish. The snail set about its tiny business, moving about with its stoic mollusk determination. Over the log, up the glass, down the glass. One day, I lifted the plastic tank lid to scatter food and found a clutch of pink eggs on the underside. Unlike many hermaphroditic snails, the apple snail is distinctly male or female, and I had a momma. The eggs would hatch in two weeks or so, and tiny little apple snails would tumble out of each. I was delighted about witnessing the genesis of life. But there was another lesson to be learned.

The snail, taken from its home and living in a sort of aquatic zoo, still wanted to propagate. Although it is near the bottom of the food chain, the animal showed a unity of purpose often foreign to humans.

When we kill our springs and lakes and rivers, we kill something in ourselves—something that nestles deep inside the spirit. Surely we will live on in some form, but at what price?

A future without the delight and solace of natural places is not one most sane humans would consciously choose. Instead, it is being chosen for us by powerful, growth-obsessed zealots who live in a sort of fantasyland of denial. Before the recession took hold, Florida was losing its natural lands at a rate of twenty acres an hour, largely thanks to the poorly planned growth known as sprawl. There's no reason to think that rate of loss won't regain its momentum once the sprawl is revitalized. Despite our human cleverness, we still haven't figured out a way to balance growth with environmental sustainability.

A snail egg isn't laid by a lizard, no matter how much we might think so. And the natural landscape of Florida isn't infinite. Its intricacies are delicate and finely geared to inextricable ecological rhythms.

Having bogarted our way to the top of the food chain in a heartbeat of time, we are just now facing the accountability that comes with the job. The apple snail, for whom all of life may be a single Zen moment of being, might have some answers for us.

But we have to stop rushing about, listen closely, and pay attention to the details, especially when they come to us in a whisper of tiny pink eggs.

3

Welcome to Midge World

I joined some friends for dinner at a little waterfront restaurant on the south shore of Lake Monroe here in Sanford the other evening. Nice breeze coming up off the dark night water and truly lovely the way late springtime in Florida can be sometimes. I arrived a bit late, so I'm just getting seated as the food arrives. We're inside a large screened porch attached to the restaurant to take full advantage of the fine weather and the liquid geography. A waitress is bustling about, saying waitress-type things, and a very animated woman I don't know is also at the table, waving her arms. But this is not the strange part.

This 1920s-era structure was once the Hotel Forrest Lake, as seen from a kayak out on Lake Monroe.

The strange part was when a truck equipped to spray insecticides drove up on the lawn next to the screened porch and started gassing us. They were actually trying to gas the midges, little fly-type insects that breed as larvae in the giant body of water outside, and then, as adults, swarm in and engulf whatever is moving. They don't bite, but since they multiply in the millions like some sort of biblical plague, they pile up in great numbers, and are slippery as hell when you step on them.

The midges, also called "blind mosquitoes," are hardy enough to survive in the sluggish, nutrient-enriched eutrophic waters. So the wise, long-term solution is to clean up this sluggish dilation in the St. Johns River known as a lake. A healthy river bottom would support a wider variety of aquatic insects and predators and the midge larva that live down there would find it harder to compete for space and food. That approach, of course, would take some long-term thought and planning. It seems so much better to default to the old Dow Chemical slogan: "Better Living Through Chemistry." So instead of ecological restoration, we resort to great plumes of pesticides since it seems so much more . . . dramatic. Those evil midges want to harass us, unleashing an insect jihad on our shores? Blow the suckers off the face of the earth.

I asked the waitress why the truck was gassing us, when clearly, we ought not to be gassed. Her answer was classic: "It's the city . . . or county spraying." Which sort of means, it's okay, because they know what they're doing. Or if they don't, we can't do anything about it anyways. Once my friend Colin, who is a physician, figured out what was happening, we all took our food and beverages and moved inside. But by then, we had a patina of pesticide about us. I also tried to study why another half dozen people continued to sit outside and feed while they were being sprayed. Perhaps they already knew the city or county had approved it.

Sanford has tried to get rid of its midge problem for years now, doing everything under the sun *except* trying to clean up the lake. In 1977, the Greater Sanford Chamber commissioned a study on the midge affliction and found that it resulted in a loss of $3 to $4 million a year in business. While the midges might be tiny, this wasn't small change. About a decade ago, the city spent approximately $100,000 to equip a large barge that would sort of suck all the midges to their teensy little bug deaths.

But a storm came and washed it ashore. Later, the midge season didn't arrive on time, and the barge sat there forlorn, bereft of midges. By the time they did come, everyone had lost hope, and the midge barge had lost funding. Now there are three small midge barges, which function like giant bug lights. Photovoltaics energize the lights by day; by night, the soft glow draws the midges like entomological sirens to their inglorious dissolution. Sort of like little singles bars for insects.

This has been going on for years now, long enough so that researchers have written papers and even chapters in books about it all. In 1987, one Florida entomologist with a sense of humor actually described the adult form of a particular species of the midge as *Dicrotendipes thanatogratus*—for Jerry Garcia's former iconic rock swarm, the Grateful Dead.

Other bug scientists have noted that, although all the general and specific types of midges in the family *Chironomidae* don't bite, they can be, well, troublesome. There is a very subjective component in this equation, and it has been described in at least one abstract as "overall midge annoyance."

"When large numbers of adults die, they can build up into malodorous piles," according to one report. Another points out that the larvae of midges—which to the nonscientific eye look a bit like mosquito larvae—are "very tolerant" of human-made pollution. Indeed, midge larvae enjoy the soup of microscopic plants called phytoplankton, also known as algae. Like most plants, this algae is also jolted into growth spurts by fertilizers.

It turns out the bug light barges are also part of another study. So far, this barge research has discovered that, indeed, midges are attracted to the lights. (I'm figuring a study of my porch light might have also revealed that.) The solution? Install lights around the lake in areas where there is little or no "recreational, business or residential activity." That is, in the swamps. When fully lit, the swamps and other wild natural areas would then "discourage migration of midge swarms to Sanford." It is assumed overall midge annoyance would be greatly reduced.

As for the lack of dissolved oxygen in Lake Monroe, the tiny midge larvae have the capacity to swirl up from the mud to the surface for a gulp of air when needed. It seems the midge is the right animal for the right place since the City of Sanford still channels its stormwater from streets and yards via underground pipes into the lake. This has the effect of both lowering the oxygen content and raising the level of algae. As evolutionary biologists would say, the midge has found its *niche*.

And of course, the chemical trucks spray toxins far and wide, even though we know by now that blasting the adult midges with toxins is lame when compared to actually correcting the conditions that make the larvae robust and happy.

However, unless you're inclined to read a text like "The Chironomidae: Biology and Ecology of Non-Biting Midges," you'll likely fall into line with folks who believe that a good dose of bug spray will cure just about anything. Years ago, when the city had its own official "Midge Patrol," that pesticide truck would participate in the annual Christmas Parade. When it did, it would get a healthy round of applause—although to the best of my knowledge, it did not actually gas the audience during the parade.

I'm wondering if eating all the mercury-enriched bass from "lakes" like this for years hasn't somehow made us more addled than the typical Floridian, and thus, unable to make good decisions about mixing insect management with *al fresco* dining. If Jerry Garcia were here, maybe I could ask him.

4

A Florida Swamp

In With the Ixia

A healthy, young bald cypress tree with its trunk fluting out into buttresses to help it anchor itself in a soggy swamp bottom.

The forest below fell away into darkness, and we went down into it.

The fire break trail my good friend Steve Phelan and I hiked to get here had taken us along the edge of a broad, flat pasture occupied by a white wooden farmhouse with a tin roof, a few Palomino horses, and a madly barking dog. The horses were fine looking and the dog was paranoid.

The trail of wild bahia and packed white sand was rimmed by a low field of saw palmettos and a narrow margin of small slash pines. Shiny wild blueberry bushes, a runt of a plant with tiny leaves, grew in the understory like well-tended bonsai. The pasture, fenced with hog wire, was just behind the pines.

It had rained last night and the imprints of animal tracks were crisp, as if a teacher had made them with a stamp for a class. The prints were mostly deer, but there was also the distinct mark of a large Florida black bear. The pad marks of its paws were so defined you could see the wrinkles in them. One of the pines had been bowed over and deeply scratched by a young male bear announcing itself. The tree had bled sap and now, amber-colored droplets of resin were frozen in mid-drip. The blueberry fruits, hard and reddish, would be ripe soon.

The trail vanished where the pasture ended; in its corner was a hunter's deer stand. It was a durable plastic hutch propped up on metal pipes, looking like a guard tower at the edge of a penitentiary. It seemed a ridiculous human-made conceit sitting out here next to the thick sub-tropical forest until I looked into the dark slits. During seasonal hunts, rifle barrels would be looking back out. Unaccountably, I sensed a certain dread, maybe the fear of an animal between the time he senses the report of a rifle and feels the deep penetration of a bullet in his flank or neck or, if he's lucky, his head. Better to go quick than to drag your wounded pelt through the woods for miles. Maybe it was my own fear; perhaps in thinking the desire to kill a deer was just a sublimated urge to shoot me, Steve, or some other shaggy, bearded granola stumbling about at the edge of the woods. It struck me that I was becoming as paranoid as the farm dog.

I thought of the bright, well-tended pasture above and the dim tangle of vegetation below, thought of how it illustrated the contrasts of our landscape here in Florida. To most, the open field would be a great relief, a symbol of progress and inviolability, proof that human dominance over the rest of nature was unquestionably virtuous. That's the way Florida has been seen for the last five hundred years by its colonists. Trees were measured in board feet, rivers and lakes in the way they could water livestock or be drained off to allow soggy land to be settled.

A few have seen it otherwise, like the eighteenth-century naturalist Billy Bartram who spent a lot of time in Florida mucking about in this same watershed, a bit to the east of here. Bartram saw God's creation realized in nature, from the plants to the wildlife, and insisted that humans had no more standing in this cosmos than an ixia or a pitcher plant. He reveled in the hidden and the cryptic, saw wisdom and instruction in wild places.

As for me, the pasture and all it represented was monotony, a place robbed of its hidden discovery—one giant loaf of white bread with precision-cut slices, full of tiny holes of air. And so I was glad when the path ended and we left the high plateau for the darker woods. I saw a narrow animal trail through the thick palmettos, and hoped it would lead us at least part of the way to the swamp below. I took it and Steve followed.

The higher land had likely been a seabottom terrace in one of Florida's distant incarnations, and, when the ocean finishes rising in another few centuries, may yet be again. As we went, it occurred to me that the slope we were following could have led a Neolithic fish down into a deeper abyss.

On an oceanographic expedition once, I rode in a submersible to 3,000 feet, watching as the sea life became more primitive as we went deeper. On the bottom, we saw the protoancestors of modern fish, glowing and blinking bioluminescence in the perpetual darkness, weird spatulate heads and tentacles not yet bred out by the efficiency of the lighted world above. I thought of the Florida swamp that way, as a sort of Devonian epoch where ferns and mosses ruled the earth, and humans were intruders from a time not yet invented. This Devonian had trees, of course, but many were bald cypress that jutted up out of the humus, broaches of soft, feather-like needles at the end of tall sticks. It was easy to think of them as giant ferns.

The animal trail ended soon enough and we had to push through a fretwork of serrated palm fronds and the spindly branches of myrtles and scrub oak. With the tangled brush and the steep descent of the slope, we had abandoned any hope of stealth and were bumbling through the woods like wounded animals. Briars of blackberry and the large thorns of the smilax vine pulled at me, and webs of tiny crab spiders stuck to my head when I wasn't quick enough to duck under them.

From somewhere in the swamp below, a woodpecker's beak hit a hollow trunk again and again. I think of how an ivory-billed was last seen in Florida in the 1920s in the upper basin of this larger watershed. It was living in the swampy bottomland of old growth hardwoods, illusive even then. Slow-growing trees like cypress sustained it, especially when they matured. But hardwoods like this were also favored by the loggers, who had been very thorough in their work.

I can't imagine that place being any wilder than the one we were entering today. The woodpecker thumping today sounded like the pileated—a look-alike cousin of the ivory-billed, and a bird adaptive enough to still exist. We moved through the woods without talking, and when I wasn't staggering into branches, I was snapping deadfall under my feet. I took comfort in knowing the ruckus would scare any self-respecting viper within hundreds of feet. I remember once walking soundlessly along the soft, spongy bottom of a dry swamp, and almost stepping on a giant moccasin curled up on the exposed root ball of a sabal palm. Its body was as large as my forearm and its eyes were alert and agile, little windows that glowed with the light of a prehuman past. I carefully stepped around it, and it carefully allowed me to do so.

Today, with our lack of stealth, I imagined myself snake-proof. The snake least likely to flee from us was the pygmy rattler, an exquisite little reptile with an intricate crosshatch pattern on its body. It was fearless but small, and its body held little venom. Every time I have seen a pygmy, a woman hiking with me has spotted it first. To me, they were all striking, vivacious women of various ages, and I vaguely wondered if female aesthetics had anything to do with the wakefulness of snakes. Were they invisible to me, or was I invisible to them?

Gators are usually back in here too. Like snakes, they are one of the great dreads that help keep the wilderness of Florida free from hoards of recreational hikers, all tricked out in their sporty L.L. Bean apparel. Since the swamp was now nearly dry, the gators that usually hunted it would have moved closer to the creek edge where it would be easier to snatch fish, turtles, wading birds, and smaller gators. Even if one was still around, our commotion would likely disturb it. Only once have I ever had a gator charge toward me, and then it was only trying to get away and I happened to be between it and deeper water.

I thought of the half-mad conquistadors busting along in their armor here five hundred years ago, clanking like giant tin cans in their fruitless search for gold and glory in the Florida swamps, sweating and cursing and nearly always lost. I figured it was a miracle they saw any animals at all. Of course, there was simply more of everything then—wildlife, water, wetlands. Panthers were here; so were great flocks of Carolina parakeets. But how fully did they see it all? If nature is only an inconvenience to a quest, there's scant room for communion. If the quest is to exploit a resource, the best way to do that is to dig and drain, slice and hack. Maybe it gets mapped or drawn, but only for that utility.

Steve, more prepared than I, as usual, had on long khaki pants. The pants were velcroed just above the knees to make them short if he wanted, but of course, he wouldn't want to today. I wore shorts because my legs moved better in them, no restraint on the knees. But the downside was obvious: already the briars and low branches had left scratches across my exposed skin and my calves were trailing lines of bright red blood.

We knew there was a creek somewhere down here. There were also at least two springs, maybe more, and we were hoping to find at least one of them. The springs were so remote that neither was marked on the quad map. Except for the few strands of faded orange plastic flagging left on trees from the last hunting season, there were few clues to the terrain. The flagging, which could be used to mark direction, meant nothing to us. It simply gave hunters reference for their territory, how to get in and out of it in order to shoot deer, turkey, and wild hog.

The quad map itself would have given us some hints about typography, if we had remembered to pack it. Isobars would have illustrated the rises and falls in the terrain, of course. But I figured that we were experiencing it ourselves, each step an informational pathway between the forest floor and our senses. I rely heavily on maps in distant places like the Everglades where the monoculture of red mangroves can easily throw you off. I'm less inclined to do so here because the habitats are diverse and distributed by common sense—scrub and sandhill are usually up; swamp and blackwater river are down. Everything else is in between. Getting lost isn't impossible, but it takes some work.

Odd, but Florida is now lived in by more than 18 million people, and visited every year by millions more tourists. I wondered how many take the little trails that lead from the light and descend into the soggy jungle-like bush. I thought about the appeal of that idea and realized it wouldn't sound so hot on a billboard or in a full-color tourist brochure. Leave the Light for the Darkness. Look for some obscure natural shit that you may or may not find.

In comparison, a large alligator on a Jungle Safari ride would be guaranteed. If real, it would be seen from a very safe distance. If automated, it might be close and actually snapping its just-pretend jaws in your face. In any case, its presence would be announced by a tour guide, and shows to see it would start and stop at a prescribed time. It would be the Cracker Jack box version of exploration, an expected and downsized surprise, the fear of real Florida places neatly excised from the experience. Sometimes, I wished I could be satisfied by performances like that, but even as a kid, I had a hard time with the contrived spin of it all.

The slope that brought us here had leveled out in the flat, dry forest floor. During the wet season, the blackwater creek would flood and flow through this bottomland, filtering and enriching itself. Watermarks on young cypress and swamp tupelo around us were nearly chest high, a visual reminder of that wet season rise. I have scuttled through Florida swamps like this in a kayak when they were inundated. It reminded me of the Amazon during its wet season when that giant of a tropical river spreads itself through its forest. Amazonia has been heavily logged, but so much of its wild heart still remains, spreading itself across that continent with great energy.

In contrast, the woods surrounding this creek are a relic, an organic monument to what all of this peninsula once was. Despite laws against trammeling wetlands, we continue to lose our swamps and marshes each year to "mitigation" where the natural system is destroyed, and then in some sorry-assed way, re-created elsewhere. The re-creations are the Frankensteins of nature, and if they work at all, it's in an odd and stilted way, and not for very long.

The swamp floor, although nearly dry, was uneven and I repeatedly stepped on small beds of twigs and branches that broke through to gullies and holes a half foot or more deep. Once, my left leg went down into a deeper depression in the humus and a thick branch snapped against the hard bone on the front of my calf. It broke the skin and left a welt that, within minutes, swelled to the size of a golf ball and bled. I cursed a bit, and stopped to put my leg up to drain the blood away.

Steve heard me yelp, and came to see if he could help. My water bottle was warm, but he had a cooler one and offered it to me, and I pressed it against the welt. I rested for a few minutes, wiping away some of the blood, and then we went on. Down here, the taller trees met above in a great canopy, blocking most of the sun. It seemed more like twilight instead of midday.

It's not unusual to see isolated stumps of logged hardwoods back in the Florida swamps. But we had now stumbled into a place that had once been a grove of bald cypress. We counted nearly a dozen stumps directly around us. They were immense; the fluted buttresses still splayed out and the distinctive knees were still upright, solid and unmoving. The wood of a live cypress is usually gray vellum, but the dead ones were colored brown like a deerskin.

Bracken ferns, wild muscadine grape vines, and swamp hickory sometimes grew out of a stump, giving it the appearance of a giant planter. While most trees had been cut four or five feet above the floor, at least one was nearly seven feet high. It must have been a magnificent specimen when alive.

Steve studied medieval literature when younger, but later in his life he came to nature literature and from there, into nature itself. He understands the history of logging hereabouts, and knows a lot about cypress. He tells me that after a tree reaches forty years, it only grows about an inch in circumference annually. Although the seeds from the cones don't germinate underwater, the tree itself needs enormous amounts of liquid to thrive. And while it hasn't been strong enough to resist the blade—what tree has?—it's so dense that the decapitated stumps, even after 75–100 years, are still durable. This is all a testimony to the iron-like strength of the inner "heart wood" of the cypress, a quality that takes a good long time to be fully realized. I think of the tree as I do a living being, with great respect for its venerability. The irony here is that the prized "maturity" of the cypress—a quality that might have helped keep any one of us alive in our human world—led to its demise.

I asked Steve to take my photo next to the largest stump and he did. He guessed most of these were once virgin timber, probably two thousand to three thousand years old when they were logged. A century ago, land was cheap enough in the Florida interior that the logging companies simply bought it instead of buying rights to its timber.

Oddly, the desire to exploit the landscape sometimes saved it: The lumber companies often held onto the land here into the 1940s and 1950s, sometimes selling large tracts to hunting clubs when the older hardwoods and longleaf were logged out. Few buyers at that time seemed interested in draining and building in the dark swamps when they could go to higher scrub and sandhills to fashion their new dream communities. Sometimes, the hunters later resold their parcels to real estate developers, and made out very well financially by doing so. But sometimes, they understood something essential about the enduring solace of nature and sold their land for use as public parks and preserves that could be enjoyed by everyone. In either case, it was an easy sell since the land was free of multiple ownership. The tract we are exploring today is a more recent add-on to a core parcel of over six thousand acres that the hunters of the Apopka Sportsmen's Club first sold to the state of Florida in the 1960s for a very modest sum, and I am very grateful for that.

The massive cypress stumps, as well as the new young trees growing nearby, gave hope the creek was close, and soon we came upon it. It was a perfectly wild little river, flowing slowly as Florida rivers are prone to do, and tangled with brush and trees that had fallen into it. It was tannic, of course, as dark as iced tea, offering a window here and there where it shoaled. In those places, the bottom was either white sand or leafy mud, and I knew from experience the mud was a boot-sucking sop that could go down several feet.

We pushed through sabal palms along the low creek banks, looking for a fallen tree trunk that might serve as a bridge to the other side. At one point, a downed sweetgum seemed to hold promise, but such things always look easier from the shore than they do up close. I mounted it and the tree-bridge took me a good five feet above the creek, and the trunk, which had seemed broad and inviting, became narrow and unsteady. I gingerly turned back when I couldn't get through a thick clutch of live branches that were still thriving from the tree's midsection. My calf was still throbbing from the injury, and I was favoring my other leg. It threw my balance off just enough to jeopardize any finesse I might otherwise have and left me not as confident as I should have been about this fording business.

We were in deep now, surrounded by the natural gothic, a place where slender piers and pointed arches and vaulted stumps were woven with the filigree of branches, hanging mosses, and vines.

Bartram was among the first to observe that birds from the American northeast would not fly to the moon or overwinter in the mud under the ice, as commonly believed. Instead, they would come here, to the swamps of La Florida. On hikes into the backcountry during the winter, I have seen migrating flocks of robins, bluebirds, and warblers, blurs of color like oil dabs on a canvas. No wonder this peninsula has been so mythic for so many, for so long. Florida and its swamps defied conventional reality, becoming the territory of the imagination.

And why not? The entire primal landscape around us could have been a workshop of cognitive shards, as if we had entered a place in the unconscious where thoughts and feelings went to be considered before they were born—a mushroom here, a lichen there, all mossy and green and pungent. Most would decay and be forgotten forever; but sometimes a sprout would flourish and something new would arise from it.

I understand the ease with which Steve, schooled as a Medievalist, made the transition to the modern literature of nature. It was far easier to do so here in Florida, in the subtropical swamp, than in a bright open prairie back on the continent. Around us, it could have been last week or the last millennium. In the swamp, we are all Medievalists.

It was early summer, and the heat of the day had warmed everything up, like a heat lamp might do in a terrarium. The temperature and humidity made it feel as if the entire landscape was on a slow simmer. Damp wood, decaying leaves, ghost lilies, bromeliads, the chlorophyll of a million leaves. I thought of that scent as a sort of primeval exhale that blended all that had ever been here before us. It occurred to me that if this swamp is gothic, it is far more than just form that makes it so. It has something to do with the dance of shadows, and the dim ochre reckoning of daylight filtered down through wood and leaf—into and out of the veined acetate of beetle wings, the ovary of an orchid bloom, the shiny varnish of a tiny mandible.

Light in the swamp is changed light, transformed by what it flows beyond to reach the bottom. I think of it as I do the illumination that reaches a deep coral reef in the sea, rendered not just less by the distance, but refracted by the invisible planktons it must pass through. It is light energized and changed by its journey. No longer bright and cheery and warm, it is enigmatic and somber, charged with the existence of where it has been.

As for us humans, I figured we moderns carry with us perceptions that are likewise filtered. Except our circuit boards are also burdened with learned templates in which we must wedge information into a certain niche, whether it belongs there or not. Technology and its need for efficiency has taught us to do this, of course. Nature has niches, too, but they are complex and not easily revealed, and the impatience of our TiVo world often misses them. It especially misses them when it comes to swamps.

I think of all those here before me, the pre-Columbian Timucua and Mayaca, and later, the Creeks who would become the Seminoles. The old naturalist Bartram knew the Creeks; he wrote of them and drew some of them in great detail. These people, he noted in his journals, ought to be deeply considered, since there was so much to be learned from them. They weren't deeply considered, of course, and now we have what remains of the Indians' world without the Indians, no instruction manual on how best to understand or sustain or commune with it. We have obliterated the stories that could have taught us so much about botany and zoology and the contemplative transect of it all in the human spirit.

Steve, a far better student than I, seems intent on this quest to recover the wisdom of nature, and he puts as much study into it as he did into his graduate work. He dawdles a lot, stopping to look, sometimes to pick up pieces of seeds and bark and roll them over in his hands. Unlike the scientists who sometimes come into places like this to survey plants or animals, he has no pretense about ever knowing it all. Instead, he has a sort of emotional confidence that allows a healthy ignorance to be forever tolerated.

In that same way, I wonder if we can also come to know a god without needing to have that god defined for us until it has no secrets left at all. And if God is not about surprises and mysteries and growth, then what kind of God can it be? The only kingdom left to it would be fenced pastures and domestic farm animals and madly barking dogs. And I suppose it is the tacit knowledge of this that somehow connects Steve and me as much as anything ever will.

There is another smell in the air, that of pure death, and we are drawn toward it. It is a deer, or what is left of one, and it is caught in some snags in the middle of the creek. The scent is so overwhelming that I must breathe out of my mouth or it will sicken me. It took a bullet in the flank and ran a long ways before it finally died. We walk beyond the deer, beyond the knowledge of its death, and finally, we stop. We have come to find springs, but have found none and now it is late.

Steve uses his GPS to point us back toward our trail. We have traveled far through the swamp and our exit will not be an easy one. We make it halfway back up a slope, to where the hardwoods end and the gridlock of saw palmettos begins. This time, though, there's not even an animal trail to follow. With no way to finesse it, I take the lead and move forcibly into the nearly impenetrable green, using pushing muscles in my arms, legs, and back. In thirty minutes of this, we cover about a hundred yards.

I am sweating heavily now, and my arms and legs are bleeding freely from the hash marks. The palmettos are so high and thick I cannot see Steve even though he is only a few yards behind me. He tells me he has taken another reading and we are somehow going in the wrong direction. I wonder about that since we can only be going up; that is the direction that should take us out of the swamp.

Then I realize this odd Florida land, underlain by soft limestone, sometimes swales in great loping windrows. The creek had oxbowed as we followed it. The slope we used for our descent is gone, replaced by other rises that flow in giant corrugations.

I take a pull on my water bottle. There's enough left for one more hit and I need to save it. It has started to rain lightly and the sky, even above the palmettos, is heavy with clouds. We are lost, no trail in sight, and as expected, it has taken some work. Steve takes yet another reading, mutters something about the GPS not working like it should. Finally, he packs his instrument away for good.

I press ahead and try to focus. I think of all the history that has come before and will come after us here. If left alone, in another thousand years the young cypress we saw might tower again, as majestic as the mother trees that once seeded them. That gives me hope, but it is a rarefied hope. The truth is I am sick to the bone of technology and all the failed promises of modern Florida and its slick-as-glass promoters. If anything will ever save me, it will be the sound of my heart against my flesh. That's all I know for sure.

I hear what sounds like a gunshot and I jump, startled. And then I realize it is a sharp crack of thunder. Fear washes through me and then ebbs, a wave on the retreat. It's okay, at least I can feel it. Maybe next I can feel how to get the hell out of here.

I trust only in movement now, and I try to make it efficient, with as much grace as I can still muster. It is raining very hard now and frogs are singing loudly, males advertising themselves. I think absently that many of them are southern leopard frogs. From the swamp below, something large crashes through the underbrush.

If the sky ever clears, the moon will rise in the east, and when it does, it will lead us home.

5

Key Largo

Where Bogie Meets Lewis Carroll

There's a bunny in the gibbous moon, a pale strobe of lightning in the clouds, and in my gut, a feeling that almost anything can happen. We are at the edge of the Gulf of Mexico, slouched around a picnic table behind the Caribbean Club, a local hangout that likes to promote itself as "where the movie *Key Largo* was filmed." The truth is a few scenics *were* actually filmed here with Bogie while most of the film was shot elsewhere. But really, who cares? The fronds of coconut palms are swaying overhead, and great flocks of ibis, the wading bird with the beak bent like a red mangrove root, are gliding across the twilight sky.

A sea turtle, as seen swimming underwater, during a dive trip to the Keys.

Back out on U.S. 1, motorists are blasting by, headed for cookie-cutter tiki bars and points south without a notion of what they may be missing here. Steve Harris, a Peter Pan of a guy who takes great wonder in discovery, is explaining why the anvil-headed vapor cloud looming above the Glades to the west is an alchemy of water and energy and light. My friends Michelle, who works for a conservation agency, and Greg, an affable Canadian-born photographer, listen and nod their heads appreciatively. Nearby is a cannon recovered from an offshore Spanish colonial wreck, forever bereft of its thunder. Yes I am a pirate, two hundred years too late. Steve could be talking about sea slugs and we would all still be absorbed, in a tropical sort of way. It's all about alchemy, really.

Steve, an excellent writer who runs a sailboat charter to make a living, will help us figure out how the natural water-driven world works in these parts. Teasing myth from reality is our job here, and to do so, we'll be sneaking under the metaphoric ledges and swim-throughs of the reefs, looking most of all for new ways to see over the next few days. Steve named his boat *Caduceus* for the magical staff wielded by Mercury, the messenger God. Mercury used the mythic rod to summon the gods of heaven to earth. Steve tells us the dreams of heaven can be right here in this moment, if we really want them to be.

To advertise his evening sailing trips under the stars, Steve has created a brochure. In it, he has written: "We identify constellations and learn the ancient myths that gave them voice." Steve enjoys a cold drink, but even more, he appreciates the sublime natural energy of his island home. "I live in paradise," Steve says of Key Largo. "You just have to know where to look, that's all."

The nearly full moon is now in full ascendancy over a tropical horizon of mangroves and water. I shift a bit on the seat of the wooden picnic table where we are sitting. I announce the fact that ancients saw a *rabbit* rather than a man in the darkness of the moon's craters, taking it as a symbol of fertility and renewal and magic. We all look more closely at the rising moon, sip from our cold drinks, inhale the tropical night air. I'm unsure if everyone actually sees the lunar bunny. But I'm confident they're all keen for the magic.

By midmorning, we meet at Steve's house on a quiet street that trails down to Key Largo Sound, beyond a tangle of gumbo limbo and Jamaican dogwood and flamboyant trees. Nearby is a state botanical park where the rare Keys tree snails, looking like hand-colored porcelain cones, still endure. Key Largo is thirty miles long and its northern half is virtually undeveloped, mostly protected as public land. Like much of the Keys, its plants washed here as seeds from the Antilles, taking root in the thin limestone rubble of the ancient reef underfoot.

With us today is Steve's friend Garl, a soft-spoken, gentle guy who is a kayak outfitter. We slide Garl's sit-atop sea kayaks in the water at nearby Garden Cove and paddle northeast into the Atlantic, our snorkeling gear stowed under bungees. We are headed toward the tip of a mangrove island mapped as Rattlesnake Key. The sky is big here, dappled with cumulus, and the calm autumn sea—lolling between tropical storms— seems to spread out forever before us.

Garl reminds us we are paddling over the sort of habitats that are often fished but seldom snorkeled or dived. "There's a lot going on down there," he says, "but few people ever see it." We float first across sea grass pastures and then "hardbottom," a distinct coral rubble landscape punctuated with sea whips, fans, and all manner of sponges. Places like these are vital to the life cycle of fish, as useful as the mangroves and reefs for feeding, breeding, hunkering down. Steve tells of a friend who caught a five-foot blacktip shark on a rod and reel here, only to have it cut in half by a much larger hammerhead before he could bring it in.

We decide to snorkel at a partially submerged wreck of an old concrete-hulled barge, anticipating almost anything. As we enter the water, a school of lookdowns—a thin, cartoonish fish that always seems to be forever looking down—swims in front of us. I count ten, then fifty, then a hundred. Before it is all done, more than five hundred pass just inches away, all looking forever down.

We fin to the old barge hull, which is encrusted with the marine patina of more than half a century. The wreck has become artificial hardbottom, studded with sponges, feather-like bryozoans, and a garden of soft corals. I fin low and peek into a dark crevice under the hull, also looking down. A half dozen spiny lobster look back, slender antennae waving to some unknown crustacean rhythm. We circle the barge, beyond blue-headed wrasses and neon gobies, juvenile Spanish hogfish and a pair of resident barracuda, and then fin out across the natural hardbottom that spreads out around it.

Fish hang vertically in the scrub-like clumps of soft corals as if each has been placed here to confound us—a scrawled cowfish, a sharpnose puffer. Garl has seen seahorses here tethered to gorgonians, but today, the most dramatic find so far is a dinner plate-sized yellow stingray, lemon-colored like a squash and just as immobile. As I watch, it darkens noticeably but doesn't move. As we fin away, I spot a single nurse shark, three feet worth of smoothly upholstered brown with a set of glassy eyes, a creature that seems more Claymation model than real shark. White sea biscuits are scattered nearby, looking like sand dollars on steroids.

We flop back into the sit-atop kayaks and paddle another three miles to shore. We are famished and dehydrated. We cartop the kayaks and our three-car caravan heads out toward U.S. 1. But before we reach it, Steve leads us onto a side road next to an old car with a giant fiberglass vulture rising out of its rooftop. We stop at a seafood restaurant in a cozy, low-slung building there, the Buzzard's Roost. Michelle orders the Buzzard Fish Sandwich, and the jolly waitress asks her, "How would you like your buzzard?" Steve quickly replies, "Scraped off the road," and we all laugh. The sandwiches—of dolphin fish, not buzzard—are excellent, the iced tea endless, and the fossilized coral canal outside the restaurant, like almost everything in Key Largo, leads to the sea.

The Largo Lodge is cool and quiet, shrouded in palms and Antillean foliage, a gaggle of retro cottages lining a shady lane that opens when it reaches the Gulf. Like other local Mom 'n Pop–run motels, it has an eccentric charm all its own. I check in at a tiny office that is surrounded outside by orchids and a busy squirrel feeder; inside are two Lava Lamps, four sparkly disco balls, and a wonderfully cluttered desk manned by a wonderfully gracious landlady with big retro hair. "It's different back here," Harriet "Hat" Stokes tells me, and indeed it is. When I awake by midmorning, the dense green wall of palms and ficus and pothos around my cottage makes it seem like the middle of the night.

We are scuba diving today with Lad Akins, who several years ago helped create an organization called REEF—Reef Environmental Education Foundation. REEF is to fish what Audubon is to birds as it encourages avid divers to identify and count individual species of fish. I am particularly looking forward to these dives because I was part of the original proto-dive team that first helped test REEF techniques here twenty years ago. Lad, an eternally good-natured guy, hands me an underwater slate and a waterproof fish ID booklet. Between our initial dives and now, over 85,000 individual fish counts have been recorded. The reports help marine park managers understand the health of fish populations, says Lad. But they also divulge surprises—such as the existence of exotic species like the Indo-Pacific batfish and the revival of the once-rare goliath grouper in the Keys.

Today, we're visiting the wreck of the *Benwood*, a Norwegian freighter sunk after a collision with another ship in 1942, and French Reef, a grotto where coral-chomping sea life have gnawed under the natural reef, leaving a unique series of ledges and swim-throughs. As we gear up, Lad says fish surveys show one of the top ten sites for fish diversity in the greater Caribbean is offshore Key Largo, including sites like this.

Down we go in slow-mo freefall to the thirty-foot bottom. Earlier, Lad told me about the jawfish that live just outside the halo of the wreck in the sand. The first thing he does is to lead me to the burrow of one. I slow down my breathing, focus my vision. Sure enough, there's a yellowhead jawfish, body the size of a fat bluish pencil, bobbing in and out of his hole, as if his tail is attached somewhere inside by a string.

We fin to the wreck, an amalgam of coral and sponges, its steel and wood thickly carpeted by the magic of its sea time. Wrecks underwater look nothing like the sort of cartoons created by Disney. After a half century of submersion, currents, storms, and saltwater mute the sharp human-made edges and the sea bottom itself seems to have rolled up and across what remains. If that's bad news for those who insist on Captain Hook visions underwater, it's good news for sea life which always looks for something hard or durable on the bottom to anchor its world. And so, with the sharp right angles left behind from the geometric precision that was once a ship, the *Benwood* is less a reef, and more a coral creation, a Moorish castle with places to hide, to feed, to rest, to breed.

In this incarnation it swarms with brightly colored tropical fish, a patch of vibrancy in an otherwise vast and empty ocean floor of sand, every bit as functional as a natural reef.

It's shallow here, so there's plenty of sunlight from above to illuminate everything, making each tiny fish glow as if it has built-in circuitry. After a few minutes of this, I have shed my dry land tensions, and allow myself to feel fully in solution with it all, absorbing the luminous sea energy that surrounds me. As I do, I remember again why I love to dive, and it has little to do with the intellect.

I snap out of my reverie and see Lad next to me using a pencil to record what he has seen on his yellow underwater plastic slate: schoolmaster, mutton and lane snapper, goldspot, and bridled goby. Lad glances up at me, and then writes "cleaning station" and points to where grouper are queuing up so the little Pederson's cleaning shrimp can do their jobs. It is an odd sort of synergy wherein larger fish—including many that might otherwise eat smaller invertebrates—move into a certain invisible nook so that their gills and even their mouths can be picked clean of parasites by the careful tiny claws of the shrimp. I find that astounding all by itself. But that's made even more so by the civility of the patrons-to-be, each large predator politely waiting its turn to be serviced. It's a food chain bargain: The shrimp gets to eat the parasite, and the bigger fish gets to go about its life, no pesky little sorrows boring into its flesh.

I drift a few yards away and see a lone spotted drum, busy with its endless pirouettes. I signal Michelle and show her the tiny fish with the giant dorsal, and she writes on my slate: "No Spots." I hand the slate to Lad, who eyeballs the fish and then writes correctly: "Juvenile." Emerson once wrote that nature and books belong to those who can *see* them. Like all great universal truths, this one still endures, even when we are using technology the old Transcendentalist could hardly imagine.

⁂

Jon Dahm's little four-seat helicopter lifts off as lightly as a Schaus swallowtail butterfly from a Frangipani blossom. Greg, the photographer, is in the front next to Jon, the passenger door off so he can shoot, and I'm in the back with Michelle. We met the pilot last night when he came over for a cooked-in crab cake dinner back at the lodge. He was with Lucy, his giant English Mastiff, the namesake of his service—Flying Dog Helicopters. We pulled out a map then to locate Carysfort Light on the reef, and this morning, that is where we are headed.

We glide atop south Key Largo and its busy highway, and then out over the ocean between the uninhabited Rodriguez and Tavernier Keys. In seconds, the geography beneath us turns to green water and coral— at first, ocher-colored clumps of patch reef, and then perforated slabs of bank, four to six miles offshore. We head north, identifying well-known reef clusters like "Molasses" and "The Elbow" by the fishing and diving boats anchored around them, like kittens nuzzling up to great platters of cat chow. The spur and groove formations of the reefs, carved long ago by the east-west flows of the tides, look as if some giant hand moved across the bottom, scraping out coral with each finger of the "grove," leaving the lateral "spurs" of coral intact. Just to the east, the rich blue waters of the Gulf Stream push in closer here, coursing across a deeper sea bottom beyond the shallow reef line.

The altimeter reads 200 feet and the world below becomes a Technicolor vision from an undersea dream. We see schools of bottlenose dolphins cresting the transparent sea, tiny buoys of lobster and stone crab traps, and three lone sea turtles on journeys known only to them. Under us, a great frigatebird soars. Soon we reach Carysfort with its gothic-looking light tower, a relic from 1852. Since the north-flowing Gulf Stream is so close, those ships that needed to sail or steam south had to squeeze through here, between the treacherous reef and the muscular current. The Spanish came here first, grounding entire flotillas of treasure galleons three hundred and more years ago. Even after the lighthouse was erected, the wood and steel hulls of ships crashed into the coral. Over the centuries, Carysfort became a repository for what archaeologists call "submerged cultural resources," corals and sponges claiming the artifacts of other years for their own. At last count, over sixty wrecks have been consumed by the reef-building marine life on Carysfort.

It's lonely out here seven miles from shore; only one private boat moored near corals that peak into giant elk and staghorn just under the surface, a Lewis Carroll vision as seen from the sky. We make one last pass over the light, low enough so I can better see its filigree of iron-pile construction, intricate but sturdy, Industrial Age ironwork securing it to the hard limestone somewhere under the coral. The crosshatch pattern of the steel reminds me vaguely of the intricate veins in the wings of a dragonfly.

There are six of these lighthouses in the Keys, between Miami and Key West, and in the days before LORAN and radar and GPS, they were absolutely essential as visual warnings of the dangerous ridges of coral just below. But their image was beyond mere utility: The fine, grid-like iron aesthetic of these lights influenced Alexandre Gustave Eiffel to build his famous tower in Paris, in a place far from any coral or Gulf Stream.

Jon turns us back toward land and soon we are above north Key Largo and its broccoli-top terrain, etched with tea-colored creeks and sloughs and linked to the mainland by the Card Sound Bridge in the distance. The largest stand of West Indian tropical forest in the Unites States is under us, populated with the last of the American crocodiles. The rare tree snail *Liguus* thrives here, speciating itself with different colors and bands, depending on the tree hammock where it lives. A single road that runs from Card Sound to U.S. 1 spines the broccoli, and abandoned harbors and canals bite into its edges.

Manic schemes in the early 1970s would have turned all of this into a congested misery of a place with 100,000 people, a monorail and hydrofoil base, golf courses, marinas, and no fewer than ten health spas. This unusually long key has great natural utility—it acts as a dam to block the southeasterly flow of turbid, nutrient-heavy, and colder waters from Florida Bay, protecting the offshore corals. Patch and bank reefs grow in greater profusion as a result. Dense settlement would have overwhelmed that function by creating its own stream of pollution that emptied directly onto the besieged northern reef with no natural barrier to block or filter it.

Building actually began with a few grand model homes and a harbor, which was scooped out of a shallow lagoon. Then a perfect storm of environmental laws and poor development strategies collided. When the smoke cleared, the state of Florida was able to purchase most of the resort-to-be, keeping the *Liguus* on the trees and the fish on the reef, gifting nature with the space and time she needed to sustain a wonderland of wildlife and plants and coral.

᠅

There is a gigantic ship beneath me, and the closer I get, the more it reveals itself. Down the mooring line I go in scuba gear, hand over hand in the stiff current until I reach the rigging at the top of the wreck.

At 130 feet, the vessel is blue, eternally blue, and it rises up majestically from the sandy bottom like a nautical mirage. This used to be an old navy ship known as the *Spiegel Grove* before being cleaned and sunk by local dive operators who are always searching for new sea bottom diversions for their clients. Ships, however they find their way to the bottom, provide a substrate that allows new reef growing to occur. Certainly, that was the case with the accidental sinking of the *Benwood*. Regardless, most human-made structures that end up on the bottom have the capacity to turn into miniature reefs, thus taking the pressure off the natural berms of coral. Once when snorkeling near Islamorada, I found a discarded refrigerator on a vast bed of sand under twenty feet of water. It was studded with tiny chunks of coral and swarming with tropicals.

But depths like this can also do serious damage if not approached with caution. Techniques for diving inside the caves of the springs of Florida can at least be taught. But diving deep challenges the human physiology in unexpected ways. Each diver's reaction to the narcosis of depth, to oxygen poisoning or another malaise, is not fully known until experienced. It's not unlike flying a one-person ultralight—you solo on your first flight, whether you want to or not. To date, at least six divers have died here, including three veteran New Jersey divers experienced with depth, cold water, and unfriendly currents.

Greg is below me next to the deck railing and Michelle just a few yards above. We are a ragtag trio respectively in swim trunks, a shorty wetsuit, and a lightly insulated "skin." It is a stark contrast to our very serious techie mates we first met on the dive boat, some of whom are using this for deep-diving training, and most of whom are encased in thick black neoprene from hood to toe. The "skin" I'm wearing is splotched with tropical version of a very light wetsuit, and it is happily splotched with great patches of yellow. Sharks are said to be particularly attracted to this color; thus, veteran divers call it "Yum Yum Yellow."

Under me, Greg and Michelle enter a deck hallway, spooking a school of muscular bar jacks that explode around me, pushing the water in a great surge of energy as they do. I duck down inside, following a permanent line along the bulkhead, floating where crewmen once walked. The metal here is covered with marine life, from barnacles to soft corals and anemones. A recent REEF study showed that fish diversity here almost tripled since the 510-foot long navy ship was sunk in the summer of 2002. The nearby Gulf Stream current transports larvae of fish and corals to it, and cruising pelagics like sharks and cobia drop by for a snack. Yum Yum Yellow.

Back outside the hallway, in open water just beyond the hull of the ship, I discover that the dynamic of the formerly slack current has changed drastically. Although I am finning as hard as I can toward the line leading to the surface, I seem to be going nowhere.

I check my air pressure gauge, and see that pushing against this newly invigorated current has cost me air I didn't plan on losing. I wonder if I will have enough left to reach the surface. I start breathing in short, shallow bursts and feel an early wave of panic wash over me. Finally, I stop finning and close my eyes. As I do, I remember the most essential rule that can ever be taught or learned about scuba: If you panic, you have no other options. I say that to myself a few times, and concentrate on breathing in slow, even breaths instead of rapid gulps.

My vision, which had narrowed, widens slightly, and it occurs to me if I sink down a few yards, it might take me out of this new lateral rip. I do, and it does. And the world around me begins to gradually brighten.

Last night, we sailed Blackwater Sound on Steve's boat, listening to a Van Morrison CD, Van singing that it's a marvelous night for a moondance. All I had to do was relax and feel the jib gently billow with the light breeze, watch as the sun dipped into the horizon, turning the sky a deep scarlet. Once, I saw dolphins playing in the pressure wake of the bow, and bent over on my knees to watch them. A young one turned his head as I peered over the gunnel, and looked me squarely in the eye before vanishing forever. I think of this now as I move slowly toward the mooring line, and my breathing slows more as each image comes back to life in my mind.

When I finally reach the line, I am breathing slow and steady once again, a welcome feeling. I inch my way hand over hand back to the surface, pausing at intervals to blow off nitrogen, just as my dive computer on my wrist tells me I should. I look down once and see the *Spiegel Grove* dissolving back into the muted blue of its own world. It dissolves as if someone has turned a dimmer switch on a light, dissolves until it is no longer a ship at all, only an everlasting field of cobalt blue.

Slightly buzzed from the experience, I think to myself that *Caduceus* may be a sailboat, a mythic desire, or the line that has carried me deep into the dreams of the sea—and then, with more grace than I thought was possible, led me back out again.

6

Roadside Wildlife

Galloping with the Mastodons

I wonder about this Florida sometimes, about the difference between where things belong and where we sometimes find them.

Nature here, with rare and wonderful exception, isn't the virgin wilderness that Ponce De Leon or the poor lost soul known as Cabeza de Vaca found five hundred years ago. Nor is it what Marjory Stoneman Douglas or Archie Carr encountered earlier in the twentieth century. It's something else entirely—a place where we often have to take our wildness wherever we can get it. Sometimes, it's neatly woven into the tapestry of a park or a preserve, close to being as much of a natural gestalt as it ever will.

But increasingly, this natural Florida greets me right smack in the middle of urbanization. When it comes to me this way, the effect is both comforting and oddly jarring, like hearing a Bach requiem in the middle of a food court at a mall. One of these hybrid visions emerged the other day when I was driving near Disney World, approaching one of those concrete cloverleafs that perpetually swirl about like streams perfectly confluxing—neither clover nor leaf nor stream. It reminded me of the message in *The Geography of Nowhere*. That book explained the delusion of efficiency and "prosperity" we've somehow bought into, and how it's compromised and fragmented our landscape, erasing any sign of individuality from it.

Still, I always search for something redemptive about this urban Florida terrain. I've gotten pretty good at looking beyond the theme world billboards and the giddy caricature-level roadside invitations to "Join Our Deckside Party Happy Hour!" (From signage like that, a

A great blue heron on a post in front of green marsh inside the Lake Woodruff National Wildlife Refuge.

visitor might imagine Florida to be one giant democratic pool, rimmed by decks and beaches, and ruled by people who make their living inserting teensy umbrellas into sugar-charged alcoholic beverages.) It's a behavior that does pay off because I've seen a fascinating array of animals and plants that sometimes edge right up to the very shore of the road easements.

And that is what I was doing, even as I approached a major concrete switchback on I-4 in central Florida. As I did, I saw upcoming on the right—at the edge of one of those geometrically perfect rectangular ponds the engineers have built for us—two long-legged wading birds.

At first, I thought: cattle egret. But these guys were much too big for that. As I got closer, I thought: great egret. But just as I did, I noticed something not so right about their heads. Finally, as I got next to them, at a speed of 65 mph in a domino-line of fellow motorists all busy streaming off to Someplace Else, I got a real good look at them. They weren't egrets at all; neither were their mottled, black heads odd— at least not for this species. These birds were actually wood storks— what native Floridians, for reasons that make wonderful visual sense, call "Iron Heads." There were two of them, and one was fishing with its beak down in the water, cattails all around, while the other one was just standing there looking, seeming very self-contained, almost like an Old World stork. She looked as if she had seen the world begin, all the time passing by in the millenniums since then. And, here she still is, carrying the genetic code of distant memory, in a place where humans exist as tiny blips on the extended time line of creation. She's a wild animal that lives, for now, in the geography of nowhere.

Perhaps the wood stork, and all the others I've seen near or above congested Florida roads—the wild turkeys, the sandhill cranes, the bald eagles, the swallowtail kites—are simply biding their time. They've surely endured here a lot longer than us, weathering ice ages and coastal reconfigurations and stealthy aborigines with chert-tipped arrows and spears. And now here they still are, grazing stoically on a roadside that once was wild natural land as herds of exotic, hairless mammals inside their well-insulated steel and fiberglass shells madly stampede up and down their hard-packed trails.

Do they smile silently to themselves, marking the time until our cleverness grinds to a halt? Are they quietly waiting for the day when we so-called upper mammals gallop off into the sunset with the camel and the mastodon and the giant sloth, leaving them to their apple snails and gambusia and crayfish, back in a quiet swamp or marsh that this lush Florida climate revitalizes for them? Are they envisioning a more advanced moment when the gods smile on them again, and they can reclaim what was once theirs—just as the Yucatan jungle reclaimed the civilization of the Mayas?

Maybe these roadside birds are more than relics of Florida's lost wilderness. Maybe they're reminders of something else, too.

7

Florida Rivers

A Confluence of Alchemy

A river sings a holy song conveying the mysterious truth that we are
a river . . . An enchanted life demands an appreciation of this flow.
Thomas Moore

That night we came to a very wide, very deep and swift river,
which we did not dare cross on rafts. . . . A horseman named Juan
Velázquez, native of Cuéllar, entered the river without waiting, and
the swift current knocked him off his horse, but he held on to the
reins, and both he and the horse drowned.
Álvar Núñez Cabeza de Vaca, on getting lost in Florida in 1528

I was paddling through the treetops of a Florida river the other day, soaring through the foliage canopy like a giant bird. Heavy limbs of ancient live oaks were flopping lazily in the current as if they were metronomes keeping time to the river's pulse. The gunnels of my kayak came within a few feet of a tattered blue jay nest still cradled in a branch. Other limbs bristled with the spiky leaves of pine bromeliads, and once, a green fly orchid, all just inches above the water.

The river was the Econlockhatchee, and a series of tropical storms had filled its valley of paleo-dunes to overflowing. A month earlier it had been a shallow, sandy-bottomed blackwater stream that you could have walked across. A year before, rain had been so sparse that it stopped flowing and was less a river and more a series of narrow sloughs. But now it was high and raging, full of eddies and little standing waves.

Like everything else in Florida, our rivers have little in common with others back on the continent—indeed, during various stages of our wet-dry seasons, they don't even seem to have much in common with themselves. Gravity makes them work, of course, but it's a distinctly

Florida-driven gravity that pushes water across barely perceptible gradients on the landscape. Its source is not glaciers or snowmelt of the mountains, but the superheated hydrological cycle of our water-bound peninsula. The liquid driving our rivers falls from the sky in extraordinary amounts. Then, it either gathers up into swamps and marshes, or seeps downward into the soft lime rock of our crust. Great wetlands like the Green Swamp brim and overflow, driving our rivers outward from it. Or the bone-white karst underfoot does likewise, its own underground rivers pushed to the surface by the unseen alchemy of hydrostatic pressure from the uplands.

Writers and poets (Harriet Beecher Stowe, William Bartram, Sidney Lanier) have variously considered our rivers wild, noble, or given the right mood, indolent. Artists have delighted in them, featuring them thematically in landscape paintings (William Morris Hunt, Winslow Homer, Herman Herzog). Musicians have been notoriously mixed on the subject. The most famous river (the Suwannee) was celebrated by a songwriter (Stephen Foster) who never saw it. Yet arguably the most

Watermarks on the trunk of cypress trees in front of my kayak help show how far the water rises with heavy rainfall on our rivers.

sublime composition (*Florida Suite*) about a Florida river (the St. Johns) had the very legitimate franchise of being romanticized by a composer (Frederick Delius) who lived on its banks and truly fell in love with it.

Rivers have influenced where humans settled in Florida and how their cultures were molded over centuries. The bounty of flowing rivers fed their imaginations as well as their appetites. Dugouts, carved first from longleaf and then from cypress, became art with great utility. Some of the earliest pottery in North America was created on the banks of the St. Johns. Artistic skills here transformed wood into eagles, owls, otters, and iconic totems symbolizing protector spirits. A few survived, hiding for centuries in the safety of the river mud.

Industrious Americans expanded the notion of river transportation, adding steam boilers and paddlewheels. Both ornate and serviceable, the baroque steamboats toured nearly every river deep enough to float them, regardless of how torturous the meanders. "Landings" for the steamboats emerged where once there had only been hardwood and palm hammocks, drawing turpentiners, timbermen, planters, and early tourist promoters.

When the steamboats gave way to railroads, the practical use of rivers waned, and settlements created by boat traffic often dissolved into the detritus of the swamp: St. Francis, Suwannee Springs, Ellaville. But this was not always true, and every now and then those settlements morphed into modern cities, like Jacksonville. At other times, they remained modest and pleasantly retro, like Welaka and White Springs.

Florida rivers are predictable only in their uncertainty. The Econ is sort of like the Suwannee in that it trickles from a swamp, courses through a distinct valley, and dramatically rises and falls with the season. But the Suwannee, like many Florida rivers, is fed by springs, whereas the Econ is not. Other rivers, like the Hillsborough, are augmented both by springs and by groundwater seeping up through fractures in its bottom. Some rivers are in fact extended spring runs—like the Ichetucknee, Alexander, Juniper, Silver, and Wekiva. But even then, many of these runs are fed seasonally by rainfall leaking out of their tannic swamps. In wet summers, spring runs like the Wekiva are tea-colored; in dry winters, they become spring-clear again.

Some rivers, like the Chatham and the Lopez in the western Glades and the Nassau above Jacksonville, are so tidal that they are pushed less by gravity than by the moon and the sea. And a few rivers are not truly rivers at all—for instance, the Indian River is a brackish lagoon that does not flow, except when driven by wind. Marjorie Stoneman Douglas called the sawgrass prairie that is the Everglades a "River of Grass" because its waters do move, although one has to stand in it for a long time to realize it.

We have more than 50,000 very nonlinear miles worth of river in Florida, which are more or less divided into 1,400 named bodies of flowing water. The process of naming a river seems less to do with its size than the opinion of the cartographer who got there first. We have no "brooks" mapped in Florida, but we have "creeks," which are sort of similar. And we have "dead rivers," which lead into aquatic cul de sacs, ending navigationally but not biologically. We don't have "bayous," but we have "sloughs," which are usually deep, unmoving patches of swamp. That is, until the wet season, and then they become a dynamic part of the river once again.

The proper names of rivers are like the waterways themselves—they are snapshots in time, changing course in the semantical landscape, not unlike a channel will reconfigure itself through its floodplain. In this way, our most historic river was variously known as Welaka (Creek), Mai (French), Rio Corrientes, San Mateo, and San Juan (Spanish), and for now, it is the St. Johns. Fortunately, an unusually large number of river names first invented by early Creeks still endure in Florida. More often than not, they describe features or animals rather than praising some European deed or conqueror: Withlacoochee (Small River), Oklawaha (Muddy), Sopchoppy (Oak Tree), Loxahatchee (Turtle Stream), Chassahowitzka (Hanging or Opening Pumpkin), Echashotee (Home of Manatee or Beaver), Pithlachascotee (Chopped Boat). Saying those names out loud sometimes restores life to the traditional myth of the river, if only for a little while.

If some names have morphed over time, the official lengths of rivers have also been altered as new information is revealed. But this is problematic: mistakes are so often repeated, they have become fact. Almost all almanacs consider the 245-mile long Suwannee the longest river when its course out of Georgia's Okefenokee Swamp is considered. Yet, the St. Johns, which is 280 miles from its navigational headwaters at Lake Hell 'n Blazes to the ocean, is longer by at least 35 miles, and it does not have to cross a state line to be so. (When its biological headwaters are considered, the St. Johns becomes at least 310 miles long—which is 65 miles longer than the entire Suwannee.)

Certainly, figuring the size of a river is tricky business all by itself: The "mainstem" or main channel of a river is usually considered its "length." But a river may have literally hundreds of miles of tributaries, branches, sloughs, and spring runs in its larger ecological system. And it is the watershed itself—all that vast terrain that drains into a river system—that is the key to its health. A challenge in appreciating rivers is to help modern Floridians understand that, although they may live miles from a channel, their actions trickle down to it through the valley-like watershed. Indeed, people who preceded them may have chosen their geographic home because of its location in the scheme of all things. In a state as wet as Florida, it was always wise to know exactly what was up and downstream.

If modern rivers suffer an identity crisis because their place in the gestalt of the landscape is often misunderstood, they must also endure a more immediate challenge. We have five "water management districts" in Florida, which seduces us into thinking our rivers are well-protected. But, while these districts have the statutory power to link growth to water availability, they seldom do so. Indeed, most of the time they only pretend to conserve water via a series of conservation plans that are not mandatory. Wealthy developers and politicians are aware of this delusion. Thus, they will allow the districts to "manage" water on their behalf, and will likely do so right up to the point where there is no water left to manage.

As the aquifer and its springs decline, some districts are now scheming to commandeer flowing river water. Yet at the same time, other agencies charged with tourism promotion are making great hay out of our aquatic assets in the name of nature tourism. This dilemma seems the best example of "negative capability"—of being able to hold two diametrically opposed ideas in your head at once and to still function. This conflicted approach to river management also takes on a spectacular twist that George Orwell would have appreciated: Rivers are classified at sequential levels according to how clean they are—Class One is drinkable, while Class Three should only be used for boating. For instance, the more rural upper St. Johns is rated "Class One," while the more congested lower river is "Class Three." Florida's Department of Environmental Protection, which also oversees the water management districts, has even proposed increasing the levels of classification in order to keep from designating more rivers as damaged or impaired. Certainly, it's far easier to indulge in "spin" than it is to protect the quality of a water body.

Confused? So was I for a long time. At some point, I decided to forsake logic—since it wasn't getting me anywhere—and to make a point to become more intimate with rivers in the hope intimacy would lead to a new way of understanding. I would stand in rivers to my chest to fly-fish, swim in them, paddle over them, snorkel and dive under them, and camp on their shores. I would experience them with friends, especially those willing to open themselves to the nuances and quirks and glories of the river's spirit. I would read of them in nonfiction books and novels, essays and poems, and scientific reports. I would delight when I found an old map that traced a meander or illustrated a branch that no longer existed.

Sometimes I would go out on a river alone, shouldering my kayak to the edge of the water at the ocher light just before dusk, and paddle until it was well after dark. Dipping my paddle sparingly to steer, I would drift downstream with the slight current, not unlike a patch of floating hyacinths. Alone in the river darkness, I would breath slowly and imagine myself as nearly invisible. Wading birds would screech from the dense riverine forest, fish would smack the surface to feed, and alligators would begin their slow patient survey of the dark primal water, reclaiming the river as completely as the night itself. Without the noise of my clumsy modern ego to drown everything out, the river would regain its preeminence and grace, and when I had the courage to allow it, it would rise up to touch my soul. If I were lucky, I could reach a singular place nurtured by the full emotional sway of bliss, of respect, of fear. It was an experience beyond the safeguard of the intellect.

Once, after spending years around a river, I wrote a book about it. In doing so, I talked to scientists and river dwellers and read everything I could find—from research papers to poetry—on the subject. Even then, I could not capture it fully, for to write about a river is not unlike sculpting clay that is never put into a kiln. The subject is malleable, something that is continually remolded over time. If we expect it to stay put, we are badly mistaken, for rivers—even those bulkheaded and channelized—tend to break loose every once in a while. Secrets, hidden well, slowly reveal themselves like totems in the benthic mud. Rivers have a mystic quality to them, a way of helping us remember something we thought we had forgotten.

The process of appreciating Florida rivers has nothing whatsoever to do with ownership or territoriality. To love a river enough to want to write about it, paint it, or compose a song to it is to have the capacity to at once hold tight to it—and, just as completely, to let it go.

8

B. B. King & Beluthahatchee
in St. Augustine

It's midday Friday, and I'm on I-95, moving upstream toward St. Augustine in an asphalt riptide. This is not a particularly comforting behavior for me, so I calm myself by slipping in a CD and listening to B.B. King. B.B. is telling of meeting the Queen of England early one morning on the streets of London. The Queen, just back from a party, rolls down the window of her limo, and—lamenting the great confusion she must face in the world—asks B.B. for some advice. The bluesmeister tells her: Better not look down if you want to keep on flying. I always figured he meant: Don't over think it, darling.

The wake of a boat I'm in at the moment churns up the tea-colored tannic river water. While this tannic water is characteristic of many rivers and creeks in Florida and the southeast, this particular shot is from the St. Johns.

And now I am passing over the rain-swollen St. Johns, traveling beyond the Tomoka—which I make a point to always see because its subtropic shores enthrall me—and then, farther north, over the spartina marsh that leads to this oldest of Florida cities. Once here, I dodge the horse-drawn tourist carriages, and at the ritzy and historic Casa Monica relinquish my car to an enthusiastic valet kid and check in.

I'm here for a writers' conference, one of those otherworldly events where people who spend an inordinate time inside their heads actually attempt to communicate with their fellow humans. The venue is Flagler College, which was once railroad czar Henry Flagler's grandiose Hotel Ponce de Leon. I leave the Casa Monica, another Flagler edifice, and head out for a session I'm to lead across the campus. On the way, I run into Stetson Kennedy. Stetson's cool, far more so than most folks one-fourth his age, a man confident enough in his abilities to not punish others with his ego. He's researched and written perceptively about Florida and its people, first in the WPA Writers' Project in the 1930s and later in a courageous book that exposed the power the Klan once had in this unreconstructed "Sunshine State." He was poking about the back roads here when he was nineteen. At this time, he's ninety-one, a little trick of time switching those digits around backward, like someday they will do for us all if we live long enough. He's in a guyabera, a small, compact guy, but with a strong sense of life engagement about him, and he's walking alone down the street, no entourage or fanfare, just Stetson as Stetson, which I figured he's always been. I embrace him, and we continue walking toward one of the Flagler buildings, where we will be in different sessions.

As a young man, Stetson roamed the state with his team of writers, talking at great length with African Americans to better understand how they saw the world. It was a brave thing to do in a time when the fiercely racist Florida was still deeply segregated. It was especially so in that one of the team members he led was Zora Neal Hurston. The richness and imagination of the oral histories was stunning, inventing safe and happy places to give solace to people who otherwise wouldn't have it. Stetson learned of mythic sanctuaries like "Beluthahatchee," a blissful refuge where "all unpleasant doings and sayings are forgiven and forgotten." Back in the 1950s, Stetson bought a remote slice of land and water south of Jacksonville to live; friends like Woody Guthrie would come and hang with him, rejoicing in the spirit that bound creative souls together against the big chill outside. Stetson named his rustic and unpretentious country retreat "Beluthahatchee."

In contrast, this Flagler College, built in the late 1800s, is as flamboyant and in-your-face as it gets, lots of fountains and steeples and cupolas and an intricate bas relief weave of fish and frogs and angels, all jammed together at once. The style is Spanish Renaissance Revival, and it was one of the first structures in the nation to be electrically wired. The sum total is a whack-upside-the-head reminder that the rich are, indeed, different from you and me. Flagler cofounded Standard Oil, and later, saw Florida as a sort of fiefdom that he would open to the rest of the world via his railroad line and his extravagant hotels. As long as his guests didn't stray too far from their accommodations, they could have an experience that—except for the sunshine—had almost nothing to do with the prevailing backwoods culture of the time. In a way, those luxury hotels were not unlike today's theme parks in that they were grafted onto the landscape, rather than woven into it. Like so many obsessed and uber-wealthy Florida folks, Flagler was way off the grid, and a tangible thread of his mania remains here, embedded in the architecture. His contemporary, the renegade cane planter Ed Watson, wanted to be the Flagler of the western Glades, but destiny would have it otherwise.

Stetson is headed off to his own workshop session, but before he goes, he grabs me gently by the arm, just to slow me down a bit so, in case I might want to, I can listen. He wants to tell me a little story about Zora. His voice lowers an octave or two, and he begins telling me of a unique-to-Florida tale that Hurston had collected from the poor and put-upon black folks of Florida's Great Depression. Within just a few moments his composure changes, and it seems as if he is channeling the spirit and even the cadence of another time. Now, Stetson is no longer ninety-one but twenty-four or twenty-five, and he remembers everything there is to be remembered: "And so, Zora says: 'One day God was on his way to Palatka, him and St. Peter, walking there. And they were so busy with the latest bunch of angels that had just arrived at the Pearly Gates, that they didn't notice the Devil who was hiding just up ahead, behind a big ol' stump. But the Devil was waiting, and right then at the last minute he jumped out from the stump and hollered 'Christmas Gift!' (There's a lot of subtext to this story, but the best I can figure is this was a Southern version of Trick-or-Treat, and that when a person was surprised in this way, he had no choice but to relinquish a gift.) So the Devil had done caught God by surprise, and God had to give him something. And God, He thinks about this for a bit, and He finally says: *Take the East Coast* (of Florida). And that's how come the Florida east coast got so many mosquitoes, and scorpions, and hurricanes, and all of that stuff—because it belongs to the Devil!'" Stetson smiles, pats me on the back, and disappears inside an ornate Flagler portal. I shake my head, realizing I've just traveled back eighty years or so to another world, not even expecting to do so, a bit of folk wisdom still vivid and alive, almost as if it all just happened. And that may be the biggest gift—for real—that anyone can give to a guy like me who's so appreciative of the values and the stories of another time.

I find my way to my own session in which writer Les Standiford and I are to talk "In Conversation." I've read Les's work—he is a skilled storyteller of both fiction and nonfiction, and I've always looked forward to chatting with him, although not necessarily in front of a group of people. A guy who impersonates Mark Twain introduces us to the audience—this is, after all, Florida, and people can be just about anything they want. And then Les and I chew the fat for forty-five minutes or so until Mark Twain asks the audience for questions. I make a point to remind folks that Kipling once wrote that the magic of literature is not in the man but in the words. Les and I chuckle at this, knowing the best of ourselves is not in this public moment but in the doing, in wanting to raise higher ideals to a place we can barely describe right now.

The session over, I walk out to sign books. An attractive, dark-haired woman in the session walks out with me and tells me of once reading an essay that I wrote about bears in the woods, a narrative that laments the way we are losing our wildness in modern Florida. She says it moved her to tears, and I thank her for having the heart to tell me that. I sign books, shake hands, go back to my fancy hotel and put on a sport coat, and return for a showing of our PBS film *In Marjorie's Wake* in the massive Flagler-era dining room. Like much of the rest of the compound, the room is over-the-top in aesthetics and its own mythology: More angels and seraphims and gargoyles and cosmic stuff in great arched domes and atop stained glass windows. When I arrive, young students from the college are finishing up their cafeteria meals. In one corner, there are inflatable plastic palm trees and sharks, and Buffett's "Fins" is playing.

I meet Holly, an enthusiastic, young undergrad who helps me set up the projector for the film screening. Students are leaving and the high-backed, ornate wooden chairs are rearranged to accommodate the newly arriving audience, which is now pushing against a rope across the wide dining room entrance. The rope opens, the crowd descends, and our movie is ready to play. I briefly introduce the documentary, explaining that it tells of a 1933 river trip author Marjorie Rawlings once made on the St. Johns with her neighbor Dessie Prescott. Then I stand back while the 150-odd folks soak it in for the next hour. I notice the plastic palm trees and sharks have deflated by now.

After the film, Betty Jean Steinshouer, an informed and animated scholar who impersonates Rawlings, spends the next forty-five minutes nailing both the mannerisms and the persona that once distinguished the mercurial Florida author; no script, just going with it from the heart. Rawlings leaves and Betty Jean returns as herself, filling in the blanks about why she is impassioned to do what she does. I think some about Rawlings, about what it took for her to not only move to Cross Creek in 1928, but to stay there and learn after her husband Charles left her. I wonder if, by courting comfortable modern lives, we have lost something essential that dwells in the spirit. If given the choice, I figure I might rather live in Rawlings's time, might rather dream of a real place like Beluthahatchee. I awake from my reverie long enough to hear Betty Jean generously praise both Stetson and myself as "national treasures," and I quietly turn a bit red from embarrassment.

The show is over, and I mingle out into the grand lobby. Several folks say very nice things about the film. One middle-aged woman—who is reminiscent of Rawlings's own description of a Cross Creek neighbor as an "efficient and angry canary"—accosts me, making fun of the "national treasure" thing. But she does so without smiling. "Does that mean you're irreplaceable?" she asks, intending to mock. "No," I say. "It means I'm recyclable." She mutters something and walks away. I remind myself that films will attract a different audience than a literary reading since attending a movie doesn't require much, just a willingness to sit quietly in the dark.

It's hot here in Florida, even at 9:00 p.m., and sweating, I stroll out by myself, over to my hotel, and standing there on the outside patio, watch the grand old Florida architecture flicker to life around me. It could be an intricate movie set for a Gatsby scene, but the solidness of the structure communicates far more to the soul. It is Florida, but like most of our place-based romantic tableaus, it is so much more—almost more than the human imagination can absorb. I think of the woods and creeks and people of Stetson's Florida, think of all those brave, off-the-grid artists and field workers with kindness in their hearts, and realize how fortunate I am to know of, and to newly meet them, every now and again.

And then I exhale big, like I always do when clearing my spirit of confusion. And I think of the blissful refuge of Beluthahatchee, think of a place where all wrongdoings are forgiven and forgotten. As I do, I remember B.B. King's own advice: Better not look down if you want to keep on flying.

9

Inside a Florida Spring
without a GPS

I always look forward to a midweek run up into the Ocala National Forest because it reminds me of how diverse our peninsula can be—and, of how far removed our interior is from the Florida vision that's often peddled to the rest of the world. On the drive today, the brilliant Florida winter sun illuminates the ancient white sand under the gentle, rolling hills and swales of pine and scrub. There are few places on earth where the landscape actually seems incandescent as it does today, paleo-sand

Fern Hammock Springs in the Ocala National Forest. Fern Hammock is a series of small boils that well up and create a stream that confluxes with the Juniper Creek a bit downstream from Juniper's headspring.

shoals glowing just like they once did when under the shallows of an emerald sea a million years ago.

In no time, I'm off of U.S. 19 and onto the old Ft. Butler Road that will lead me to the entrance of Juniper Springs Recreational Area. Although I was here to paddle the run of Juniper not so long ago, I've actually spent little time poking around in the hammocks around it. Unlike so many of our springs that are recharged in uplands soaked with fertilizers and septic leaks, Juniper is not afflicted with nutrient loads that can turn spring waters light green. Tucked away in the forest here, Juniper is fed by the pure rainwater that seeps down through the healthy, intact scrub, tiny bits of silica polishing the water until it's so pure it seems distilled. The St. Johns River Water Management District, entrusted to care for these springs and all others within its region, contends Juniper has lower "dissolved solids" than most Florida springs, thus allowing for a clearer, more bluish water. *Dissolved solids* is a nice way of saying what-happens-when-humans-step-heavy-on-the-earth.

If the transparent waters of Juniper Creek can be considered a theater, then I'm headed backstage to better understand the dynamics— the natural rigging and scaffolding and lighting that bring this sweet spring system to life. Today is special for another reason: I'm looking forward to meeting Margaret Ross Tolbert here, an artist who has, over the last twenty-five years, literally immersed herself in the springs of north Florida. Back on dry land, she paints what she has seen below, transporting her subaquatic vision to the terrestrial world, brush strokes and splashes and feathering that translate the spring through the language of its reflection and its sensory *pull*.

On my way in, I get directions from the ranger at the gate that will take me beyond the main headspring of Juniper to another set of springs— Fern Hammock—that are a bit farther back in the woods. It is where Margaret suggested we meet. I park and walk down there, up and over a little arching bridge to a low wooden bench. Unlike the larger headspring, Fern Hammock is not bulkheaded nor is it as open. The oaks and sweetgums and sabal palms here close in overhead on the transparency below, as if protecting it. A run or "branch" carries the spring waters off for about six hundred feet, where it meets the Juniper Springs creek;

from there, they'll flow another ten miles or so through the vast Juniper Prairie Wilderness to the St. Johns River at Lake George.

Fern Hammock is actually not one single large spring, but some twenty-five smaller ones, and they arise not from dark limestone "vents" but emerge as sand boils. Some seem as blue as Windex, others white from the fine sand that roils up from the soft rocky karst far below. It looks almost like a diorama someone dreamed, so electric it seems plugged in. The water management folks periodically measure the age of water that naturally pumps out of springs in their district. Fern Hammock, they figure, has an "adjusted carbon-14 age of approximately 2,000 years." If that's accurate, then that also explains why the water here is so clear and blue: The preindustrial humans who lived or traveled across the recharge hills for these springs did so in a time when stepping lightly was the only option they had.

Margaret arrives soon enough after a drive down from Gainesville. Our plan today is to come up with a strategy for a joint presentation we're to give on the springs of the St. Johns. We figure it makes a lot more sense to meet outdoors at a spring than in some human-built structure. She's a striking woman with black hair and dark eyes, a talented artist who also has a wonderful sense of humor about where we are on earth, just now for this moment. We sit on a wooden bench at the edge of Fern Hammock, and I think the many little springs in front of us seem to be re-creating themselves, painting their lives into existence with water and color and light. We chat some, share some ideas. I know several brilliant artists who paint nature—some are wonderfully enriched souls who render their singular visions of landscapes onto canvas with great verve and style. But I've never met one of this quality who also has the spirit to go *inside*.

I guess I've done this with my own research, snorkeling and diving into springs and the rocky chasms that funnel water to them. But like Margaret, I've done this only as a means—as a tool—to understand, to feel the pulse of an ever-changing world that seems at once real and make-believe. This seems a rare and lonely business because most of those I know who go into springs and caves as divers are more often than not obsessed with the technical logistics of the exercise rather than examining what the art of the experience reveals. It is not unlike those paddlers who make arduous topside journeys on our rivers. For those folks, a GPS coordinate has far more meaning than a metaphor.

Art and poetry return human passion to the experience, reminding us of the universal bond of nature and the soul. Philosopher Joseph Campbell has told of exploring this bond, of forging a journey not just into an unknown landscape—but also into the collective unconscious where myths endure. This is the "Hero's Journey," made not just for the sake of chest-pounding or trinket-buying, but for returning with a gift, a story, a shard of a myth—something to allow the community you left behind valuable insight into that secret and difficult place. It is so much more than scrutinizing digital numbers and lines on a tiny screen.

This all fascinates me, and I figure just hanging out some should be a dandy reinforcement for my own senses. Stuck here in the world of words, I never learned to paint anything more than wood on a house. Nevertheless, being able to look at magic anew always stirs me. Beyond her impressionistic grasp of the ever-shifting vibrancy of springs, Margaret has also invented a "supernatural" being to help us take ordinary ideas underwater—and, by doing so, to make them extraordinary. That being is named "Sirena"—for the mythic sirens, and indirectly, for the family of manatees that bring us so much delight. Of Sirena, Tolbert has written: "Rarely sighted, when seen she seems preoccupied with everyday pursuits. Sometimes, we see her in the midst of more fabulous exploits . . . poised on the abyss before another contest with the unknown."

Like all great artistic and natural mysteries, Sirena can never be fully captured, because the mystery will cease to be so, and she will vanish. She is the essence of the springs herself, at once both fragile and dynamic, charged with the movement of light. Sirena's face is never fully seen in the series of underwater photos that try to capture her, and of course, that makes her even more mythic. To say Sirena is Margaret's alter ego would be presumptuous; perhaps Margaret is Sirena's alter ego.

And so, Sirena exists only underwater inside a spring. And because Margaret has a wonderful freewheeling sense of humor, Sirena also appears at different times with an umbrella, with a clock, with a tennis racquet. Often she is wearing a long dress, shoes, and even a straw hat. She is slender, elegant, her face always turned away, searching. Today, Margaret bought some heavy wooden bowling pins from eBay and wants to see if they will stay put on the bottom, along with the lawn bowling ball. (The ball does; the pins don't.) And so, in her next emergence, Sirena will bowl.

Although the eventual photos of Sirena are captivating and mysterious, the actual moment of creation can sometimes be . . . discordant . . . for those who are there simply to recreate. "It's funny," she says, smiling, "whenever people see us getting into the water with the dress and tennis racquets and all the other stuff, they immediately get out."

I think of this some more, and then we walk about, looking for new containers of liquid light hidden away in the dark green gloom of the subtropical forest. Margaret uses a word I have never heard to describe our springs, and it is a very good one. The word is *aleotropic*, which means "having all properties, at once." They absorb, reflect, and liquefy, all the while seeming both real and not. To dive into a spring is also to dive into a cloud, a shaft of sunlight, a tree canopy. We see little bream, hanging in place like mobiles over the transparency; see more sand boils, roiling, like the ones that Marjorie Kinnan Rawlings once used at Silver Glen to spin the flutter wheel of little Jody Baxter. We see mysticism come to life, and light refracted in ways only God could have ever imagined. We feel that special Florida mythology of ancient wonder, where a hidden energy bores its way out of the soft rock and sand below us and imbues the natural world with its touch, just for now.

And then we leave, returning home to our words and our brushes and our imaginations. And when we go, we take just a little bit of the magic with us, determined and certain that one day we will again pull it back out of where it lives in our hearts and return it to the world. And, it will be made somehow different by its travels within.

A week after I return home, Margaret sends me photos of Sirena on another adventure. In this one, she uses an old manual sewing machine on the sandy bottom of a spring to sew a long, flowing fabric of some sort. In one frame, Sirena is shown in the cusp of the clear spring water, right where the red-brown tannins of the river meet the ether of the spring. It suggests a place where the light meets—and is swallowed by—the unknown.

I write back and say perhaps Sirena is now trying to stitch together the Jungian unconscious with the conscious, to make all whole and righteous. I think of the timelessness of spring water that has been in the dark rock for two thousand years, and how fleeting our own human thoughts and actions can seem in comparison. Then I add: "Then again, maybe Sirena is simply saying: *Sew What?*"

10

What the Road
to Nowhere Reveals

The "Bridge to Nowhere" was built across the Wekiva River back in the 1950s as part of a development scheme to construct an international jetport and a virtual city inside the heart of the swamp of this river. The plan stalled, and was then abandoned. The road that was to cross the bridge and swamp was thankfully never built. Thus, we have the "bridge to nowhere." In this way, it's symbolic of the grow-at-all-cost mentality that swept across Florida over the last half of the twentieth century—regardless of laws against damage to wetlands, the aquifer, the springs, and so on.

Early this morning, I drive out to Rock Springs Run State Reserve for a solo walk-about. SR 46, once a quiet two-lane country road, takes me there, out beyond the fancy sprawl of "Dunwoody Commons" and the gated upscale community named "Bella Foresta." Sure sounds like Florida, eh? Along the way, I pass the sign reminding me I have entered the "Wekiva River Basin," zip across one bridge over the river, and another smaller one that allows black bears to cross under it instead of becoming roadkill on the asphalt atop it. That's because this once-quiet country road has increased tenfold in traffic over just a few years, and has become ground zero for road-killed bears in the state. The sprawl of the oddly named "European" shopping plazas and walled developments have done this, as if the insatiable, greedy need to slather the native landscape with an overblown McMansion lifestyle is justified as long as it sounds remotely exotic.

I turn into an old paved road with faded orange median strips at the state reserve. Back in the late 1950s, real estate developers built this 1.8-mile road with the idea of staging a megacommercial center here. A bridge across the Wekiva near the old marina on the other side of the river would connect with the road, and a dandy new jetport would have become what the Orlando airport is today. Except it all would have been smack in the middle of the spectacularly diverse biological terrain that cradles the Wekiva River. The fact that this did not happen makes me believe there is hope, even here, and that maniacal schemes placing giant airports and fast money above wildlife and swamps and springs don't always prevail.

I park where the developer's old road dead-ends into a little grassy lot next to a trailhead kiosk, shoulder my backpack, and continue heading southward, except now on foot. It is early February in Florida, bright sun overhead and almost no breeze. Even the clouds seem motionless in the deep blue sky above. The trail takes me past a restored sand pine scrub community, the earth so white it seems like it was kicked up by waves just yesterday. Like other scrub communities, it is higher than most everything else, the steep rise of its ancient dune still prevailing.

Although a sign back on the kiosk warns hikers to stay on the trail so they don't get lost, I take every chance I can to get off of it, following narrow animal paths through thick bushes of wild blueberry and gallberry, beyond head-high stands of saw palmettos, through now-dry ephemeral ponds, brittle grasses crackling underfoot.

A couple miles of this leads me to a series of fire break roads, and I take the second one because I want to see how some hooded pitcher plants that live there are doing. The gullies in the road are almost always soggy with rainwater, allowing bog-loving plants to migrate out of the wet flatwoods and onto the path. I start spotting the carnivorous plants soon enough, and am not surprised they have been battered by the dormancy of winter. I stoop down and pick up one dead stem, peeling the throat of the plant back with the blade of my small pen knife. As I do, I see the residue left from a banquet of insects—indigested shards of fly wing, beetle leg, a glimmer of a tiny carapace. On the ground nearby, I see a lone sundew, another meat-eater, one that uses the sticky cilia on its flattened leaves to do the same work of the pitcher plant. When Bartram stumbled across the sundew during his visits to Florida, he called them "sportive vegetables," and I chuckle at that notion.

The water on the trail, just a few puddles at first, deepens and finally makes it impassable. I turn around, headed for a dry fire break road to the south that promises to transport me deeper into the low flatwoods. As I do, I hear the song of a familiar bird, one I know from my childhood growing up on the Eastern Shore of Maryland. It's a robin, and I stop in my tracks and look closer at a large sand pine. There's a dozen or so of the birds in the tree, and another dozen nearby. They're migrating, heading back north so they can be there when all the little boys who love nature can spot the First Robin of Spring by early March, and then excited by the discovery, run in and tell their moms, just like I used to do.

I keep up a good pace, stopping only now and then for a swig of water or to snap a photo of something that strikes me. In the nearby understory, I spot something shiny and blue, neither of which are natural qualities for an object of this size. I approach it cautiously and see that it is a dead balloon, drifted away during a moment of distant childhood party joy and, finally bereft of gas, settled down here for its final landing. Lost helium balloons will drift anywhere, of course. But when they settle in a more heavily populated landscape, they are swept up, run over, or stuck in the trash. Here, in a place where no one lives and few visit, they fall from trees down onto the ground, and there they usually stay.

There are few animal tracks today and only a lone pile of bear scat. I have seen bears before, although rarely; more common are white-tailed deer, wild turkey, even hogs. Once a small yearling deer, spooked by a hiking partner twenty or so yards in front of me, ran as fast as it could to escape, and despite its relatively small size, I could feel the intensity of its terror and strength as it brushed me.

Plants have always fascinated me, and I marvel at how they change with the landscape, not unlike how human cultures change with geography, languages and beliefs transformed over thousands of years by the presence—or absence—of rivers and mountains and islands. As the flatwoods around me also become more flooded, I veer off onto another slightly higher animal trail and end up inside a stand of sawgrass, stopping to run my fingers along the sharp serrations of the blades. It is a tactile acknowledgment of the plant's name, a sedge with blades of tiny organic saws. I muddle about some, jumping from one unmarked wildlife trail to another, and stumble over more pitcher plants. This time, some state biologist with enough savvy to get a grant has marked each with little flags on a metal pin; sometimes, the flags have labels with indented numbers. I see two: 529 and 530, and I hope they started counting at one and not at 500.

Pitcher plants are rare and protected in Florida; that's because the special acidic bogs where they like to spend their lives are often in the country where developers find cheap, soggy real estate to squander. With a promise to "mitigate" and rebuild these wetlands elsewhere, they often get away with whatever they can. However, re-created bogs often need decades of time to readjust their chemistry to create the special conditions carnivorous plants like this require. With their capacity to capture their own nitrogen on the hoof, the pitcher plants prefer bogs with low nitrogen. That allows them to better compete for space in the terrain with other plants that are not dependent on the same needs. I stop, sit on my haunches, drink more water. I'm about five miles back in now. I'm confident the brilliant winter day will allow me a good two hours of sun to hike back out before darkness begins to settle atop this remote Florida landscape. Funny, but while I much enjoy the company of others on the trails, I feel somehow buoyed that I am here alone, responsible fully for my own devices, my own happiness. It is something to know enough of the land and the movement of the sun so you can find your own way, sometimes without consulting maps or even compasses. I'm confident it's instinct that guides me in such matters, a trusting of the genetic coding that will guide us all, if we stop long enough to allow it to be heard.

I turn to go, but spot an old fire break road that looks familiar. I go to it and walk a ways down, far enough to see it has been abandoned and is no longer maintained like the others. Sabal palms and small oaks are growing in the middle of it, but compared to the untrimmed woods, it's easy to navigate. As I walk along, something that has been hidden in my heart rises up and I feel a lump in the back of my throat. It is the trail I once took three or four years ago when hiking with my buddy Steve, and my best animal friend, Shep, a sensitive, intrepid sheltie that seemed always on the verge of wanting to speak. Shep loved these trails as much as any dog can love anything on earth. He would trot a dozen yards or more ahead, stopping once in a while to look over his shoulder at us, panting, wagging his tail, a dog made so happy with a moment and place, knowing his humans were close behind.

Shep is gone now. But the feeling he is here at this moment on this trail is so strong that it mimics reality, like a morning dream when images and experiences seem more real than life itself. I see his eyes now, looking up at me, expecting me to always be the best I can be. For that is what good dogs expect of their human companions.

I walk along, quiet in my thoughts as the sun dips lower toward the tree tops. The songs of a flock of migrating birds, anxiously preparing a roost for the evening, seem somehow more pronounced than ever. I hear a distant call of a barred owl coming from somewhere on the trail I have just left. Like the roosting migrants, it too seems amplified. A light wind picks up and moves through the tops of the sand pine and myrtle and scrub oak, softly rustling the branches, needles, and leaves as if they were strips of velvet. I have burrowed so far inside myself that nature is left to rejoice without the heavy weight of my humanity.

It is not until I have covered almost another five miles and come within sight of the trailhead kiosk just before dusk that I realize I have turned inward because I have been praying. I have been praying for my now-gone little sheltie, praying for all those trails where his spirit once led us—sometimes with others, sometimes just ourselves. Absently, I think if I had otherworldly powers, I could chart those memory trails across the heartscape of my own soul, just as a topo map charts the features in the landscape. In this way, I could map out the isobars of every sensory moment—each scent of a wildflower and waft of a breeze, each eager smile of discovery, each tail-wag of pure joy. And then I realize I just have.

11

Why You Should Care About a Little Cabin in the Woods

An old Cracker-style cabin built by the family of the renowned Florida naturalist Archie Carr. Carr's father had it built outside of Umatilla not long after the family first moved to Florida. It was used as a retreat for hunting, fishing, and just relaxing in the solitude of the Florida wilderness. When complete, the restoration will allow the U.S. Forestry Service to use the iconic cabin to help visitors better understand the Carr's knowledge of natural Florida.

It took a journey to Nicaragua some years ago to remind me how important the great naturalist Archie Carr and his work had been to the preservation of wild places—wild places in Florida, in Nicaragua, everywhere. I was there to write a magazine story, and although I had a working knowledge of ecology, it didn't dawn on me to focus on a single species to help others understand concepts like animal migration, habitat protection, and the need to use environmental boundaries—and not political ones—to "manage" our natural world.

Dr. Jeanne Mortimer, who had studied herpetology under Carr at the University of Florida, was working there at the time with the Miskito Indians of Nicaragua's Caribbean coast. The Miskitos, known locally as the "Turtle People" because they hunted sea turtles, were involved in a project to set up a massive marine preserve along the coast. Rather than excluding indigenous people from such management plans—as many otherwise well-meaning programs will do—this one meant to more fully include them. However, poor countries like Nicaragua have little money to help support such high-minded strategies; when you're hungry, a turtle is no different than a grouper or a lobster or a queen conch. It provides immediate food, and for a certain overseas market, cold cash.

"Sea turtles are very political," Mortimer told me one day in Puerto Cabezas, pushing her matted blonde hair back from her face. It was hot and we were both sweating. We were having lunch in a little bodega-like restaurant with no windows, and a barefoot young man was going table to table, trying to sell us some green turtle eggs in a plastic bowl. The eggs, with a leather-like texture, were as white as alabaster; sand from their nest still clung to the shells. The egg vendor didn't faze Mortimer. "It's a poor country," she said. "People have to eat." By night, this Puerto Cabezas was lawless, sometimes marked by gunfire. One day, I walked the dusty main street and saw a shop owner on the ground outside his store, picking out maggots from his supply of dry rice.

As for the "politics" of the sea turtle, the biologist explained that a species that migrated such vast distances to feed, breed, and nest was a working example of ecology. "Turtles depend on a multitude of geographic places to survive," Mortimer said. Despite the turtle hunting along the Miskito Coast, it was more likely that very wealthy people elsewhere were contributing to the demise of the sea turtle by building seafront homes on beaches where the animal had historically nested, and polluting the waters in which the turtles spent most of their lives.

Fast-forward to today and to an unexpected call I just received from Ray Willis. Ray's a good ol' Florida boy who also happens to have a doctorate in archaeology from the University of Florida. I met Ray a few years ago at Silver Glen Springs in the Ocala National Forest while producing a state PBS film on the early naturalist Billy Bartram and his travels to Florida. I had earlier called the United States Forest Service office and asked if there was anyone around who could speak about the history of Florida on camera. A woman with a soft drawl told me the entire USFS archaeological staff would be glad to help me out. And then she chuckled. The entire archaeological staff turned out to be Ray.

We walked around the edge of Silver Glen Spring later that day, and Ray helped me understand the lifeways of the native people who had lived there long before the Europeans arrived. Ray had always struck me as someone who cared very much about Florida, someone who wanted others to understand a state that was so often misunderstood. Like well-educated good ol' boys will sometimes do, Ray also hid a brilliant and perceptive intelligence inside a persona outfitted in khaki and camo.

Today, Ray told of a situation that was both a dilemma and a blessing. A little Cracker-style cabin and forty-six acres of land in a corner of the Ocala National Forest had been donated to the USFS by Dr. Tom Carr, a noted physicist and, at ninety-one, the surviving brother of Archie. The tin-roofed cabin near Lake Nicotoon was built in 1938 by the parents of Tom and Archie a few years after they first moved to Florida. Indeed, pastor Archie Carr Sr. came here with his wife and family to serve as minister for the local Presbyterian church in Umatilla. After their arrival, Mrs. Carr played the piano in the church and taught music to local children, while Pastor Carr ministered to his flock and got to know the lay of the land. There were less than two million people living in Florida then and most of them were in towns and resorts scattered along the coast. The interior of Florida was a more tropical slice of the deeply rural South—Alabama and South Carolina—where the Carrs had lived earlier.

Pastor Carr, an avid hunter and fisherman, continued to develop his love of the outdoors, and with his wife, helped introduce the Florida version of it to the five Carr children via the cabin retreat. Like many of the lakes in the forest, the one-square mile Lake Nicotoon was clear and sandy bottomed, and it was barely a hundred yards from the front door stoop. The pastor built small wooden rowboats by hand, and the Carrs fished from them. Sometimes, Archie Jr. would come out and row the boat by himself around Nicotoon. Archie later became known as an excellent nonfiction writer who could tell a great story that made science sound exciting and down to earth, but then, he was just learning the craft. When he began to write, one of his first stories was about deer hunting. It melded the sportsman's passion for the woods and the animals with his own growing knowledge of the nuances of science. Entitled "Hound Magic," it explained how deer could actually switch off their scent during a pursuit if they froze still and didn't move. The article was sold to *Field & Stream* for $100. The money paid for a screened porch on the front of the cabin, facing the lake.

Even though this was well into the twentieth century, much of this untraveled peninsula seemed as wild as it had ever been. Animals like panthers and bears and deer roamed across the rugged landscape of scrub, pine, and oak hammock. During the lifetime of the cabin, three generations of Carrs spent a great deal of time here, using it as a sort of refuge—a place to relax, reflect, and study the unique nature of Florida. It was part Thoreau's cabin at Walden, part Aldo Leopold's "shack" in the woods of Wisconsin. Although as an adult, Archie later had his own family home on Wewa Pond in Micanopy, this early Florida forest retreat gifted him, his wife Marjorie Harris Carr, and his children with the opportunity to deeply experience the subtleties of the singular Florida wilderness without the filter of civilization.

Archie earned his doctorate in zoology from UF in 1937. Although he later traveled widely through Latin America and the Antilles following his beloved sea turtles on the "windward roads" of distant shores, the little cabin in the Ocala woods could be thought of as the place where the spirit and ethic of the larger Carr family was nurtured, a place where a cypress-and-pine-boarded cabin, its brick fireplace, and its wooden-shuttered windows kept the rest of the world in context.

Of the need for preservation, Archie once wrote: "If this difficult saving is done, it will be because man is a creature who preserves things that stir him." And, as Ray Willis explained to me, that is what this little cracker cabin in the woods needs today—for the people who were stirred by Archie's legacy to come to its rescue. It is not unlike what a different band of pilgrims have done for another author's Florida house not so far away at Cross Creek.

When I first went out to visit the cabin with Ray, I was astounded the structure was so dilapidated. "Well," said Ray, "I've never seen a structure in that bad shape that was still standing upright . . . I'm figuring all the vines and bushes growing around it held it up." When Florida began to experience its modern growth boom in the early 1970s, the cabin seemed lost in a state rushing head-on into the future. Then, after a poorly considered causeway was built by the state to put a road across the distant edges of Lake Nicotoon, it turned out the lake was actually fed by a sheet flow of water upstream of the causeway. And then Nicotoon began to dry, and the cabin was virtually abandoned. What Ray Willis has in mind for the structure is no less than a resurrection, a regenerative act that will carefully restore the cabin using the skills of a local Cracker carpenter, augmented with the guidance of heritage preservation specialists. But funding is needed to do this right, and Ray is hoping that all those who've ever appreciated how the Carrs fought for the authenticity and natural integrity of Florida will help.

Certainly, I can be counted among this affected group because Archie's writing has surely stirred me. When I was researching a book on the St. Johns River a few years ago, I sifted through hundreds of articles and research abstracts on the river and its science, and talked to scores of people throughout the river basin. Archie's insight on the St. Johns stood out like a wild river iris in a dark swamp because it both moved and humored me. And it also did what every great teacher wants the students of the world to do—it made me think. Archie was not just a good teacher; he was a courageous man who broke away from the herd, and that's an increasingly rare action in our feel-good modern world. It would have been far safer to have simply inhabited the world of natural history, where the animal itself could be examined, considered, and celebrated without the troublesome real world challenges of government and culture. Nonetheless, Archie joined others in examining these ideas until the pragmatic and whole notion of "Conservation Biology" was born.

And so, today, the complete ecological visions that fully consider ethics, art, geography, culture, and science have come home to roost. Like his wide-roaming sea turtles, these ideals have migrated between Silver Glen Springs, Nicaragua, the Antilles, and now Lake Nicotoon in the Ocala National Forest. The little Carr cabin in the woods hasn't moved an inch over the last seventy-five years, of course. But the ideas nurtured there have been around the world uncounted times inside the hearts of every scientist and writer who ever truly cared enough to stand their ground.

And like a star you wish on at night as a kid, this little dilapidated physical structure provides a steady beacon in our crazy, ever-shifting modern world—and it does so as a place where the very best elements of the human spirit, caring and imagination, reside.

It's the sort of illumination that anyone who cares about our besieged natural Florida can hardly do without.

12

Cedar Key

Scuttling with the Mermaids

I'd been skirting the edges of Florida's "Big Bend" for years, figuring the backwater villages scattered along the geographic armpit of the Panhandle were more than retro enough for my taste. Then I discovered there was a whole new world here, one more natural and wild than I ever imagined. This world is given over to scores of offshore islands protected inside several water-slogged wildlife refuges, a liquid place physically apart from the more accessible mainland. I was hoping a trip inside the refuges might open some new doors, maybe even reveal a secret or two—always a good thing.

It's fitting that naturalist John Muir ended his "1,000-mile walk to the Gulf" here. Alighting somewhere near the "Cedar Keys" in 1867, Muir described the "many gems of palmy islets called keys." Following Muir's lead, I head for the epicenter of the Bend, where several of these

Historic 1884 map of Cedar Key and nearby Atsena Otie Key.

islets are now linked by a series of bridges and causeways that dead-end into the modern day Cedar Key.

The causeway transports me off the mainland, out to where I'm surrounded by water and marsh grass on both sides. As I drive along, mullet splash and brown pelicans cruise, looking for a meal on the hoof. Some wondrous funk catches my attention, and I make a sharp detour at the "Mermaid Landing Cottages." The little Mom-and-Pop compound is all blue and lime-green, lots of whimsical mermaid stuff scattered everywhere, as if some kid with a great imagination has been at play. It seems to teeter precariously on a thin, low slab of land between the roadway and the Gulf. In the midst of everything, I see a handmade sign advertising "kayak rentals." If I'm lucky I can get both a room and a kayak here.

Muir, some say, was whoop-headed from malaria when he finally arrived—which might explain his reported sighting of a *mermaid* with "glistening green scales and the flash of golden hair." Perhaps he even heard music, the siren's ephemeral call. Several years ago, I had a vision like that late one night in the bar of the old wood-framed Island Hotel on Cedar Key, sitting on a stool across from the mural of Neptune, who was cavorting with a blonde sea nymph or two. The longer I was there, the more the bartendress looked like the seductive girl-fish in the mural. The possibilities seemed endless, but . . . you know how such visions often turn out.

At Mermaid's Landing, I walk into what I think is the kayak rental office, and finding no one there, wander through what turns out to be someone's home, beyond an empty wine bottle and a kitty litter box. I'm figuring excursions like this might get you shot in some places in Florida. Back outside, I find an affable fellow who doesn't seem to mind that I've just come out of the front door to his house. He's happy to fix me up with a single kayak for the day, and to top it off, will even rent me a cottage that backs up to the Gulf. The fellow is bearded, lean, lined from the sun, a bit Muir-esque himself. I want to ask about the mermaid thing, but I let it go. I unload my overnight bag in my room and stuff my jug of water and snacks into my backpack. Outside, I stow my pack behind the seat of my rented kayak and climb down into the little boat. Kayaks sit lower in the water than canoes, and generally, allow for much better tracking. Nonetheless, I often feel as if I'm *wearing* a kayak rather than sitting in one.

The springtime day around me is luminous and I'm anxious to get a firsthand look at Muir's "gems of palmy islets." My plan is to paddle out into the Gulf and explore as many of the islands as I can within the Cedar Keys National Wildlife Refuge, and then return before dark. Although the refuge surrounds some of the bridged islands and mainland, I am far more intrigued by the thirteen cays that are off the grid out in the Gulf—wild patches of sand, mangrove, and palms ranging in size from one to 165 acres. As I push off, the mermaid wrangler advises me to avoid returning on low tide when nearly all the water will ebb away from the launch site, leaving me stranded on the mud flats. He also suggests I "keep an eye on the sky." It doesn't take me long to figure he wants me to pay close attention to the potential for thunderheads, which in the warmer months can quickly rise up from the great billowing cumulus and turn the otherwise placid Gulf into a frothing, wave-rolling sea.

An easy forty-five-minute paddle takes me around the southern edge of Cedar Key, winding in and out of mangrove-rimmed creeks, past shabby docks where working clam boats are berthed, and beyond at least two half-sunken wrecks. As I emerge from the labyrinth of water and mud flats, the Gulf of Mexico stretches out before me like a great endless sea, radiant in the sunlight. To my left is the flat Dog Island, and barely a mile ahead, the heavily forested island known as Atsena Otie, the site of the original Cedar Key settlement.

I pause at the edge of the flats, swig down some water, and then point my bow into a steadily growing ridge of incoming waves, heading for Atsena. The horizon, under a warming Florida summer sun, quivers and then dissolves entirely, making the other offshore islands—Seahorse, Grassy, Snake, Deadman's—seem to levitate atop the flat green waters. Overhead, a magnificent frigate soars like an ancient pterodactyl. Brown pelicans dive for fish, and on the shore of Atsena Otie, a yellow-crowned night heron patrols the sliver of feral beach.

Birds don't exist in an ecological vacuum, and their presence here is a clue that the local waters are still healthy enough to keep them happy. As an affirmation of this, a small pod of bottlenose dolphins arch through the water just in front of me, scattering the school of fingerling mullet they're chasing. Approaching Atsena Otie, I pass several sport fishermen who are busy working the island shore from the decks of their small boats, drawn here by the abundance of fish, just like the dolphins. As early as 1818, Atsena was home to a trading post. As the village grew, a rail line and a road spanned bridges to the island, and the Faber company built a mill here to cut lumber for the pencils it made. An 1895 census showed over fifty families living on the key. Some harvested oysters, fish, and green sea turtles; others worked at the Faber mill. But a powerful hurricane blew through in 1896, whacking the mill and most everything else. Foundations of buildings and a cemetery are still here somewhere, phantoms hiding back in the thick hammock of trees.

Wild scrubs and grasses push up to the edge of the island, and I follow along as close to the shore as I can get without grounding. Suddenly, the foliage opens up to reveal a deep, narrow channel, and I paddle into it, having no idea where I might end up. The channel turns out to be a tidal creek that takes me deeper into the middle of the key where it spreads into an expansive, shallow lagoon. It's quiet back in here, a place fully removed from the rest of time. Giant schools of redfish, tailing over oyster beds, scatter in a frenzy of copper colored fins. Mullet seemingly jump for joy, sunlight reflecting off their silver scales like a disco ball from the seventies. I paddle to a thicket of black mangrove bushes, air roots spiking the mud under them. Like the tropical frigates overhead, these stunted wetland trees are in the northernmost limit of their range.

I sit here for a while, savoring the wild solitude, until finally the tide begins to fall, ever so gradually. As it does, it exposes the smaller "coon oysters" growing on the mangrove limbs. The mollusks slam their shells shut, spitting as they do, until the entire lagoon is alive with the soft timpani of the oysters on ebb. The scent of salt and sea and sun-warmed mangroves and sea purslane is palbable. At the top of the tree line, an osprey returns to her giant twig nest with a fish in her talons. These are the sort of moments I live for, unexpected trysts of discovery that both comfort and excite me.

Finally, I turn and paddle back out, following a different creek that delivers me to the windward shore of Atsena, foot-high waves on a steady roll out here. As I move along, a six- to seven-foot shark cruises a few yards away, its dorsal slicing the surface, likely more curious than anything. I figured there was a reason the local high school athletic teams are called the "Cedar Key Sharks."

I paddle north toward Seahorse, passing the low-lying Grassy and the more predominant Snake Key. Seahorse rises dramatically up from its narrow beach, a fifty-two-foot-high relic dune left over from the Pleistocene when the Florida coast extended far out into the Gulf. It's been the home to a lighthouse here since 1854, but unlike the towering lights of Florida's Atlantic coast, this one is squat, benefiting from the elevation of the old dune. In Muir's day, Seahorse was becoming one of the busiest commercial ports on the Gulf. Ships from the nearby Suwannee River regularly steamed through here with cargos of cotton, sugar, and lumber. But when geography is built on sand, fame is fleeting: A deepwater port was dredged in Tampa, and the clear-cutting of cedar decimated the local forests. The 1896 storm that devastated Atsena did the same to Seashore. Islanders left in droves. By 1913 the light was decommissioned.

I put ashore, shake out my arms and legs to free them of cramps from the tight cockpit, and walk to the bottom of the steep dune where "No Trespassing" signs flank the slope. At the top, the stout brick lighthouse is connected to a house-like structure of wood and tin, a gutter from the roof leading to a cistern. The cottage and light have been commandeered by the University of Florida as a marine lab since 1951. The facility's open to the public only a couple days a year during a seafood festival back on Cedar Key. I was here once during this brief time window, and hiked the trail up to the light, under a foliage canopy of live oak, sabal palm and red bay, beyond an understory of wild olive, prickly pear and saw palmetto. I saw a small cemetery with graves for island settlers and light keepers dating to the late 1800s. This islet was originally occupied by pre-Columbians thousands of years ago, and during the Second Seminole War, used as a detention camp for Indians. I wondered how many unmarked native burials might also be here.

Today, I hear a raucous sound coming from the foliage on the dune slope, and looking up, see scores of juvenile brown pelicans—feathers sprouting like thin weeds from their heads—still on their nest. In no time, the salt marsh mosquitoes start to bear down on me like they do in the Glades. I waste no time getting back into my kayak and pushing off.

Back out in the Gulf, I discover the wind has calmed and the once-rolling surface has turned into a large, flat mirror that stretches as far as I can see to the west. The water has also become clear enough that I can look through it, can see the islands that I paddle near are rimmed by halos of shallow seagrass. Together with the oyster bars, salt marshes, sand, and mud flats, it's a great place to be a fish. I remember reviewing an inventory of marine life during my earlier visit to Seahorse: permit roam here, as do grunts, sea trout, barracuda, a dwarf seahorse, and four species of pipefish—which is essentially a seahorse straightened out. The shark I saw earlier could have been a black tip, an Atlantic sharpnose, or a scalloped hammerhead. Minnow-like fish such as silver-side anchovies thrive, as do scallops, lobsters, stone crabs, and anemones. If plants and trees create habitat for wildlife back ashore, their underwater counterparts do the same here, anchoring a larger food chain of life that goes far beyond the water's surface. No wonder Seahorse is also a rookery and a roost for over fifty thousand birds. If there were a mermaid or two about in John Muir's time, I can think of few better habitats where they might want to live.

I turn and paddle hard now, back toward my own temporary habitat on the edge of the sea. The giant torch of a late afternoon sun touches the Gulf waters, backlighting a low bank of cumulus with its burnt umber glow. I move steadily beyond these old keys in a bluish furrow of my own making, back toward a modest civilization of roads and bridges and cars, back to the present tense.

The tide that first began to move when I was in the lagoon on Atsena is getting close to full ebb; a few times, the plastic hull of my kayak scrapes over the top edges of hidden oyster beds. When it does, it scatters schools of thumb-sized baitfish that explode from the shallows in great flashes, like shiny strips of aluminum. Just beyond Atsena, I pass an exposed white sandbar where fiddler crabs scuttle, large claws flexing back and forth. They seem to be forever strumming a miniature song from the salty air, perhaps creating a melody heard only by other fiddlers. I haven't walked a thousand miles, but I have spent most of the day in a small boat in a big sea by myself, and it has been exhilarating.

There are only a few inches of water left atop the mud as I close in on my lime-green mermaid cottage at the edge of the Gulf of Mexico, but for now, it's enough. I realize there *is* music out here on these isolated keys. I think of it less as a siren's song or a fiddler's tune than as a sacred natural hymn. It is music replete with possibilities.

13

Ft. Drum Creek

Monasteries and Baboons in the Map

Ft. Drum Creek is starting to feel a bit mythic, like a Greek god, the Tooth Fairy, or an honest Florida politician. You want to believe it's real, but you're having trouble proving it. The creek—which exists only in theory for now—is a ways from where I live, and not terribly far from the northeastern shores of the gargantuan Lake Okeechobee. By most historic accounts, this Ft. Drum Creek births the north-flowing St. Johns. But more than a century of slicing, dicing, and draining the

Michelle Thatcher trying to get her compass bearings near Ft. Drum Creek just northeast of Lake Okeechobee.

countryside has severed that connection. There are ditches and canals south of Blue Cypress Lake that will lead you into the St. Johns system. But Ft. Drum and its meager flow seem to be stranded from them by a swath of pastures and fields. Maps illustrate this, depicting the dried-out land in white, sometimes gridded by red, geometrically straight lines that represent roads and platted lots.

When he once wrote a book about the Everglades, naturalist Archie Carr imagined following a tiny gambusia, our native mosquitofish, as it navigated its way south of a chain of lakes outside Orlando—downstream through the Kissimmee River, in and out of Lake Okeechobee, and southwest into the Glades—since that is how the "river of grass" historically flowed. I'm suspecting a gambusia with a yen to go north might make it from Ft. Drum into Blue Cypress, Hell 'n Blazes, and then all the way to Jacksonville. But he'd either have to grow legs very quickly or wait to launch his odyssey after a hurricane or series of tropical storms soaks the dried out savannas and marshes in between.

Earlier in the nineteenth century, when Florida's wetlands were intact and the peninsula was literally brimming over with water, a season of plentiful rains raised the rivers, swamps, and creeks everywhere, sometimes inundating the higher berm-like escarpments of compacted shell and sand formed by ancient coastlines. One such north-south scarp divides the south-flowing Kissimmee to the west from the creeks and branches of the north-flowing St. Johns to the east. Another twenty-seven-foot-high scarp a bit south of Ft. Drum Creek separates the headwaters of the St. Johns from the surface hydrology of the Glades.

During particularly wet years on the peninsula before the introduction of dredging, rains might even inundate that particular east-west scarp, allowing a watery connection between Ft. Drum and the Taylor Creek-Okeechobee-Glades system below. In those times, Native Americans from both the Glades and the St. Johns could then paddle far beyond their own territories. A very ambitious gambusia, in turn, could cover the entire state between what is now Jacksonville and Flamingo, at the tip of the southerly Florida cape. Indeed, before it was corseted with the marvels of engineering—canals, permanent ditches, and locks—there was no telling what this wet and warm peninsula might do. Or, as the observant J.W.P. Jenks wrote in *Hunting in Florida* in 1874:

"Though the area of Florida compares with that of New England . . . three fourths of its surface is much of the year under water. The great rains of summer (overflow the marshes) and the sources of the northern flowing St. Johns are confounded with that of the southern flowing Kissimmee. None but wild Indians, cattle-rangers, and naturalists can be expected to wade through its swamps, risk its miasma and brave its dangerous animals."

I am enduring this peculiar miasma today because I have been talked into helping a friend navigate her way from the historic but not-so-wet headwaters of the St. Johns to a place soggy and deep enough to actually float her kayak. From that deeper sluice, she would then spend the next few months paddling northward through the main river system by herself. But, if following this river north to its confluence with the sea east of Jacksonville seems daunting, navigating Ft. Drum Creek today is no less so. Before we drove down here, I spent several evenings examining topographical maps to understand where Ft. Drum starts and stops. Often the river is traced across the sparsely populated landscape by a narrow, winding corridor of green, like a felt tip marker that's lost most of its ink. Sometimes the felt tip creek splits away into a new waterway; sometimes it fades into the cartographical whiteness of nothingness.

Much of the terrain here was historically prairie, Florida's version of a broad, grassy savanna. With the exception of upland sandhills and scrub, most everything on this nearly sea level peninsula could become soggy with the monsoon-like rains of the wet season. But that was before draglines and linear ditches and the slogan "drain to grade" descended on Florida, siphoning off water and drying out most of the "wet prairies." Even the rugged and remote "Allapattah Flats" that historic novelist Patrick Smith once used as a backdrop for his moving stories about Cracker lifeways in the dense interior have become stamped with the red, right angle geometry of man.

Back on the rest of the continent, water cascades down from old volcanic mountains and hills to a lower point, sometimes in the crease of steep valleys. But in Florida, where the prehistoric ocean has more subtlety shaped the land, the direction of any flow is far less certain. Roads and causeways, "old railroad grades," and ditches from years of fragmented "flood control" change all the rules. Sometimes, sloughs and even creeks begin and end with no clear connection to another body of water. To the east, the topo map shows thin scribbles of blue charted as Nubbin and Myrtle Slough, Taylor and Van Swearingen Creek. To the west are Mosquito and Lemkin (likely a phonetic word for "Limpkin") Creeks, Popash Slough, and the once-great Kissimmee River, which is mostly constricted inside an arrow-straight channel known as C-38. It is the Monte Python version of surface water hydrology, a man-imposed science bereft of reason, wherein slivers of water flow until, with no warning, they suddenly vanish as if swallowed up by an impromptu skit.

So here we are, having driven south of YeeHaw Junction across the middle of Florida, passing roads named "Hololo"—a Creek word for roseate spoonbill—and beyond the sites of old Seminole War forts. Most of the forts were situated so a garrison of soldiers could leave one fortress and hike to another in one full day. The modest fort known as Drum was built sometime during the second Seminole Wars in the 1840s, and was located at the crossroads of two military paths leading to Forts Basinger and Vinton, and Forts Kissimmee and Jupiter.

For those who had never seen the dark interior heartland of Florida, this subtropical peninsula and its wild Indians seemed fearsome and exotic, a place where—faced with uncertainty—you could simply make stuff up. "The Knockabout Club in the Everglades," a wonderfully baroque chronicle written in 1887, tells the story of its intrepid party searching for the elusive Lake Okeechobee. This "Great Lake" seemed a Shangri-La sort of place, distinguished with "ruins of castles and monasteries, with carved and ornamental pillars, ruins of Indian cities, dens of pirates containing untold treasures." If that wasn't enough to get the blood flowing, the writers added an extra flourish: "indeed, some ubiquitous party had [once] explored the lake and had found monkeys and baboons."

The real life, hardscrabble village that eventually arose near the site of Ft. Drum after the Civil War had a school and a railroad station and a few pioneer homesteads. Today, while other former "forts" have realized much grander ambitions—Lauderdale, Myers, Pierce—the village of Ft. Drum remains every bit as obscure as it ever was as a fort: At what is mapped as "Ft. Drum" there is a diner, a general store, and a bit down the road, a cemetery. There are also natural features nearby that remind us of the special sea-driven geology of our peninsula. The most obvious is a site once called "Ruck's Pit Quarry" where rock hounds would pay $30 to chisel away at an ancient coastal ridge of Pleistocene-era minerals and seabed fossils. Not surprisingly, "Ruck's Pit" bores down into the escarpment that once defined an ancient lagoon shore, the same shore that today functions as the gently sloping rise that births the St. Johns.

I exit U.S. 441 where Ft. Drum is marked on the map, and drive east toward the creek. Within a few miles, we come to a narrow roadside bridge that marks our starting point. Many bridges—even those that cross spring runs and sloughs—include the name of the water body cut into their concrete walls. But Ft. Drum Creek isn't even accorded that. It's secretive, a haunt of a rill that puddles up under the bridge, and then in a flat vein of tea-colored water, flows off into a thickly wooded swamp hung with vines and moss. We get out and look. It seems to be dense, impenetrable, a hideaway jungle likely complete with its own special brand of miasma. From the bridge, we can see no more than ten yards inside the wall of foliage. If we knew better, we'd get back into my vehicle and drive to the Ft. Drum Diner, maybe drink some sweet iced tea and chow down on some fried catfish with corn puppies on the side. Then, we'd look at the map, laugh at the idea of finding our way down a creek that—even when charted—seems monumentally unsure of itself.

We would do that if we were normal people, but of course, we are not. We are "naturalists" and—along with "wild Indians and cattle-rangers"—we will accept the historic prerogative to "wade through its swamps, risk its miasma and brave its dangerous animals." And so, we unload a kayak from the roof racks of my car, holster up our backpacks, and stumble down the steep berm to the dark water with the kayak in tow. Ft. Drum Creek is actually flowing, ever so slightly, and it is moving north, aiming for its historic destiny with the headwater sawgrass marsh of the great St. Johns River. There's a turnpike, a great expanse of marsh, and even some dry prairies between here and there. I'm figuring no one's yet bothered to tell the little creek that it just might not make it these days.

Then again, no one's told us, either. And so by forging and following this little hidden creek, we are hoping to learn something about the way rivers work here in Florida, about how a green or blue line on a map is not necessarily a green or blue line on the ground—and most of all, how the intricate weave of ecology is often hidden from easy reckoning. At the base of the berm that holds the bridge, I push the kayak to the edge of the water. My friend gets in and paddles up to and under the bridge, and back. Although we don't know it now, this is the deepest patch of creek for miles. South of here, the subtle rise in the landscape that pushes the creek northward gets little of the attention afforded other key natural features around Florida—the Glades, the Green Swamp, the springs that arise from the deep Floridan Aquifer. Yet, that ridge was the eastern paleo-shoreline of an inland bay over two million years ago. Geologists and amateur rock hunters chiseling down into the ridge around "Rucks Pit" there have recovered scads of fossilized sharks teeth, geodes, and one of the largest beds of calcite-bearing clamshells anywhere.

As she scups about, I stop and breathe deeply and slowly to relax, just as I do when I first enter the water with scuba tanks offshore. As I do, I feel my modern, fast-road tensions dissolve, feel my senses open, just a bit. The stream is wild, solemn, alone. I can imagine it being the archetype for all the seldom-seen little tropical creeks in the entire world. It seems to exhale, and its scent is that of cooked swamp, wild vanilla, leaf humus, palmetto blossoms. The immediacy of the moment grabs me hard, and I begin to think: This is really pretty cool. Maybe I can pretend it's 1874 again, and we're exploring a place that few others have ever seen, maybe even find some floating islands of monasteries strewn with pirate treasure.

Then, I look down and see rutted, freshly turned black earth at my feet, the sign of large, feral boars at work. They are animals with bad teeth and an attitude to match. My swoon with the romance of make-believe history becomes less so. The hogs, imported centuries ago by the Spanish, can wreck havoc on a delicate natural system in their quest for roots and tubers, snorting about like miniature bulldozers. More to the point, the large males, with sharp incisors curling ominously out of their mouths, have also been known to attack humans. Earlier, my friend had also told me wild hogs are distinguished from other animals by their capacity to hold a grudge. I wonder to myself how she knows this. Then I remember I know the names of all the original Four Tops. Sometimes, there just isn't any good reason for some things.

Nonetheless, I am wondering what a grudge-holding, 250-pound, half-mad pig would do if he found me standing on his prize root pantry. Just as I am conjuring that one up, a noise from the distance jars me. It is the report of a high-powered rifle, the kind that fires bullets that zing for a couple miles through the woods. And I remember it is also hunting season down here. My wild boar moment is replaced by the image of a nearsighted hog hunter, who—after sipping from his flask of Jack Daniels all morning—is making his way steadily toward us, just waiting for the large hairless mammal up on his two hind legs in the rut to snort at him. If he shot me, I figure I'd likely hold a grudge, too. Can't really blame the hog, after all.

After my pig revelation, I look downstream a bit to see my friend encountering her first "portage." It is a massive fretwork of downed trees and limbs that not only block the kayak, but in fact, have blocked most anything that's floated this way for the last year or so—a few plastic soda bottles, a Styrofoam cooler, a lid to a PVC bucket. I help drag the kayak out of the water and around the brush pile. On the other side, the creek seems to have diminished in size; worse, another brush pile is less than fifty feet away. We decide to simply drag the kayak through the jungle until we can find a place where the little boat—which barely draws four inches—will float. And so we slosh onward, ducking under fallen trees and trying to sidestep large swales of muck, the kayak in tow. We do this over and over again in slightly different variations. I think of the mythical Sisyphus pushing his large rock up the hill, only to have it tumble back down, over and over again. As I think of this, I imagine myself saying to the ever-thwarted Greek: *I get it now, bro.*

By now, shafts of golden sunlight burn through the foliage canopy above like spots on a theater stage. Blood is trailing down from my neck, arms, and forehead in tiny rivulets from encounters with assorted briars and thorns. Although sparse, the little tea-colored creek flows off into the fretwork of wild landscape, deadfalls of trees, and limbs every few yards. Now that we are deeper in, the vines and muck, briars and needle palms make it almost impossible to follow along the shore of the creek.

Kayaking is out of the question, so we finally leave the little boat and try to forge ahead as far as we can on foot. As we slog along, I think of the "Knockabout Club" some more, remembering their first real "sighting" of the swamp that held Ft. Drum Creek: "How well I remember that dark green clump, for that was the first landmark known to my guide when we were lost here two years ago." And then, "We saw what looked like a river, but what in reality, was only *fog.*"

This image becomes more vivid as we push through the fox grape and briars and bromeliads, trailing along next to whatever looks wet. When we catch a glimpse of the blackwater gathering up inside a natural furrow, we are nearly ecstatic. But each time, the water-filled depression disappears within just a few yards, as if it is only fog. I'm figuring monkeys and baboons are right around the next corner, and I wonder what sort of grudge those primates might be holding.

The subtropical, water-fed vegetation of South Florida has done its work well. We have finally reached a point where the foliage is so thick we can't even see beyond it, can only stumble along in slow motion through a barricade of vines and fronds, plants that are no longer our pastoral friends, but which seem lifted from a bad B-grade movie in which nature comes alive and torments the poor, misled humans until they go quite mad.

Finally we come to what passes for a "clearing." It's the size of a small bedroom. Here, my friend sets up her camera tripod and shoots some giant bromeliads in resplendent red bloom. I sit on a rotting log and swill water from my backpack, using some of it to wipe away the sweat and blood, which seems to be coagulating nicely. I run my hands through my hair, and find an entire diorama there—tiny leaves, twigs, the silk of a spider web, an empty carapace of a bug, and finally, a little crab spider. As I disentangle the swamp from my head, I glance down to see a five-foot-long snake skin, translucent scale-like impressions where the animal used to be. Looking around, I notice several clutches of narrow strap ferns spilling out of tree branches, and realize I seldom see this particular epiphyte back in northern Florida. I go to take a gulp from my water bottle and find it empty. Heat, dehydration, blood, thirst, and a few well-placed insect bites have done a dandy job of filtering reality for me.

Somehow, a thread of the adult in me prevails, and I admit out loud that we probably won't be able to get much deeper in today. Although she's also close to being out of drinking water and no less scraped or soaked than I, my friend disagrees with this strategy. By now, I am thinking to myself she was likely the sort of kid who ran with scissors, just because you told her not to. On the promise that I will come back soon and accompany her with hiking and camping gear for as long as it takes, we retreat to higher ground. There, we follow the tree line that enfolds the relic confusion of Ft. Drum Creek, its miasma, and dangerous animals. The sun lays lower in the sky, and I'm hoping we reach the bridge before dark.

We do, and as we scramble up the embankment with the kayak in tow, a large American pickup truck coasts to a stop next to us. I walk a few steps and look inside the cab. A good 'ole boy is at the wheel, grinning from ear to ear. "Did you all go back in there?" he drawls, and I say, yep, we sure did. He asks me if the creek opens up, maybe turns into a good fishing hole somewhere downstream, and I assure him it does not. "Man," he says, shaking his head, "I don't know anyone who's ever tried that with one of those little boats." I want to tell him there's probably a good reason for that. Instead I wave goodbye, and we load up the kayak. From here, we finally drive to the Ft. Drum Diner where we eat immense platters of fried catfish and hush puppies, washed down with sweet tea. It's a meal I've been fantasizing about for the last several hours. It's not a monastery laden with treasure, but it feels like one.

I sit here in the diner, enthralled with the notion of not being lost in a swamp for the night. And, in my newly found, Southern fried comfort, I think clearly for the first time today. As I do, it occurs to me that Ft. Drum Creek has always known exactly where it is flowing. It is only we humans who were confused.

14

Florida Fantasyland

Bella Foresta

She's a brute of a reptile, as large as my kayak, and she's up on all four legs, running toward me like a giant lumbering dog. I'm wedged into the cockpit of my small craft, its bow grounded atop the mud at the edge of her bulrush hideaway. I'm holding my paddle in a white-knuckled death grip, but am otherwise paralyzed. My only reaction is to exhale in a low distressed groan, of the sort bad movie actors use when mutant zombies have a full-face grip on their heads.

A young two-to-three-foot long alligator floats motionless in the water just behind some cypress knees.

As the gator reaches the edge of the low bank she actually launches herself toward me, becoming airborne for the briefest moment. Then she belly flops into the river, splashing me with water and duckweed and mud. Within seconds, she disappears beneath the surface, only the swirl of small eddies—and the thump-thump of my heart—left to remind me she was here at all. My intellect tells me I frightened her and she was only trying to escape to deep water. But my gut tells me I was almost toast.

Around me on this spring-fed subtropical river, bald cypresses are bursting with soft needles and the blooms of the river iris are glowing like neon in the green understory. I am deep inside an east central Florida landscape that seems as wild as the day it was birthed from the sea. Ironically, there are dozens of contrived theme park "experiences" not so very far away that promise to scare the living bejesus out of you in exchange for pricey admission fees. But there is no scare like the real scare, and no aesthetic like the one the native Florida terrain can deliver.

I didn't come here for the scare, of course. That's the realm of extreme sporters who are in it just for the thrill. While I've done my share of diving inside the lime rock of springs and onto deep, current-driven sites far offshore, I did so for the revelations of seldom-seen places. And it's this promise of discovery that keeps me here, that allows me to believe the natural world still has a chance to prevail inside a peninsula that is busy reshaping itself so that it resembles something other than its true nature.

The truth is that Florida is a wonderfully odd and biologically diverse state that, from time to time, finds itself run by a bunch of well-dressed and coifed screwballs who are big on spin but dangerously out of touch with real world constraints. Although the state is one of the few to require local cities and counties to devise growth management plans to balance use with preservation, the powerful growth industry has rendered it useless by pressuring local officials to exempt such laws when their own short-term needs are at stake. With no realistic plan to guide growth, Florida is open game to all manner of schemes that end up grafting illusion onto its landscape. To get to this Wekiva River system, I drove past a gauntlet of just-pretend places that had Jabberwocky written all over them. There were the synthetic chain restaurants that could have been anywhere—Joe's Crab Shack (mock fish net floats that will never see water and frozen Alaskan king crabs) and Don Pablo's Mexican Kitchen (intentionally distressed stucco without a Mexican in sight).

The most ludicrous modernism was a new walled-in development that, after the native baywood and sweetgum were clear-cut and clay was piled atop the rich black wetland earth, became the "Bella Foresta," an enclave of ritzy new homes guarded by a gate. Like other developments that are named for wildlife they displaced—Eagle Ridge, Black Bear Estates, etcetera—Bella Foresta is simply one more fancy name that has no real meaning here. It is as if the just-pretend illusion of Disney has spilled over its fence and rolled pell-mell over the countryside.

But here's the kicker: Florida also has a large chunk of its landscape protected as parks and preserves, thanks to ambitious land buying programs. So there's enough of its extraordinary subtropical terrain left to still deliver an authentic wilderness punch. Experiences like this allow you to bore into its relic geography. I can do that by visiting those water-logged time capsules that have changed the least since the gentle naturalist William Bartram first journeyed into the peninsula over 240 years ago.

And so, after driving past the make-believe Bella Foresta, I am now deep inside the real one, an enchanted place surrounded by over a hundred square miles of scrub and forest, river and swamp. It is a wilderness with alligators and coral snakes and bears, only a few miserly miles from one of the most gridded-out and congested fantasylands in all the world. One single major asphalt road runs through it all, and it is lined with Bear Crossing signs that, sometimes, are not too far away from little kiosks selling knockoff designer sunglasses. If this surrealism didn't exist, Gabriel Garcia Marquez would have to make it up.

After my gator encounter, I continue paddling downstream on the Wekiva, past the remnant Indian midden mounds still packed tight with the snail shells and manatee ribs and rattlesnake vertebrae, headed toward the mouth of the Blackwater Creek. This was once the territory of the ancient pre-Columbian Timucua Kingdom of the Sun. Nature and the wildlife that populated it were revered. The lives of the Timucua were woven into the environment, and not separate from it. The natural world of what would become Florida evoked awe, beauty, respect, and fear. It cost nothing to get in, except an appreciation for its sacredness.

Five more miles and I find the mouth of the Blackwater, tucked away under a foliage canopy on the opposite shore, modest and unassuming for a waterway nearly twenty miles long. I poke my bow into it, stop for a granola break, check the time. The sun is dipping toward the tops of the highest cypresses now, and the osprey are flying back home to roost in the golden light. Once, on an earlier trip here with a friend, one of the raptors soared right over us with a huge mullet in her talons. She landed on a tall cypress branch to get a better grip and when we looked up, all we could see was the large mullet tail flapping from the tree tops.

On I go, pushing against the outflow of the gentle current, spring-fed like the larger Wekiva, but tea-colored from the tannins leaking out of the surrounding swamp. Alone back here, I listen closely for sounds: The barking of tree frogs in anticipation of the night, the call of the pileated woodpecker, the rustling of a large mammal—bear, coyote, boar?—from somewhere back in the woods. The golden light has changed to a burnt umber, and I breathe slowly, using my paddle sparingly so I make almost no sound. A wading bird known as a limpkin screams like a panther from around the next bend. Bartram first described this bird almost 250 years ago, and I smile to myself, knowing that he heard this same cry. "There is a very curious bird, called by an Indian name (Ephouskyca) which signifies in our language, the crying bird," he wrote in *Travels*. "It is about the size of a large domestic hen: every feather edged or tipped with white . . ." After describing the limpkin, Bartram—then likely as hungry as I am right now—shot, roasted, and ate it.

Bartram's sensibilities were far closer to those of the Native Americans who lived here along the rivers and springs. Wildlife was to be respected, admired, and when necessary, prepared for dinner. Gods usually took the shape of predatory animals to stave off the fear of the unknown. The Timucua carved totems to these gods, and planted them at the edge of their mounds on the shores to protect them, iconic light against the vast darkness.

Wilderness areas like the one that now surrounds me are among the last repositories for the sacredness that once guided entire lives, that forged everlasting bonds between mortals and the gods of the natural world on this peninsula. I paddle deeper in now, paddle until it is full dark, until I am safely beyond the contradictions of modern Florida.

I am in wonder and awe at the evanescent quality of this real bella foresta, a place that truly seems on the verge of dissolving into vapor. I have finally broken through the artificial surrealism of the fantasy worlds, and found my way to one that mindfully threads its way through time. Back here, everything seems to make sense. Mullet in the tree tops, alligators soaring through the air, wildflowers glowing as if lit from within. Awe, beauty, respect, fear.

I pretend I need to do nothing more in this world than acknowledge the iconic light. And for all the many hours back home, right up until I reach my take-out, I succeed. There, with my kayak tied to the top of my car, I drive out of the relic Florida and back into the asphalt of the human-built one, the warmth of my own delusion vanishing in a volley of oncoming headlights and the nervous bleat of horns.

15

Following the Unseen

A trail leading into a thick, dark subtropical hardwood tree hammock.

The forecast was for rain later today, so I got some work out of the way early on and headed for the woods. The plan was to walk an hour in and an hour back out, no more than five or so miles, but of course that doesn't include the dawdling so integral to sauntering.

The woods here are easy to figure: To the west, there's a well-marked mile-long loop trail through the longleaf; to the east, a rutted dirt jeep path leads you to a series of unmarked firebreak roads that wind back deep into an impressive tangle of palmetto and pine, and later, through an oak hammock with a few wild orange trees. At the trailhead kiosk, the map shows only the loop trail; the great bulk of this state preserve is not managed for people, since the expense would be too great for the meager state park budget. The best way to keep folks from poking about places like this is to simply leave them off the public map. And so, the unmapped parcel is always my choice: It's seldom used by other hikers; it offers a better chance to see wildlife—or at least signs of them; and, it allows you the opportunity to get lost. If you follow it long enough, it'll put you back closer to the edge of the St. Johns, the flatwoods and then open prairie finally giving way to a canopy of oak and bald cypress, gnarly knees poking up like little goblins back in the river's swamp.

I decided to go on the spur of the moment, and didn't bother to try to roust up a hiking bud. A few years ago, Shep would have joined me, his boundless sheltie enthusiasm as unbridled as Bartram's own eighteenth-century expression of the wonders that La Florida would gift to our souls. The course-setting is easy, no compass needed. This is a trail I have walked many times before and while it has a certain familiarity, it also changes dramatically by season, time of day, weather, and sheer happenstance.

The first couple hundred yards takes me to the edge of a deep sinkhole, usually empty to its steep bottom when dry. I walk back through the myrtle and sweetgum to see if it might be holding water after a few weeks of heavy rains. In this way, I suppose I use it as a giant rain gauge, trying to figure how much water has settled into its enormous V-like funnel in the terrain. Today, it's nearly two-thirds full, a good twenty feet or so of normally dry bottom inundated, duckweed floating on the surface and a great egret nagging at the edges. Overhead, dark patches of clouds sometimes obscure the sun, cooling the air just a bit now and again.

The dirt road I follow beyond it is as walkable as it will ever be, packed down by the rain and the tire treads of a park service vehicle of some sort. At trail side, the smallish trumpet-like white flower known as creeping morning glory begins to appear, as does the lizard's tail, its name fully realized in an appendage of pale white. A tiny pea-like orange bud I can't identify shines from the understory here and there, as do scads of narrow-leaved sabatia, a five-lobed little wildflower that revels in the moisture of the seasonally wet piney woods. It's a flatwoods here, so everything seems to be in place, little ecological pronouncements of plants and landscape ready for the listening.

I look to the west for the bald eagle nest that should be near the top of a certain longleaf, and am comforted as always when I see it there. I raise my binoculars for a closer look. No one's home, but just knowing the nest is being maintained is enough for now. The fragrance of pine and wild soggy prairie is replaced by a strong odor of burnt vegetation. As I round the next bend I see the charred remnants of a prescribed burn, thick stalks of saw palmettos looking like the blackened limbs of some prehistoric animal. I survey the burn and see scores of white sand piles, each marking the pitched-up earth from gopher tortoise burrows. If the burn hadn't pulled back the curtain, all I would see would be a vast unyielding field of green.

I take a path that I know will lead me to a slough just behind the main branch of the lower Wekiva. In other hikes here, I have always been able to find a downed tree that will let me ford the little bayou. But today is different: The slough is wide and deep, only a shoal of white sand from an erosional creek interrupting the green blur of duckweed floating atop the water. I carefully pick my way along the steep banks, looking for the place where a mama gator usually tends her brood, but today, nothing. Farther along on the shore, I see the distinctive bleached white snail shell (*Viviparous* sp.) that creates most of the bulk of Native American midden mounds along Florida rivers. I figure the Indians who once lived here would feel blessed by the strong coursing of water, uplifted by the way the rains reopen old creeks and branches closed by the drought. In a landscape dominated by water, every new aquatic portal meant a chance to gather more food, animals, and plants. I won't be able to make it across to the mainstem bank of the Wekiva today, but that's alright. The imagined cheer of long departed Timucua and Mayaca is more than enough.

I turn to go, fascinated by the way the heavy rainfall has inscribed itself in the soft earth. At some point, the already soggy flatwoods brimmed over with the rains, sending little transient creeks surging down to the lower river. As they flowed along, they gathered into one, and then cut down deep into the soft earth, leaving behind a large, empty gully several feet deep, a Florida version of a western arroyo. I walk beside it, looking more closely now: small, isolated puddles of tea-colored water lie in deeper ruts here and there, tiny swamps of water-blood dissolved from the decay of humus. Intermittently along the walls of the gully, it seems the white sand has not just eroded, but has actually melted, flowing layers of soil caught just for now in a freeze frame of time like candle wax, perhaps to become sedimentary rock a millennia from now.

Walking out from the gridlock of trees, I feel the first drops of the day's rain. I am sweating now, and it feels good on my skin. Other than a deer track here and there, the only imprint on the packed sand is the one I left coming in; on the way back out, I try my best to retrace those incoming steps.

I think of those who have walked this trail with me before—all good-hearted women and men intent on plumbing the solace natural places allow. And one little dog who could never get enough of the woods, and the scent it left for him. The visceral knowledge of having been with them all is redemptive, for I have led most of them here, over time. I think fondly of each of them, think of how fully and how differently they were able to respond to the mystery of this Florida landscape. Like Shep, the scent is here for me as well—except it's not an olfactory one. It's one I react to deep in my gut, projected as images that allow me to relive each journey I've ever taken on this trail.

Just ahead, two white-tailed deer barely beyond the yearling age spook, bounding off in different directions. I stop in my tracks, not wanting to scare them any more, and even though the rain is becoming harder, I decide to take a longer trail spur back. As I do, I pass a pile of osprey feathers, and wonder what other animal has been strong and swift enough to have done this—an eagle, a stealthy bobcat, a coyote?

Just as I'm prepared to cut across an open pine forest of wiregrass and small turkey oak, I see a pile of what seem to be bones and go to it. It's the pieces of a once-large gopher tortoise, the topical scutes pealing back from the heavier calcium, little vertebrae scattered about. I wonder at the narrative of this animal, of its beginning and its end. As I do, I realize once more how the landscape brims with sacred stories it has to tell of its wildlife, its plants and trees, its seasons, its people. The lineage is long, extending from those who once gathered snail shells and slept next to the earth, to those of us who walk through it for a day. Having done so, we open our hearts to it, cherishing the way its lessons settle down on us, as real as any tonic.

It is raining hard enough to cloak me in a sort of white mist now, and I quicken my pace, back to the beginning. I am soaking wet, but I am sorry to go, to leave all the little stories behind. I promise when I get home I will write down notes of what I've seen today, of how the wild Florida landscape has gifted me once more with a memory yarn. In doing so, it imprints me with arroyo-like moments that are etched into my spirit, just as the water has etched its own way down into the earth.

16

A Tropical Storm Is Coming

Another Noir Day in Paradise

It's hurricane season here in Florida, that special time when the big blows rise up out of the Antilles and travel through the Torrid Zone for a visit. Like blizzards up north, tropical storms and 'canes are a way of life here, something you sort of try to work around. Still, there's something very . . . unreal and conflicting about it all. My point? Bad guy Edward G. Robinson made it in the vintage film noir flick *Key Largo*. When told a hurricane was coming his way, he was amazed to learn that storms

My fenced-in backyard, which has been converted from a monoculture of St. Augustine grass to a certified wildlife habitat.

like that had hammered the Keys in the past. Robinson growls incredulously: You mean to tell me that a hurricane hit here before—and people still live here???

I knew something was up late yesterday when I came home. I walked through the long and narrow screened back porch and headed for the fenced yard. As I did I noticed two very still and strange objects on the top of the cypress fence. I stopped inside the porch and saw it was two red-shouldered hawks, positioned about three feet from each other. They were wonderfully intent on studying the fish pond just below them, so much so that they almost completely ignored me.

I walked carefully back into the house, grabbed a digital camera, and came back, shooting as much as I could at a distance, and then slowly moving toward them. I got to the other edge of the pond before they even noticed me. At that point, there was only about seven or eight feet between us. I continued to happily click away and they continued to happily ignore me. There are a couple large comet goldfish in the pond, fish I had bought as inch-long culls from the aquarium store, and let loose many months ago. With the sunshine and rain and dissolved oxygen, they grew fast, and were now almost ten inches long, plump from grazing on the underwater plants and algae in the pond. There were also countless tadpoles from a bullfrog and a southern leopard frog, along with scores of gambusia spawned by a few tiny mamas I brought back from the St. Johns just a couple months ago.

While I'd seen the hawks around before, and often heard them calling from the thick canopy of live oaks overhead, it was strange for them to be so close and not reacting to my presence. Then I realized what was happening: I tapped the glass on the barometer in the porch and saw the needle plummet like the GPA of a FSU lineman. And it was summer. I didn't even have to turn on the self-consciously melodramatic Fox News to know a tropical disturbance of some sort was on its way.

But I did turn on Fox for the theater value, and it was as expected, the usual scare-the-bejesus-out-of-the-audience sort of performance weather people in Florida love to indulge in, a journalistic train wreck in slow motion. The screen was full of charts and maps and pretty green and yellow splotches that were spinning about, headed toward the Keys and South Florida. A route was already predicted, and the tropical storm known as Fay was eagerly moving along it, churning its way up into central Florida. The Fox reporters remind us that outsiders still refer to Florida as the "plywood state" as the result of heavy damage from a series of back-to-back 'canes a few years ago. I saw clips of manic consumers south of here eagerly buying everything manic merchants would sell them, stuff having to do with batteries, bottled water, plywood, canned goods, and so on.

I resisted the urge to go back out myself and buy such stuff, since with all the camping gear and stoves and freeze-dried food I have on hand, I was already set. After all, life in the Torrid Zone is distinguished by nothing if not the capacity to be able to camp out in your own home. Nonetheless, I wondered if the hawks had been watching Fox News, and knowing their prey would be lying low over the next few days, were out doing their own version of hurricane hoarding, courtesy of the comets in my pond.

In the house, I checked out the aquarium where I keep a bunch of wild goldenhorn marissa snails, some native aquatic plants, and two separate species of bluegill, known locally as "bream." The two bream, who don't get along all that well under normal conditions, react oddly when the barometer falls and the pressure changes. Since they're wild fish and not reared in a tank from birth, they respond as they'd likely respond in the river: they huddle back in a bottom corner and position themselves, one looking one way, and one the other, as if to cover their butts—or in this case, their caudal fins—from whatever disaster might come their way.

By the following day, the morning was cheery and bright, but by late afternoon, a thick band of rain and winds washed over us, a weather surge so pervasive it made everything outside look white. The rain continued into the night, and the wind picked up good with gusts up to 40 mph. A large dead limb from my neighbor's wild cherry tree fell onto my fence, and by the following morning, the yard was full of smaller branches and moss. I tried to drive downtown, but even the main highway, U.S. 17-92, was flooded. Lake Monroe, a quiet and domestic looking megapond on most days, was raging like a little sea, waves heaving themselves up with the wind and coursing northward with the current. Boats anchored outside the marina's breakwater were thrashing around, and at least one houseboat had sunk.

At least there was no water in the house, like there had been over on the coast. I felt bad for the local homeless folks, though, and also couldn't help but wonder how the wildlife would fare if we had much more of this. Developers don't create tropical storms, of course, but they distort the landscape so fully that water ends up in places where nature didn't intend for it to be. Wetlands that have historically stored such stormwater simply aren't available anymore for that function. And the human-made retention ponds and canals, which often try to do the work of wetlands, simply hold water until that special moment when they overflow. Growth management plans and future "Land Use Maps" usually study the local landscape for potential flooding, and then try to direct development elsewhere. But "amendments" to those plans—also known as exemptions—are granted routinely by elected city and county officials. This is not against the statutory law, of course, but it's certainly an affront to land use ethics everywhere. You may think "corruption" too strong a word for these exemptions. But on a larger philosophical scale, corruption is exactly what has happened because—once corrupted—the natural assets of our landscape no longer function as they should.

I thought about the film noir thing some more, and although that genre had mostly to do with the American gangster flicks of the forties and fifties, it's also relevant to Florida today, with or without hurricanes. We have morally conflicted protagonists, lots of femme fatales (beautiful but treacherous women), crimes of passion or money, ill-fated relationships, paranoia, and corruption—all portrayed in a subtropical landscape of high contrast lighting and distorted shadows. Florida, at once the "plywood state" and a tropical wonderland, is film noir, alive and well.

It sounds a bit like another day in noir paradise, where hawks hunt comets, homes without electricity turn into large tents, and real estate developers distort reality so that it all sounds just so darn romantic you have to resist the urge to go out and do something corrupt, just to fit in.

17

A Mythic Feast

Lobster on the Swanee

On an early Saturday morning, the air is crisp and the river black at our roadside put-in on the Suwannee River. Oaks, black willow, water locust, and a thick understory of green push in close to the shore everywhere but right here at this concrete ramp. If the river seems serene, inviting, the ramp is hyper with movement, crammed with the camping and paddling gear of what must be a dozen Boy Scouts and their adult leaders. We move more quickly than usual to stow our own tents and food in the

The spring house at White Springs, Fla., on the Suwannee.

dry hatches of our kayaks, and to launch as fast as we can, leaving the chatter behind. I was a Boy Scout when I was a kid, and while the scouting fellowship had some great moments, I was usually a lot happier just being outdoors in the quiet woods with my dad.

The plan is to paddle a couple of days from here downstream through White Springs, Florida, beyond its old springhouse, under a bridge or two, and through a terrain as wonderfully peculiar as any I have ever seen.

The water is Georgia-cold, rising out of the Okefenokee Swamp, where my favorite childhood cartoon possum, Pogo, once lived. Even though it's well inside the Sunshine State now, it's not cutting us any slack. I'm guessing the temperature of the river under us is somewhere in the fifties.

Off we go, paddle blades rising and falling from the blackwater, dripping sepia. It's late November and brisk, so most critters—including gators—are laying low somewhere. That's okay because we didn't come expecting to see an ark of wildlife. Although the black bears are moving about more now, getting ready for the dormancy of mid-winter, they're likely to be deeper in the woods. And the cold-blooded animals don't usually show themselves, except during the warmest of days. What we're really hoping for is a float through time, following the slight drift of a river that's taken a million years to painstakingly carve its way down through the earth and lime rock of northern Florida. Time is of particular interest to me—the longer anything has been shaped or transformed by it, the better. There are four of us, two men and two women. We've all paddled long distances before, but the point of this two-day outing is to take our time, let the landscape sink in through our own topography, as deep as it will go.

The banks of the Suwannee bulge up around us, making this more of a true valley than what most other rivers are allowed in Florida. Limestone boulders begin to appear on one side and snow-white sandy shoals on the other. The dwarf-like Ogeechee tupelos, trees that—like the cypress—need water to flourish, appear here and there, their swollen roots entwined like vipers as they cling tenaciously to the alluvial terrain of the shore. This is the edge of the Florida range for this most southern of trees, and the beekeepers hereabouts must be happy for it: its mild, fine tasting honey brings a much higher value than other plants. Van Morrison sang about it, and the beekeeper in the independent film *Ulee's Gold* sold it. When I see these trees, it makes me feel good, as if some part of the river and swamp is speaking to me. Biologists describe those living things that need to be in a certain place for at least part of their lives as "obligate species," and I realize I am that sort of person, an obligate species that belongs in or around a river, a swamp, a spring.

One of the women paddles in front of me and then, a hundred feet away, rounds into a sharp turn under a low-hanging river tree with Spanish moss, frame frozen just for now. With the luminous morning light, it looks for all the world like a William Morris Hunt landscape painting from the nineteenth century, except with a kayaker airbrushed in.

We're aiming to camp on the low banks of the river this evening. Since I've been on the Suwannee before, I'm relatively sure we can find a place to lay our heads—especially when the river is low like this. A higher river would simply fill up its valley, inundating the walls and springs and white sandy shoals. The soft shoals are true paleo-dunes; sleeping on a Suwannee River shoal is like sleeping on a beach.

We are outfitted like most other paddling campers, except for one major difference: I have had more than my fill of campfire rations over the years, eating everything from freeze-dried stew and thin sheets of cassava in a dry tropical forest in the Dominican Republic, to Noodles-in-a-Cup and beef jerky in the Everglades. As a result, we've packed along two immense lobster tails and two filet mignons in a soft cooler of ice, and I will cook them over our campfire tonight. And so smack in the middle of one of Florida's most mythic rivers—a river known more by its celebrated name than by direct experience—we'll be hunkered over a mythic feast. I think of the steamboats that once traveled upstream on this river and the St. Johns, fine linen and silverware and food as tasty as that in any good restaurant of the time. Those floating boxes were insular, separate from the raw Cracker landscape in so many ways, and perhaps we are, too.

We pass a few other kayakers, and then, all is quiet. We've just had a cold snap, so the thermometer is expected to dip down into the high thirties tonight. The sun is now atop the tree line and, for now, its radiant warmth is welcome. Florida, gloriously different from most other places back on the continent, is also different from itself, depending on where you are. Even though naturalist Bartram visited here in the 1760s and referred to the Suwannee as the "Little San Juan" (Little St. Johns), there's little in common between the two waterways.

To begin with, there's the limestone here, which not only rises from boulders into small cliffs, but also lurks just under the surface, creating riffles and sometimes tiny standing waves. Upstream of our launch was Big Shoals, the single largest water-churning site in all of Florida, where the river actually drops several feet from an ancient scarp and maytags itself up into a sort of rapids-like frenzy. When rains have been heavy and the river and current are running high, the shoals will hit a Class III whitewater rating. But in very low waters like we have now, much of the sharp limestone underbelly would be exposed and we'd be forced to portage our kayaks and gear around it. Indeed, one of the reasons we decided to put in downstream of the Shoals was for this very reason.

Unlike older, consolidated northern rock, the younger karst limestone is a wonderful compression of sea memories—sand, coral, bone, shell. And it will continue to be more evident as we go. Tomorrow afternoon, when the limestone shores become higher, we'll even find tiny sea biscuit fossils scattered in the rock, reminders of a sea that hid all of Florida over 40 million years ago.

For now, we stroke steadily onward, reveling in the way the sunlight hits the water and strobes up on the white rock in gentle, rhythmic waves. We turn another corner, and just ahead, the old reconstructed spring house at White Springs rises up from the tea-colored river, a tall, Victorian edifice of tabby surrounding a natural spring. It was a place Yankees came to be cured of everything from insomnia to dandruff to tuberculosis, back in the nineteenth century when the springs and other natural features in the Florida landscape were its most popular tourist destinations.

We pull our 'yaks ashore here, and walk up a sloping terrain to where a stairway leads to a verandah-like porch that encircles the springs down below. An interpretive sign back by the foot of the stairs displays an archival photo of "White Sulfur Springs" in its heyday. Then, four tiers of porch-like ledges encircled the inside of the spring house, places where bathers and "patients" could take of the healing springs, moving up or down on a higher or lower tier according to the level of the river outside. In 1906, you could stay here for $3.50 a night, including "excellent meals." The magnitude of the spring was "second"—which means it could have flowed up to 64 million gallons a day.

When I first paddled this river years ago, I actually snorkeled the little spring, finning down in ten feet or so of transparent water to its limestone vent. It was still flowing well then, cresting out and over a stone rill and into the Suwannee. But today, the vision from the top is grim: there's a large puddle of stagnant water down in the limestone where the spring used to be. Clearly, the spring has lost the hydrostatic pressure it needs to stay alive, at least for now. Perhaps we've taken too much from the vein of the aquifer that feeds it—or maybe the upland rainfall recharge for it has simply been compromised by hard surface. There is a phosphate mining operation nearby, a process that requires a great deal of water to do its business. The loss of treasures like this is a reminder of how little we know about the complex, labyrinthine flow systems down in the rock beneath us. We take great pride in our human dominance over nature, cooling our homes artificially and gassing insects with toxins, giving us the delusion we're in command. But clearly, we haven't yet acquired the wisdom to "manage" ecology as well as Mother Nature herself.

Back on the river, we paddle beyond the carillon bells of the Stephen Foster park nearby, which sounds out "Old Folks at Home" every half hour, just in case you forget what river you're on. This is Florida's state song, and has brought attention to the Suwannee since Foster wrote it in 1851. The opening lyric, "Way Down Upon de Swanee Riber" gave this river a sort of celebrity, even a mystique, and surely helped with early promotional efforts to lure prototourists to Florida and its "medicinal" springs. Imagination is a big part of what Florida has been about for so long, and if it sometimes stretches the truth, well then, that's simply a part of its tradition of make-believe.

Despite all the natural places that Florida has lost, the state had the foresight to buy as much land as it could along the shores of the Suwannee over the years. Florida's interior—except for anomalies like Disney and other corporate theme parks—has few economic engines, and the Panhandle has even fewer. The water management district here figured a strong eco-heritage campaign to draw folks to the rural river basin via a well-mapped "Suwannee River Wilderness Trail" could bring a bit of economic prosperity—but without the traditional by-products of pollution. That might stimulate the economy without harming the river. I have noticed more paddlers on this river than I have ever seen before. Certainly, this is not the retro Suwannee of two decades ago, where you were more likely to see locals in overalls and straw hats fishing with cane poles along the shore than you were to see other water tourists. But that's a small price to pay compared to what could have happened to this river in the way of trendy exploitation that has swept over so much of this state.

The Suwannee also has some natural restrictions that function as aquatic speed bumps: if a motor boat came in from the Gulf at the mouth of this river, it would have no problem making its way up to the midsection, say, around Branford. But after that, inundated limestone rocks and shoals begin to appear more frequently, each with the potential to clip off a spinning propeller in the blink of an eye. But there's more: the upper river where we are now is more defined by distinct banks, creating a true geological valley. When I look more closely at the tall bald cypress rimming the edges of the river, I see distinct watermarks on their trunks twenty feet and more above my head. Seasonal rains can raise the water level at least that much, pouring in through deep, V-shaped furrows in the banks. With only the great upstream Georgia swamp to function as a giant organic sponge, this river rises and falls dramatically as it has for thousands of years, with no human flood control structure to restrict it. Anyone foolish enough to build even a hut down next to the river in the dry season would be swamped by the rise of the wet season that follows. Indeed, the Suwannee magnifies the climatic wet-dry realities of Florida, reminding us that it's a peninsula historically driven by rain.

In addition to new eco-heritage strategies and old geological realities, this old river still promises just enough offbeat menace to keep you guessing. One guidebook warns: "Please note, as with any wild area, you might encounter dangerous animals and plants." I'm figuring the gators and the water moccasins—like anywhere else in Florida—would play the role of menacing wildlife pretty well. But I wonder about the "dangerous plants." I think about this a bit, and then imagine an Ogeechee tupelo coming alive by night in a Dr. Seuss sort of way, using its medusa-like roots to create all sorts of vegetative havoc.

It is later in the day now, the sun dipping just atop the cypresses and live oaks and maples at the top of this steep river valley, putting us in shadows when it does. The shadows carry a mini-clime with them, a good twenty degrees cooler than the sunlight. It reminds me of the need to find a camp site soon. Ahead, we have one tall bridge to get under, and then a ways to go to escape the traffic noise from it. As we head beyond it, one of the other paddlers points to a clear sluice of water cascading through a rocky crevice to the river. I look at the map and see it charted as "Swift Creek." Unlike other clefts that channel rainwater into the river, this one carries the runoff from some upland springs. The great Florida naturalist Archie Carr spent a lot of time on this river, studying turtles and fish. But he was as much in awe of the springs as Bartram had been: "Each spring is different from all the others," he wrote. "But in the intensity of its grace and color, each is a little ecological jewel in which geology and biology have created a masterwork of natural art."

Well beyond the bridge, we find a long strand of white shoaly sand, and pull ashore. Tents go up quickly, and a fire is lit from moss, dry twigs, and dead branches. Soon the fire is blazing, just in time for the full dark. I begin to cook our meal over it, carefully rearranging the food in two pans atop the ever-shifting heat so it doesn't burn the meat. I have squeezed lime atop the lobster with some good soy sauce and a bottle of dry seasonings I earlier mixed—basel, oregano, even a touch of curry. It sizzles in its little vat of butter and olive oil and freshly chopped garlic, and soon it is ready. We sit back, sip wine, the deep cold of the river valley pushing us closer to the fire. And there, cross-legged in the sand of a million-year-old dune, we enjoy our mythic feast on this mythic "riber."

The stars push out above into the pitch-black quilt that is the Suwannee River night, and soon, the horizon is jammed with them from end to end, constellations of the sort I have only seen in far, remote places undiluted by urban light: the upper Amazon; northeastern Australia; the Everglades; the isolated landscape I once knew as an eight-year-old on the lower Eastern Shore of Maryland. For anyone who cares about our natural places in Florida, there is something about all of this that is redemptive, that offers hope, even in the midst of great loss. Being deep inside it makes me feel somehow reassured, awestruck by the magnitude and the timeless glory of it all, an obligate species safe for now in his special place.

The "medicinal cures" of another century still do work here, and that makes me glad in my heart. Thanksgiving will be upon us soon, and I celebrate it now, offering gratitude for the true friendship and deep magnanimity of all who care—and for a real river that carves its way out of mythology, seeping into a singularly rich and true moment from a make-believe past.

18

So You Want to Be a Nature Writer?

A diver entering the V-like crevice that leads to the main spring vent at Wekiwa Springs.

I don't think I'd trade this for anything in the world. Certainly not the field work, the discovery, the actual mind-to-cosmos-and-back process of writing, and the opportunity to do what I actually love for a job. But there are those times when it seems as if I've just walked onstage in the middle of a three-act play—one that takes equal parts from a sublime Elizabeth Bishop poem, a vintage episode of *Wild Kingdom*, and one of those baroque nineteenth-century brochures hyping Florida because it is so "salubrious" it will cure everything from heartburn to heartbreak.

Last weekend I sat at a festival celebrating the Wekiva River for five hours behind a table with my books on it. People walked by like they do oils or pastels in an art show, looking at my books like they were exotic trinkets, but unsure how they might fit into the decor. A few had expressions on their faces that I imagine they might also affect if they unexpectedly strolled by a burning bush, or a monkey banging away at a typewriter. Most seemed curious, but not enough to want to come too close. My saving grace was that I was just uphill from the enormous headspring for the Wekiva River; and, my neighboring table-mates were Fred and Linda Hitt, really fine friends who, respectively, are a talented writer and an accomplished wildlife artist. And so, during my down time, I tried to think of ten reasons why "irony" ought to be packaged as a subject and taught in elementary school, instead of being delayed until college or adulthood:

1. Of all the exhibits, the guy who was a beekeeper was the most popular. It was because he had live bees inside a sort of ant farm hive thing under glass and the kids loved it. He also made great honey, although I know for a fact that he didn't really make it. The bees did. At any rate, I am thinking of bringing a live bee display to my next outdoor book signing.

2. Many thumbed through my books looking for pictures. Not finding any, most moved on. I am thinking seriously about creating a Classic Comic book about the natural wonders of Florida. I'd need a super hero, and it could be author Carl Hiaasen's Skink. That's about as close to a hero as Florida's going to get. Except maybe for Carl, a stand-up guy who makes degenerate politics and greed sound like fun.

3. Three young women were hovering around several of my books, making dove-like sounds, as if something was caught in their throats. I

looked up, hopeful they might actually enjoy stories about nature. The alpha girl spoke. She had picked up a little slice of a small log being used for a paperweight on a stack of *River of Lakes*. She wanted to know how much the tiny log was. One of her friends asked if I would give a discount if they bought three of the little logs all at once.

4. I wrote a piece once about the spring-fed Suwannee River, ending with a lyric from the old Stephen Foster anthem ("Old Folks at Home"), which also happens to be our official state song: The lyric was "*Way down upon de Swanee Riber.*" The newspaper copy editor actually changed the lyric to read "Way down upon the Suwannee River" because she felt the line was racist, and was likely to be smoothed over and updated soon. That had struck me as mildly delusional. By glossing over a misdeed in the name of political correctness, the gritty reality of the song's era went missing. I figure if newspapers go down the tubes, delusions like this will be part of the reason since they symbolize what is fundamentally wrong when subjective humans pretend to report the "truth" objectively. Fabricated "ethics" like this will only get worse as corporate newspapers—in this new virtual world of information—continue on a downward trajectory that purges the most competent and experienced of the editorial staffs. Since any need to be objective will be lost, the emphasis to stress "appearance" will trump most everything and the public's "right to know" will be a relic of another time.

Just as I finished mulling through this memory, a swallow-tailed kite swooped low over the spring, just back from South America. I realized more fully the transitory nature of life and the surprises that nature allows. As the kite soared, rising and falling in the light eddies of the wind, so did my spirits. I wondered some about the Redneck Chinese Puzzle that is my life. But most of all, I was filled with gratification that a soaring raptor like that could bring me so much solace.

5. Not so long ago, I was asked to speak to a group of "community leaders" who were participating in some "leadership training" in a county not far from where I live in Florida. Since I am a nature writer, the topic was nature and, well, conservation. The seminar turned out to be a giant love fest for chamber of commerce types who wanted to "network"—that is, drum up business and brag about themselves. A tall, skinny fellow with a vague resemblance to a Disney character caught me

off guard. I had asked the group if they had any idea how much land was being lost to development each hour in Florida. No one knew, except for this fellow, who was also a minor elected official in that county. He raised his hand, and answered: "Zero." The real answer was twenty acres an hour. It's a reality that's squeezing the natural heart and cultural soul out of our state—a factoid with very little humor attached. But clearly, this fellow regarded the session as a sort of parlor game. I asked him why he thought "zero" was the appropriate answer, and he replied: "When you ask a trivial question, you get a trivial answer. Like in Trivial Pursuit." Then he became so giddy I thought he might dissolve before my eyes. I thought a bit about that and realized I hadn't heard anything that truly inane since I was fourteen or fifteen. I had grown up on a rural peninsula isolated from much of the world. It was a retro place where folks worked hard and long and insults were settled in a forthright sort of way. We learned not to say or do anything we couldn't own up to. Or, as a friend once advised: *You don't go selling tickets to the wolf if you don't have the wolf.* Later, I learned the trivial player was the poster child for a local, highly partisan political organization, a growth-at-all-cost coalition that prominently features a drug-abusing, reactionary talk show host on its website—along with the American flag. I'm figuring that tragic sort of irony was likely punishment enough for anybody.

6. Mary McKey was there. She is one of the kindest and most gentle souls I have ever met. On this day she was selling little photo note cards of the Wekiva River system from a tiny table. She is an excellent photographer and I bought twenty cards from her. I picked out the ones that showed the Wekiva in its most romantic light—-sun dappled palms and ferns and wading birds, sometimes with the vanishing mist of dawn making the beaks and fronds and fiddleheads fuzzy. For me, her photos were—and are—a very direct and visual way to capture the sacredness of nature, to help us all revel in what John Muir once described as a "cathedral." During a river cleanup over a decade ago, I paddled the stern of a big, battered aluminum canoe with Mary in the bow. We recovered a lot of trash from the river, and we talked some. Mary wondered why anyone would want to soil our Mother Earth in such a way. I guess, in the long haul, I was calmed by her spirit. She was in her mid-sixties then.

7. A young woman who was a teacher stopped by and introduced herself. She told me she'd been using one of my books in her classes for the last couple of years. She complimented me on the "language." She seemed sincere and I was honestly flattered. "Words really do have power," she said. "You seem to understand that." I thanked her, from the heart. I wanted to tell her that language is under siege, now more than ever—and that the words that arise from technology and business simply aren't able to describe the fullness of life. I thought more about the philosopher and educator David W. Orr. I met Orr when I was on a panel of writers at a book festival in St. Petersburg once. Like all men and women with greatness in their hearts, he was modest but very sure. In his work, Orr has written that we are losing the vernacular places where real language grows. Memory, tradition, and devotion to place mean far less in our go-fast world than they once did, and words to describe those experiences are fading from use. As a result, the ability of language to describe the role of a full and rich life in the higher moral ecology is impoverished. Life is made real by people like Mary McKey, but her power goes virtually unrecognized. The Disneyesque character and his buds, on the other hand, have far more power than any cartoon deserves.

8. I've always enjoyed listening to stories. When I was a little boy, some of my fondest early memories were of my grandmother, Mom Mom, reading storybooks out loud to me while I sat in the great protective sanctuary of her lap. When I think of what I admire the most in other writers today, I realize it's their capacity to communicate rare insight—without making a big deal about doing so. Not so long ago, my hiking buddy Steve and I drove with the fine nature writer Barry Lopez up to nearby Blue Spring. Lopez, who lives in Oregon, was here as part of a winter literary program over at Rollins College. But that day, it was just us, talking like old friends about manatees and scuba diving and the larger power of culture to tell the full story of nature. Lopez has said that he likes to use the word *Isumatug*, from eastern Arctic Eskimo dialect, to explain the role of a writer. The word means "the person who creates the atmosphere in which wisdom reveals itself." The writer's job, says Lopez, is "not to be brilliant, or to be the person who always knows, but . . . to be the one who recognizes the patterns that remind us of our

obligations and our dreams." Around us down in the spring run, the giant manatees moved slowly, either drifting in the gentle current or moving up and down as if they were giant balloons floating in a sub-aquatic holiday parade. They seemed to have all the time in the world.

9–10. A guy was playing some music down next to the Wekiva spring and every once in a while, I could hear a didgeridoo. It's an ancient reed-type instrument without the reed, a hollow branch really, and it produces a visceral throat-gut animal sound. Once I heard some half-naked aboriginal blokes playing it, and dancing out the lyrics to old tribal myths at the edge of the jungle at the tent compound of the Croco-dilus Jungle Lodge north of Port Douglas, Australia, on the northern Queensland coast. One folk myth-dance was "Crocodile Making Love to Woman." That was pretty surreal, all by itself.

Afterwards, I met my neighboring tent mate, a friendly Aussie with a killer smile and blonde hair pulled back in a ponytail. She asked me if I wanted to join her for some rum in her tent, which had walls and was quite large. But being obtuse to come-on's, having a distance to travel the next day, and not really having a clue as to where I was, I begged off. When I got inside my own large tent, wallabies were jumping up and down on my cot. I figured that was a special treat for them, so I slept on the floor and the soft thumping on the cot lulled me into a deep, dream-enriched sleep. When I woke up the wallabies and the sweet Aussie were gone and there was a large scorpion-like bug in one of my shoes. Over in the canteen, I choked down some Vegemite on crackers, drank coffee, and then got into my battered rental car and drove north to the shore of the Daintree River where a sign warned of the possibility of crocodile at-tacks. Another sign warned that rental cars were not to go beyond that point. I got out and peeled off the bumper sticker with the name of the rental car company on it. From there, I rode across the river on a small open ferry, and then went on north by myself.

I was writing a story about nature at the time, so I guess that last entry qualifies for the list. It also reminds me that biological diversity and cultural diversity usually ride the same horse—or in this case, the same ferry boat. And, since there were more than two great ironies in that description, that rounds out the list to ten.

19

An Aquatic Burden of Dreams

Lake Woodruff

Bobby's four-stroke Honda 90 gurgles its way to life, pushing his flats boat away from the dock and out into the main-stem of the St. Johns. We've launched at a marina near where SR 44 bridges the St. Johns, heading north for the Lake Woodruff National Wildlife Refuge. On the opposite bank, the Shady Oaks restaurant sits precariously on old wooden pilings, its screened porch barely above the edge of the flowing

Jaws of gators for sale inside the fish camp marina, Highland Park, to the east of the Lake Woodruff National Wildlife Refuge.

river. Last month, the adjacent dock where boaters usually moor was underwater. But the river has fallen a couple feet since then, so all is business as usual.

Instead of following the channel all the way up to Woodruff, we duck inside the tight mouth of a creek that leads us to the Norris Dead River, broader and deeper. The creek mimics the larger St. Johns, flowing northward through a landscape of hardwood swamp, edged with native duck potatoes and spadderdock lilies. Both Bob and I marvel at the isolation of the creek, reveling in the quietude of the place. Even here in winter, there are still a few tiny white flowers blooming at the end of the long duck potato stems, along with great clumps of lavender-colored Carolina aster and a cluster of what looks like a marsh bidens, yellow petals encircling a black center eye.

The remaining leaves on the trees are turning color, but it's nuanced in the way of our Florida seasons.

It's a great day to be on a great river, and without a need to be a grown-up cardiologist or a writer today, we turn our lives over to the moment, counting only the things that really matter: the brilliantly white egrets and little blues hunting at the water's edge; the belted kingfisher squawking from overhead; a red-shouldered hawk calling from somewhere inside the fretwork of cypress and maple, sweet gum, and sabal palm. We're moving along at a good clip now, and since I'm used to kayaking, I have to readjust my sensibilities to the fast-forward nature of our journey. Bob's a fine river companion: affable, bright, and with a genuine streak for adventure. He majored in English as an undergrad, so we also share a love for literature that speaks to the larger experience in nature. Soon, Bob turns the boat helm over to me and picks up his camera, capturing images as precise as any lyric along the natural shore.

It's warm enough so that we don't need jackets. Bob wears a baseball cap with "Vanderbilt School of Medicine" on it. With no hat, I allow myself to enjoy the way the light wind blows through my hair. Little official government signs with the logo of a flying goose mark both shores as part of the wildlife refuge. Created in 1964 expressly to protect migratory birds, the refuge and its 22,000 acres of water and land has one of the most diverse bird populations in all of Florida. Inside Woodruff, some 215 species have been counted; a colony of some 400 Swallow-tailed kites will even nest here later in the spring. Intact landscapes like this are chock full of food for both local birds and seasonal migrants who either over-winter here or pass through on their way south. The expansive wilderness is an avian Valhalla in the midst of a state that has a hard time controlling its appetite to build new stuff atop old landscapes, simply because it can.

Our backwater "road" will lead us all the way up to the southwest edge of Lake Woodruff, where I'm anxious to cruise the shore of Tick Island there. As we go, I recall the archaeological significance of Tick, which is essentially a 270-acre shell midden tucked in between Woodruff and, to the west, Lake Dexter. Native Americans lived on this island for almost six thousand years, harvesting wildlife, fish, and snails made plentiful by the zest of the flowing river and creeks. The abundance of nearby food allowed them to wander less, to ponder a bit more. Villages were built, mythology evoked, sacred ceremonies invented. Dreams and visions were imprinted on shell and bone ornaments and pottery, which had previously been spartan and bare.

A small wooden sign marking the canal entrance to Highland Park Fish Camp appears, and we turn into the old cut, heading to the camp for a way stop. Bob traveled here by road not long ago and was impressed with the cultural integrity of the place. Like manatees and short-nosed sturgeon, Florida fish camps are also endangered, at the mercy of those who would much rather see fancy upscale waterfront condos than a ramshackle store selling live bait and floating plastic bobbers.

The camp materializes ahead and I slow the boat to a crawl and nose it into one of the slips under a corrugated tin roof. We tie up and head inside where we find a personable young woman behind a counter full of almost every type of freshwater fishing tackle I could ever imagine: bobbers, sinkers, monofilament, leaders, swivels, hooks, and so on. She tells us her family has owned the place for almost a half a century now. We look around, soaking up the grit of authentic river funk. An ancient canoe with a sign identifying this as a "Timucua dugout" hangs above a door. Walls and shelves haphazardly display what amounts to a virtual zoo full of taxidermied animals: white-tailed deer and wild boar and largemouth bass, a dozen tiny gator heads, and one very convincing stuffed bobcat that seems as if it might come back to life at any moment. "A half century of roadkill," says Bobby, smiling.

We grab some cold sodas and sit in a corner on a couple of comfy old sofas, behind the rack with the small alligator heads. Next to me is a shelf with animal skulls and large jars, sort of like those used for pickled eggs and pig knuckles. Except these are full of whole pickled animals: coral snakes and rattlesnakes, and something small with legs I can't quite identify. "Fetus of a river otter," says Bobby.

We finish our drinks and climb back in our flats boat, driving it back out of the canal and into the large creek that will deliver us to Woodruff. Norris Dead River leads us on a miraculous meander through the soggy floodplain, passing a few other creeks like "Alligator Lake" along the way before dumping us into the southerly shore of Woodruff. As with most other "lakes" on the St. Johns, this one is less a lake and more a large expanse in the flowing river. If we traveled out of it to the northeast, we could trace Spring Garden Creek there for several miles to Ponce DeLeon spring itself. But we're headed for the heart of the refuge and Tick Island, so we go west. It's mild and sunny, just a few clouds in the sky, and for now, we're the only boat on the entire lake. We aim for the corner where the lip of Lake Dexter wraps around the north shore of Tick Island, encircling a little creek with the unlikely name of "Eph" as it does. A map we bought back at the fish camp charts a "Bennett Landing" on the edge of the island nearest us. But the landing, like almost all the others that once allowed steamships to service the St. Johns, is long gone. We maneuver into Dexter, looking for a dry shore on the island, but so far all we see is swamp, cordgrass, and sawgrass at its edge. Finally, we come to a higher flat berm that leads back into the woods, perhaps the remains of an old tramway. We tie up here, and follow the trail back for several hundred yards. As we do, the earth rises ever so slightly and the hardwoods are replaced by pines and other upland trees.

After the Timucua and Mayaca Indians were driven off in the early 1700s, white settlers came here, farming and growing citrus. The soil, enriched by the massive shell midden mounds, must have nurtured hearty fruits and vegetables. Archaeologist Jeffries Wyman traveled to

Tick Island in the early 1870s and wrote about it in his book *Freshwater Shell Middens of the St. Johns River*. Wyman reported that the artifacts found in mounds twenty feet high were crafted by a complex culture, a people who had time to consider the gods of nature and to embrace their own place in it. They carved shell plummets to anchor the bottoms of their hand-woven nets, and created pottery, hair pins, and other ornaments incised with the symbols of their sacred stories. At least 150 of those Indians were buried here, ordained for a plentiful afterlife with deer antler headgear, projectile points, and knives.

Like the Cuna (also Kuna) Indians of the San Blas Islands of Panama, many of the native people of Florida also believed that heaven would be not unlike their own landscape—in this case, subtropical cypress swamps and springs, fish and wildlife, all of it encased in a balance that was harmonic and pure. As Florida began to boom in the 1920s, the middens took on another life: in a sandy peninsula, they provided a rare, durable material to underpin new roads and homes. Draglines were brought to the island on barges, scooping up the shells and shards and ornaments to use for road fill, even drainage fields for septic tanks. As archaeologists scrambled to make sense of what was left, tour boats from Ponce DeLeon Spring routinely brought tourists here in the 1960s, giving the passengers not just a look at the eviscerated middens, but promising each a pottery shard to take home.

We would need most of the day to fully explore Tick Island, and we don't have that luxury right now. We return to the boat and push off. As we head back through Dexter, I notice little "no trespassing" signs posted at strategic landings around the island, and think "whoops." We move out into Lake Dexter, not far from what is now mapped as Idlewilde Point, the real place where the spiritual naturalist Billy Bartram once fought off gators at his "Battle Lagoon" in 1774. Bartram, our original protohippy, cared far more about the power of nature than left-brained control and pretense. Those gentle-minded spirits who appreciate the same today have given the naturalist a new life via books and conferences and even art. In *The Flower Hunter* by artist Jackson Walker, a young and strong Bartram is portrayed alone, deep inside the rich subtropical landscape, happily sketching away from his small wooden boat.

Finally, we reach the south-north mainstem of the river itself, and follow the red and green channel markers south, congratulating ourselves on the sublime journey the backwater creeks and streams allowed us today.

I think of all the damage that has been done to this entire river over time, think of those who would simply manipulate it for their own gain without any concern for the shared "commons." This is a Sunday and so I also give a silent and grateful thanks that wild—almost mythic—places like this still exist in Florida at all. It occurs to me that it's all in the seeing: depending on the way you approach it, a clue from an earlier time might be a deer antler decorated with the mystical twists and turns of five thousand years worth of spiritual memory, a sacred covenant passed to us from another dimension. To those like Bartram, who came to commune and to learn, Florida has—and will always have—sweet mystery hidden away along its shores. To others who came to transform thousand-year-old trees into board feet and to pave roads with the residue of prehistoric art, it will have another meaning.

Those who wholly embrace the deep and sacred feelings of mythology bear a burden of dreams. To do so, they make room in their hearts for the wisdom of myths that have reached out to us over time. And, once acknowledged, can they ever be denied? The sun is warm now as we return, running our little boat south against both the wind and the current, navigating the river as if it is boundary, a narrow temporal cusp between the then and the now.

20

Underneath Where
the River Used to Be

There is a river in Florida called the Ocklawaha. It is a poem of a river, blackwater, subtropical, enfolded in a very long and rich history. When early tourists came to Florida for amusement, they often booked passage on paddlewheelers that took them south on the St. Johns and then, at the village of Welaka, delivered them west into the mouth of the Ocklawaha. Most didn't know it at the time, but they were coursing through territory that was older than much of peninsular Florida, traveling beyond and even atop places where some of the earliest natives

A portion of the ancient hardwood forest that once lined the historic channel of the Ocklawaha River was inundated when the Rodman Reservoir was created. I paddled here during a draw-down of the reservoir, and this is the "forest" that I saw.

had lived, middens now sloughed off into the river bottom. Early travelogues, such as *The Highways and Byways of Florida* (1918) bragged of the Ocklawaha that "the voyage is a visit to fairyland." It promised that "no trip to Florida is complete which does not include an outing on this romantic stream with its ever-changing scenes and its tonic air laden with the balsamic odors of the forest. . . . There is scarcely a house to be seen along its course . . . but now and then a landing, with its rich freights of cotton, sugar, oranges . . . It is the most singular river."

The great poet Sidney Lanier, nearly always broke as good poets usually are, was convinced to write a guidebook about Florida and what a steamboat passenger might see on this river. To do so, he rode a narrow, boxy paddlewheeler more than a hundred miles upstream to where the springs of the Silver River confluxed with it. There, the boat entered the eight-mile run of the Silver, the liquid turquoise of the deep aquifer melting into the tea of the Ocklawaha. For Lanier, it was "as if God had turned into water and trees the recollections of some meditative ramble through the lonely seclusion of His own soul." Why don't we say such things about rivers today? Has this sacredness gone away, or has our ability to acknowledge it?

I usually paddle the Ocklawaha in from Welaka, crossing the broad St. Johns and aiming for Bear Creek, a canopied meander that trails upstream, just south of the mouth of that tributary. Low branches reach out from trunks and snags routinely poke up from the surface, creating a tighter, untrimmed version of the wider Ocklawaha. It's fun to pretend I'm following the old liquid trail the early steamboats once used to take them upstream to Silver Springs. The catch is that I can only go as far as to where the Rodman Dam and Reservoir rises up from the Ocklawaha. There, my illusion quickly dissolves because the 1968-era dam interrupts the historic prerogative of this old river journey.

Today I'm trying a different approach. With a friend, I'm going to visit the old meandering river channel the reservoir usually covers. I can do this not because I'm delusional, but because the reservoir is drawn down every three to four years. The reason for the draw-down is to dry out and, ideally, kill the invasive exotic water weeds that have clogged the Rodman more or less since it was built. Then, when the dam is refilled to its eighteen-foot depth, there will—theoretically—be less water hyacinth, water lettuce, and hydrilla. Perhaps the native submerged plants like eelgrass, coontail, and southern naiad will even make a bit of a comeback. And, just for a while, the absurd, human-engineered reservoir that covers nine-thousand acres of floodplain forest, twenty springs, and sixteen miles of historic river channel, will pretend to function like a natural system. But it won't last long, of course, and the entire cycle will be repeated again in another three to four years.

The only real good news about all of this draining business is it does allow a brief two- or three-week window in which to actually see *under* the reservoir, down to where the river and some of its springs used to be. Perhaps it will even allow a vague reminder of Lanier's imaginings of God's meditative ramble. And so, just after dawn we load the kayaks and go, driving up into the Ocala National Forest and swerving off onto a dirt road to a site mapped as Kenwood on the northwest shore of the now-diminished reservoir. A couple days earlier, I had chatted with Capt. Erika Ritter, a Florida native several times over who guides an eco-tour pontoon boat on the river, showing off the intact portions of the Ocklawaha upstream of the dam. Erika really cares, a lot, and while the concept of the reservoir bothers her, she is also eager to help folks see what the river underneath the dam looks like. She wants us all to remember. To this ends, she had suggested the Kenwood put-in, describing how to get into the old river channel from there.

With Erika's advice stowed away, my paddling partner and I launch at the Kenwood site by mid morning, driving down to a temporary dirt ramp that would normally be inundated by the giant reservoir. Sport fishermen flock in here like wading birds to an ephemeral pond that is entering the dry season. The draw-down has the same effect by concentrating most of the remaining fish in scattered sloughs and ponds, flowing springs, and oxbows of the historic channel. Once in the water, we paddle out of the straight canal with the motor-boating fishermen and after a couple of false starts, finally make our way into the meanders that cradle the historic river. The "Rodman Pool" is down by 80 percent of its usual volume, about seven to eight feet more shallow as a result.

We paddle twists and turns of the original hardwood forest—except the shoreline trees that remain around us are dead, only their grey-brown trunks still standing, smooth and tempered like driftwood. It is like paddling through a petrified forest. I look closely and make out the curves and lines that once defined cypress buttresses and knees, even the skinny round trunks of the sabal palms. I'm figuring some of the other trees are sweetgum and swamp tupelo and sweet bay, just like I see on the wild stretch of the river upstream from Welaka. Regardless of how majestic the tree was in its lifetime, the surface water level of the Rodman is the great equalizer. This "forest" around us is uniformly six and seven feet high, its phantom trunks forever bereft of their canopies, which have been eroded away by the surface waters of the reservoir.

As always, it is the springs that most fascinate me. Between chatting with Capt. Erika and reviewing a chart of the drowned springs from the local water management district, I have sketched a rough map of where the main ones still exist. We head first for Blue since, of all those covered by the reservoir, it is one of the most venerable. A resort and landing once existed here, a place where steamboats would stop on their upstream journey, maybe to drop off some passengers or pick up some firewood and crates of citrus. A narrow strand of water leads us out of the historic channel toward Blue, and I'm guessing this is its old run, a stream once known as "Indian Creek."

As we approach the actual spring, the darker tannins of the river clear and I see a roiling of water on the surface, the dynamic marking the upwelling from below. Nearby is an old wooden dock, the remnants of a resort that once brought nineteenth-century bathers to Blue. Like all else, the dock and spring will again become submerged when the reservoir is refilled. After being covered with the enormous weight of the reservoir waters for all this time, Blue still flows, but only at the rate of 7 million gallons a day. At least one study estimates that, if the reservoir was removed, the spring would gradually revitalize itself until it was again flowing at a rate of 26 million gallons a day. Once we're atop the roil, I use my polarized glasses to cut the surface glare, staring down to the darker bottom, limestone walls sloping toward the vent like a giant funnel. We sit atop the roil for a while, me trying to imagine little kids in full bathing suits of another century splashing and laughing here.

Finally, we hear the faint hum of a sport fishing boat powered by an electric trolling motor moving toward us. Two fishermen wearing camo are standing on the deck, both with cocked crossbows, looking intently down into the clear spring water for any fish large enough to shoot. I see a stringer hanging from the side of the boat with tilapia, the large African exotic imported by the Florida game and fish commission years ago as a "new" sport fish. A few species of tilapia (also called Nile perch) will bite a hook, but most are herbivores. One of the sure ways to catch them is to snag them with a hook, or shoot them with an arrow. Growing five to ten pounds in size, the hefty fish are usually slow moving, making easy targets for predators from above. The archers are serious, intent, barely noticing us as they go stoically about their quest. But I think this is a good thing: no one wants a happy-go-lucky, lackadaisical crossbow hunter lurching about on the deck of an unsteady boat when you're nearby in what amounts to a plastic dugout with a limited capacity to avoid an errant shot.

Blue Springs was celebrated in its time, but for now, it's time is gone. Likewise for other springs such as Alcorn, Canon, Big Rack Road, Hasty Greene, and more. Before the dam interrupted the flow of this river, manatees would swim upstream to some of the larger springs when the waters of the St. Johns turned colder. At least thirteen different kinds of fish also migrated up and down the Ocklawaha—mullet, striped bass, shad, and channel catfish that weighed forty pounds or more. Firsthand reports had these migrants that were isolated on the upstream side of the Rodman surviving until the 1970s, but by 1980, almost all had disappeared.

Wildlife biologists today estimate that, if Blue Springs were intact, the springhead and its spring run could safely "overwinter" up to 150 manatees, taking the pressure off of other natural thermal sanctuaries like the Blue Spring on the St. Johns near Orange City. Other larger limestone vents, like Hasty Greene, could over-winter a hundred. Restoring the river for this reason alone would offer sanctuary to several hundred manatees each winter. Now that outdated utility plants around Florida are being decommissioned or converted so they no longer provide the heated effluent for artificial refuges, natural thermal sanctuaries are more vital than ever.

Taken wholly, these drowned springs are the sum total of poor judgment, another version of when really bad things happen to really good places. The Ocklawaha, refurbished with locks and canals, its natural crookedness made straight, was to be a "Cross Florida Barge Canal." The incision had been imagined by half-mad schemers for centuries. It dated to the bloodthirsty conquistador Menendez who envisioned a waterway across the peninsula in order to eliminate the risky Florida Straits from the business of shipping stolen treasures back to Spain. Actual work along the canal route had stopped and started since the 1930s, and the giddy daydream almost came true when the Rodman was finished in 1968. If the entire thirty-foot-deep canal and its locks were complete, barges from Jacksonville would travel through the interior of Florida to the Gulf coast, and the savings in fuel and other shipping costs would be enormous. Nonetheless, the complete lack of concern for the natural landscape—and the aquifer under it—was astonishing. The scheme was actually halted during the Nixon administration for the damage it would do by breaching the top of the aquifer. The action set a precedent that required all federally funded developments nationally to prepare and to abide by environmental impact statements. And it did something else that no one had ever been able to accomplish in Florida: it galvanized the nascent and highly fractionalized environmental movement under one resolute banner for the first time. It was biologist Marjorie Harris Carr, the wife of the naturalist Archie Carr, who led this charge. She has been fondly remembered for that selfless effort, and a state greenway near the river has been named for her.

Today, we see Capt. Erika's pontoon boat in the distance with several passengers aboard, and paddle over to it. I see her boat is named the *Anhinga Sprit* for the water bird that makes a good living diving into rivers and lakes for fish. It is great to finally meet Erika, and we hang there holding onto her boat and chat a bit. Erika, animated and expressive, tells us they have seen migratory warblers and limpkins, and of course, anhingas. One of Erika's clients has studied Marjorie Kinnan Rawlings, and we consider how well the author understood this complex Florida landscape, and how she grounded her fiction in real geography: in *The Yearling*, Penny Baxter exclaims that "My words was straight, but my intentions was crooked as the Ocklawaha River." Inconsolable after the death of his pet deer, Jody Baxter floats down the Ocklawaha from the Big Scrub in an old dugout, until he finally reaches the St. Johns. In *South Moon Under*, the author described life along steamboat "landings" on the Ocklawaha that no longer exist—Sunday Bluff, Cedar, Iola, Palmetto.

The sun is falling lower in the sky, and the light is beginning to change. We say goodbye and paddle some more, stopping to absorb the golden world around us. As we go, we see a flock of some two hundred migratory white pelicans, now turned bronze by the late afternoon light. Like the native ibises and wood storks and egrets—like the camo-wearing archers—the pelicans are here especially to feast on the fish concentrated by the drawdown. I think of the poignant Oliver Sacks book *The Awakening* in which comatose patients miraculously regain consciousness—remembering how they once lived, vague at first, and then with more confidence and desire. That seems to be happening here, the historic magic of a spring revealed just for now, almost as if it's reaffirming its timeless hydrological life. But like the subjects in Sacks' book, all will soon return to a watery unconsciousness, drowned again by the very real weight of time.

We paddle until all the motor boats crank up and zoom back to the ramp, turning the arrow-straight canal into an aquatic dragway. When the air is quiet, we move across the last few meanders of the old river, pushing hard at a bicep-driven speed of three knots, inside a creek lined with the wooden skeletons of what was once a magnificent forest. As we go, our hulls each leave dark V's in our wakes, large ripples destined to live only a few seconds before dissolving into the ink the water has become. I think finally of how one nineteenth-century guidebook writer described the Ocklawaha as "this liquid silent forest aisle." When the writer used the word "silent," he had no idea how inextricably quiet the heart of this river would one day become. By the time we reach our take-out at Kenwood, I see almost all the motorized fishermen have loaded their boats onto trailers and are driving away, most with their headlights on. We are the last ones to leave the river.

My friend and I fumble to tie down the kayaks on my cartop racks in the new dusk, and drive back up the temporary ramp. I stop once and look over my shoulder, but the great valley is quiet and black now, just a few shadows dancing here and there, the ghosts of the old river hidden in the liquid silent forest aisle. It is underneath where the river known as the Ocklawaha used to be.

21

Cayo Hueso

Burrowing into the Core

In the twilight of Key West, I can almost feel the weight of its outlandish island dreams settling around me here on Duval Street. Roots of sapodilla trees push up through cracks in the sidewalk, and fuchsia petals of bougainvillea lay like confetti on the street. Overhead, frigate birds soar in and out of the scarlet clouds.

Down here on the thin limestone crust of the island, the nightly pub bacchanal known as the "Duval Crawl" is underway. Neon bar signs

A picket fence in the Bahama Village neighborhood of Key West, Fla., reflects the funky nature of the place itself. Photo by Michelle Thatcher.

glow, music thrums, and mopeds buzz like giant salt marsh mosquitoes. It seems as if the ground itself is vibrating under me. Old bodegas and buildings where Cubans once rolled cigars by hand morph into souvenir shops, pubs, and designer clothing stores, almost overnight. I get the odd feeling that I'm atop a tiny raft bobbing unsteadily in the warm turquoise sea—a raft that at once holds a carnival, a maritime museum, and a giant t-shirt shop. Some of my favorite authors have walked these same streets during the last century, from novelists Ernest Hemingway and Tom McGuane to poets James Merrill and Elizabeth Bishop. The trick is to resist the hype that would have visitors seeing them all here at once, on command.

Surely, this modern Key West is nothing if not richly tiered. Its decades of tinsel and tawdriness seem stacked, each upon the other, like an untidy layer cake. Once, novelist and poet Jim Harrison, who lived on the island, returned to Key West after being away for years. He roamed the streets with his friend McGuane, trying to figure out what old funk had been replaced by the new. "It was like a drunken 'Songlines,'" Harrison said, referencing the Bruce Chatwin book about Australia and aboriginal myth.

Shorty's, a downtown diner catering to locals—sometimes to the exclusion of tourists who were simply locked out—has now become a shop for tourist geegaws. The last time I checked, El Cacique, my favorite Cuban restaurant, had moved out to "Sears Town" because the rent was too high, taking its café con leche and generous plates of picadillo with it.

I exited with my friend Michelle from a small plane on the tarmac of the tiny "international" airport just two days ago, walking under a large official sign welcoming us to the "Conch Republic." During the next few days, I'll be off on a Songline quest of my own, a Walkabout that lets me burrow deeper into the spirit of this mythic old island town. Despite the over-the-top marketing hype, there's something very compelling that still draws me here and I want to identify it, once and for all.

The city of Key West, which sports a pink-lipped queen conch shell on its official seal, "seceded" from the Union back in the 1980s via an official city proclamation. After doing so, it declared "war" on the United States, and then one full minute later, the mayor surrendered and requested foreign aid. This actually happened, even though the federal government chose to ignore it.

Earlier today, Michelle and I were at a local party for the grassroots conservation group Reef Relief out near Garrison Bight. There, we met the "secretary-general" of the Conch Republic, one Sir Peter Anderson, a tall good-natured fellow who enjoys pontificating about the "state of mind" that Key West commands. Sir Peter has a real office with a real flag, issues passports for a fee, and even implies a very real diplomatic immunity might even be achieved—if you really, really believe. The Republic's motto is: "We seceded where others failed." There's a strong tendency to want to play along, especially since the Republic back on the mainland doesn't seem to be having a whole lot of fun these days.

We're here in the hurricane season, which means that at any given time, a tropical storm can swell up and then cuisinart its way over the top of this flat, two-by-four-mile island with little effort. If this was anywhere else in Florida, TV weather people would be scaring the bejesus out of us with thunderstorm alerts. But the big news here is about the forthcoming Hemingway Look-Alike Contest—followed by ongoing reports about the status of the "gypsy chickens of Key West," a heady issue that appears to have divided the town into pro and con poultry camps. (A chicken catcher was once hired to corral the fowl, but no one is sure what has become of him.) Meanwhile, at the Chicken Store on Duval, I can sign a petition to "hold dear the heart-stoppingly beautiful wild chickens of the City of Key West and ask they be preserved here forever."

The sovereignty of the Conch Republic, ruled by Sir Peter and inhabited by anyone with a sense for the idiosyncratic, implies immunity to just about all higher forces—from tropical storms to rigid normalcy. At Greene Street, Michelle and I dodge the Conch Train tour, a cartoonish mini-locomotive trailing along open cars full of brightly dressed tourists like a mechanized conga line. I notice some of the passengers are actually taking photos and home video of us as we stand on the curb, waiting to cross. It occurs to me that an "attraction" in this old island town is just about anything that fits inside a viewfinder.

During hurricane season, the sea seems as if it has come ashore in one languorous tide of moisture and torpor and sweat. The air is so thick you may as well be underwater. It was the sea, after all, that first defined this place—that rare fusion of Gulf Stream and coral reef and mangrove-fringed shoal. When Miami was still a coastal swamp, Key West was the wealthiest city in all of Florida, thanks to pirates and wreckers who ransacked the ships that grounded just offshore. Opportunism has prevailed ever since.

On Greene Street, we duck under a sign with a giant grouper into Capt. Tony's Saloon, where a couple of decades ago, I remember spending a leisurely summer afternoon chatting with the good captain himself. Tony told me that before buying the bar, he captained sport fishing boats that cruised the offshore Gulf Stream, and otherwise used his boat to haul whatever needed to be hauled. Someone once wrote of Capt. Tony that he seemed "like a drop out from a Hemingway novel" and Tony liked that so much he had it printed on the cover of match packs that advertised the saloon. A few years ago, Tony sold his saloon to rich folks from the mainland who were not dropouts from anything.

Not so long ago, a conch-slinging feud erupted when the new owners of Tony's were sued by the new owners of Sloppy Joe's, just a few lurches away on Duval. The current Sloppy's relies heavily on promoting itself as "Hemingway's Favorite Bar," although the original pub was actually in the building where Tony's sits today. Little signs are now posted in both bars that clarify when and where Hemingway actually drank, putting an end to the litigious spat.

Built in an old morgue, Tony's still has that fecund and decadent feel that once marked all of this old town of pirates and wreckers, spongers and shrimpers. And Tony's was the place where Papa met his third wife, Martha Gellhorn, in 1934. If you squint into the dark cavern of the bar, past the trunk of a banyan tree growing through the ceiling, beyond the bras and thousand shards of notes and money tacked to the walls, you can still imagine Papa, sunburnt from fishing out on the Gulf Stream, with the brainy and striking Gellhorn, hunkered down on the wooden bar stools.

Back out on the street, we stop in Sloppy Joe's where a clutch of white-haired cruise ship passengers is huddled around a table under a stuffed billfish and a large photo of Papa. Onstage, some tattooed slackers are banging out a rock cover song that is so discordant I can't even identify it. I notice the air conditioning is blasting away, even with the doors swung wide open. Ceiling fans spin, but only as an accessory. For now, one can purchase a "Papa-Rita" for $8 and buy more than three hundred pieces of merchandise with the bar's logo in the adjacent retail store, including golf balls. It's very difficult for me to picture Papa spending much time in Sloppy Joe's today, unless it was to start unloading on the patrons with one of his elephant guns.

The band mercifully breaks, and I look up on the stage and see Michelle hunched over and shooting photos of the crowd. Some of the crowd is shooting photos of her shooting photos. Behind me, a "Sloppy's Bar Cam" also captures her on giant screen, just in case you missed it the first two or three times. Umberto Eco was right about thrice-removed reality seeming more real to Americans than reality itself.

Out we go into the balmy tropical evening, heading for the Schooner Wharf bar, which edges up to the waters of the Key West Bight, the historic harbor of the island. Not so long ago, working shrimp trawlers berthed here, so thick you could walk the entire harbor from one deck to another, ducking below the nets and outriggers. Faced with a gentrifying harbor with costly docking fees, the raw, picturesque boats and their raw, picturesque crews moved north to Stock Island. Today, the Bight is full of expensive yachts and sightseeing charters.

The poet Elizabeth Bishop, who lived on nearby White Street in the 1930s, once wrote "The Bight," a poem that was elegant and searingly precise. Some of her images still remain true today:

Black and white man-of-war birds soar
    on impalpable drafts

And:

At low tide like this how sheer the water is.
    White, crumbling ribs of marl protrude and glare.

But other images have not fared as well:

The frowsy sponge boats keep coming in
    with the obliging air of retrievers

Except for one room with a pool table, there are no walls at the Schooner Wharf, just a bunch of frond-covered huts. The Bight, where tarpon still come and roll under the soaring man-of-war birds, is just a few feet away. There is a large dog sitting at the bar, drinking a beverage from a cup held up to him by a pretty woman. Next to her is a guy who looks like an accountant—with glasses, button down shirt, and pressed slacks, but who is wearing a pink tutu. A few yards away, a lean, dangerously tanned guy in tight shorts and a plaid fanny pack is gyrating to the music on the gravel and dirt floor, alone. His eyes seem to be focused on some point that is far, far away.

⁂

Captain Victoria Impallomeni guides her center console boat carefully through a canal cut into the lime rock of Stock Island, headed for a rare place where ancient reefs and mangrove islands of the backcountry conspire to create an Other World. Fossilized corals and oolitic limestone form the canal walls, transparent water allowing me to see its composition nearly to the bottom. We're floating on air, just for now.

Stock is the first island north of Key West, just over the Cow Creek Channel. It's gritty in the way working waterfronts can be when not coifed up. Most of the commercial fish and shrimp trawlers migrated up here years ago, along with a few backcountry guides like Victoria. Laid back hangouts, like the Hogfish Bar & Grill, have followed, advertising themselves as "The Way Key West Used to Be."

I haven't seen Victoria for three years, but her sensibilities are so closely attuned to my own that it seems that just yesterday I was standing next to her at the center console, headed out into the Gulf, anticipating most anything. We've done some cool things together over the years, and it's always come back to the water, that great magical swath of turquoise that ebbs and flows around the archipelago of the Keys. I spent Christmas Eve on this strange island once, shooting pool in the Green Parrot bar with a black Rasta guy, dressed in a Santa suit, dreads and all. Then early the next morning, while all of Key West was sleeping in, I headed out for the mangroves with Victoria.

After a couple days trouncing about the streets of Key West, I begin to feel as if the vernacular island architecture, its out-of-plumb culture and baroque hype have settled onto my senses like lime rock dust settles on my skin. The romantic history being peddled is illusive, more like déjà vu than a flesh and blood experience. There's only so much a shot of tequila in a bar at 4:00 a.m. will reveal, regardless of what famous writer sat on the same stool fifty years before you.

Safely out of the canal, Victoria trims the tabs of the motor and pushes the throttle forward, and soon we are skimming over water barely eighteen inches deep, cool now from the salty wind in our faces. Aboard are Susan, a publisher of a magazine in the Keys; Christian, an attorney from Seattle; and my friend Michelle. The three women seem vibrant, engaged. Christian, soft spoken, looks as if he just emerged from an extended rain, and he likely has. I'm grinning from ear to ear, happy to be where I am for the moment. We zoom toward the bridge for the Overseas Highway, and once under it—encouraged by our captain—we howl like wolves, letting our voices reverberate in the concrete tunnel.

The backcountry here is comprised of all the hundreds of low, uninhabited cays that spread out to the westerly horizon. The shape of each usually mimics that of the Atlantic's "spur and grove" coral reefs, with sand-covered limestone shoals carved into finger islands by the tides. Before being first linked by a railroad, and then a series of bridges and causeways, this is how all of the Keys once looked. Key West, at the tail, was the largest southerly island, underlain by just enough hard rock to keep it a few feet above water.

Victoria's been taking charters out here for thirty-two years, and in that time has morphed from a flats fishing guide to a sort of New Age sea priestess. True believers seeking transcendence rely on her to show them the way, mind melding with curious dolphins or meditating in the warm tropical waters. She sometimes drops speakers under the surface, playing reggae, blues, even polkas. Bottlenose dolphins regularly approach her boat, and she's convinced they're drawn in by the music. When I press her on the legitimacy of the rest of the New Age stuff, she smiles and says, "It's just good thoughts. It can't hurt."

Unlike the Tarot and palm readers back on Duval Street, the cosmos isn't dogmatically packaged either. On the last outing, Victoria dragged me behind her boat in deeper water on a ski rope, and I gripped a wooden tow board that allowed me to dive and spin like a giant human fish, more of a rush than a revelation. Other times, we've fished and even scuba dived.

Like most native "Conchs," she's also one hell of a navigator. Tourist boaters unfamiliar with the shallows around Key West often run aground or become stranded in a falling tide. Beyond the bridge, we glide across the shallow bottom, aiming for some offshore keys. I look at the map and see islands named Woman, Man, Ballast, Joe Ingram, Little Mullet, Crawfish. Most are a fret of red mangroves with little solid land, but some are rimmed with white sand, and a few larger ones hold pine rockland and tropical hardwood hammocks.

As we approach the first island, Victoria throttles back and we skim around the edges at idle speed so as not to disturb any of the wading birds that nest here. Victoria points out a sandy shore where she once had a tree house, cruising out here at age ten in a boat her dad built for her. Ospreys swoop overhead, and I notice their plumage is much more vibrant than the ones I know back home in Sanford on the St. Johns River. We spook a large southern stingray, and it swims away, undulating its wings like a large underwater bird. At the surface, a half dozen Atlantic needlefish flit nervously, and a few feet below, a school of silverside anchovies flash in one great unified movement. Sharks will follow the tide into the mangroves to hunt, as opportunistic as the pirates and wreckers ever were.

The mangroves anchor this backcountry, dropping leaves to provide food for microscopic animals, creating a sort of primal "soup" that feeds so much of what lives here. "The creator wrapped the world in a belt of mangroves," says Victoria, to no one in particular. And she is right: a distinctly tropical plant, mangroves splay out from the equator, but not so very far. In Florida, they trail off north of the latitude that warms New Symrna Beach and Tampa Bay.

We head for the "Mermaid Pool," a deep tidal creek that runs through one of the clutch of mangrove islands in the distance. Playing the straight man, I ask Victoria if the mermaids will be there, and she says: "They're always there when I'm there."

There are two massive wildlife refuges here that together protect more than six hundred square miles of water and ephemeral land, ranging north to Marathon and west to the Marquesas, not far from where trea-sure hunter Mel Fisher discovered the *Atocha*. We zigzag through the shallow water to avoid grounding, Victoria reminding me of this reality in a wonderfully subtle pun: "You can't get anywhere in Key West by following a straight line. You never go straight; you go forward."

On the horizon, the mangrove isles seem disembodied, floating in perfect mirages just above the water. The Spanish first charted these keys as "Los Martires" for the suffering martyrs who lost their heads back in the Old World, a trick of illusion informing geography.

Susan, an avid scuba diver, tells me she now sees a flamboyant spe-cies known as the lion fish out on the local reefs, a saltwater aquarium import from the Pacific now gone wild after being released here. It's a wonderfully gilded animal, as ornate as the passion flower back ashore. But it's loaded with neurotoxins and a sting can pack a powerful punch. Key West, says Susan, is full of such exotics, some of them underwater, and some of them on the streets and in the bars.

Inside the tidal creek, Victoria noses the boat into a natural hurricane hole where we tie off to a mangrove. Beneath us is the berm of limestone that was once a coral reef during an earlier geological epoch; the top of it is now covered with a marine community known as hardbottom—sponges and bryozoans and star corals, all studded with algal plants in the form of little feathers and trees. At ten to fifteen feet, it's shallow enough to snorkel, and so we all gear up to do so, no need to clank about with heavy tanks and weights.

Victoria tells us of folks who like to announce their food chain pre-eminence by splashing loudly overboard, simply because they can. "How would you like it if someone jumped into your bedroom unannounced?" she says. Clearly, Victoria's tenacious as hell—but she's also gentle enough to care about the consequences of our visit. "We're guests out here," she adds, smiling. "So we ought to be polite about it."

The five of us slip easily over the gunnels of the boat wearing masks, snorkels, and fins, taking care to disturb the water under us as little as possible. Besides simply being "polite," we're also far more likely to see marine critters if we don't thrash about. As soon as I'm in the water, I gently fin down a narrow slough under low mangrove prop roots, an aquatic alley that's too tight for our boat to even enter. The creek is a netherworld of its own making, as secretive as the offshore waters holding the deeper reefs. A school of silversides swarms around us, moving as one, and for the first time, I notice how blunt their noses are. Susan, who is next to me, points to a miniature barracuda, sized down and camouflaged, acutely attentive to our every move. Reddish sea stars appear, some strolling with great invertebrate purpose on the sand.

I duck out of the deeper creek and pull my way through the bow-like roots, back to shallow water where the light is amber. I see small mangrove snapper in schools, pinfish, porkfish, a juvenile snook. Two hermit crabs war with each other over their shells. A huge Atlantic spadefish hangs nearby, so out of scale that it seems like a balloon in a holiday parade.

It's quiet down here; the only sound is the one the snapping shrimp makes as its flicks its tail in a series of repetitive clicks. I hold my breath and swim to the bottom, past the tips of the prop roots covered with blue and red sponges, down to the ancient reef itself. The antenna of a large spiny lobster wave at me from a ledge, and a queen angelfish flips her body sideways as if to show me her bright colors.

This fossilized reef seems like a sprawling, low-slung castle from a kid's dream, parapets and archways and bastions of ancient calcium, bright-colored gobies and damsels floating in and out of it all.

When I descend again, the underside of the soft earth under the mangroves opens up like a large organic cave. I poke inside as far as I can and see a basket-sized hole letting in a bright ray of sun, a sort of natural skylight. Susan is following, while the others have taken another channel, leading who knows where.

I take my head out of the water and remove my mask. In the far distance, I see a flats guide poling his small boat in inches of water, trying to sneak up on feeding bonefish and permit that move between pastures of seagrass and open sand. Key West is only three miles away but Duval Street might as well be on another planet.

Once, a poet by the name of George Murphy rode with Victoria into the backcountry and later wrote "Rounding Ballast Key" about it all. Any few lines are part nature study, part metaphor:

> . . . I stood in your wake, sinking
> in that mud, its surface webbed with turtle grass
> and calcareous algae rising on my calves.
> About us the conch crawled from green to brighter green,
> the sea turtles lolled the miles across the keys from Tortuga,
> and tarpon and porpoise broke the surface at the edge

We fin back toward the others and climb aboard the dive platform on the stern of Victoria's boat, and she hoses us each down with fresh water. It is wonderfully exhilarating. I feel myself finally breathing deeply, inhaling the scent of sun-warmed mangrove and sea purslane and salt air, happy to be alive in a rare place where rays glide like giant birds and lobsters wave from archways in fossilized castles of coral.

I think of the way perceptions arrive on the ebb of a slow motion slog back ashore. It finally strikes me that experiences here oscillate, almost like an old fan: sometimes, they give visitors what they think they want; sometimes they acknowledge the pure sensory joy of a once-in-a-lifetime moment. I feel myself shift, however imperceptibly, and my senses open one more notch on the aperture. Figuring out the true Key West is illusion wrangling—like sorting a perfect mirage from the geography, a sea turtle migration from a metaphoric loll. But I realize now what I had forgotten: it probably always was.

22

What if the Shaman Is a Snail?

There are certainly more charismatic animals than the snail. But few have the sheer versatility to function with as much aplomb—if, indeed, a tiny mollusk in a tiny suit of calcium can be said to have such a quality. Perhaps it's the shell that does it, allowing for at least an appearance of stoic composure. This may be no different from local TV news anchors shielding themselves inside a theatrical armor of suits, fancy dresses, and coifs. Unless they stumble over a word on the teleprompter, they will seem the perfect model of self assurance and erudition.

There are Old World myths about snails, and perhaps the pre-Columbians on the peninsula of La Florida and throughout the Antilles even

Close up of the top of a Native American shell midden along a Florida river that shows pot shards and snail shells.

had their own stories about the iconic value of the little guys. We know the gods of these "earth people" were many, and reigned over very specific chores on their cosmic playing fields—to bring rain and hurricanes, to grow cassava, to bring fish into hand-woven fiber nets, and of course, to right some terrible wrong. Gods usually had their own totems, like Chac the rain god of the Maya, which was carved into temples and sacrificial altars. Back home here on the St. Johns, we see totemic sculptures like the owl, pelican, and otter found in the benthic mud near Hontoon Island.

The totems of river gods here were often skillful predators in real life—animals that morphed into protector spirits that stealthily maneuvered the Netherworld on behalf of their clan. In this case, the diminutive and cryptic nature of the snail may have kept it from that particular high-profile utility.

Nevertheless, we know most of the midden mounds along this river—a river that held more middens than any other in North America—were comprised mostly of snail shells. The reasoning is simple: snails like the mystery silt snail (*Viviparus georgianus*) were simply easy to harvest. While I have found shards of the much larger apple snail in these mounds along with pieces of freshwater mussels, it is the harder shell of *Viviparus* that weathers time the best.

When I was in Amazonia researching a magazine story about freshwater dolphins upstream of Iquitos, our old clunky riverboat sometimes stopped at villages, huts of wood and thatch atop the high muddy banks of the ever-surging Amazon. During one stop, I saw a small mango tree hung with a dozen or so of the empty shells of an apple snail—clearly a much larger species than the one I see back in Florida. I asked about it, and was told it was an act of sacrament, one intended to make the tree bear an abundance of fruit.

A few years later in Florida, I was paddling on the Withlacoochee River with a grad class from USF to help teach a course about the literature of rivers. That river rose up from the great Green Swamp, a complex system of seasonally wet flatwoods, swamps, and marshes that also births three other rivers, sending each off into different directions in the Florida landscape. It was on that paddle that I first saw the clues of an exotic snail in the form of a splotch of brightly colored eggs on a cypress stump. This was the giant channeled apple snail, an exotic import that was becoming increasingly troublesome. Not only did it aggressively elbow its way into the natural Florida habitat, it upped the ante a few notches: it ate its native brethren.

I have collected aquatic snails from Florida rivers before and brought them back to my aquarium and to my backyard pond. Once in the pond, they usually vanish from sight and go happily on their way, quietly realizing their snaildom. But the aquarium has that wonderful ant farm quality about it wherein nearly everything that goes on is visible, whether it wants to be or not. I consulted a guidebook to Florida snails by the noted malacologist Dr. Fred Thompson and learned most of my snails were called goldenhorn marissa (*Marissa cornuaurietus*). Their flattened shell looked like a teensy ram's horn in the way it encircled itself. Like many snails, they seemed content with their lot in life, grazing algae and moving patiently about.

But, as with most other snails—including the giant sea snail known as the queen conch—the goldenhorns had a secret that was seldom seen: they came into the world not as pint-size miniatures of their mommas, but as eggs that hatched into free-swimming larva. Like the queen conch, the larva of the goldenhorn evolved through several stages before finally metamorphosing into a shell-wearing snail the size of a pin head. Then they settled down to the bottom, from where they would navigate through the rest of their lives.

In a way, that transformation was captured in an old Chinese fable retold in the book *How the Snail Got Its Shell*: In ancient times, the snail was not slow at all—indeed, it had no shell, and was one of the fastest animals on earth. Then one fateful day, as the butterflies, ants, and bees went about their righteous business out in the rice field, the sky turned gray and pelted the earth with heavy rain and mud. The snail, being quicker than the others, saw an empty shell and made a run for it, comfortably waiting out the storm inside. Other critters coveted the shell and the safety it provided, but the snail would not relinquish it. When the storm finally ended, the snail stayed in his shell for fear others would commandeer it. He stayed and stayed, until finally, he and the shell were one. The world went on, with the snail in it. But now he had to drag his home around with him, and his agility and quickness were forever lost. A Faustian trade? I'm guessing only the snail knows for sure, and he isn't talking—with or without a teleprompter.

Snails serve other symbolic functions, too, and the one most of us here in Florida should care about is their ability to function as barometers, indicator species that tell us whether the water in which they live is healthy or not. A few years ago, I followed Dr. Thompson around in the backwaters of the Wekiva River basin in order to film a segment of a documentary about that river. We went to Sharks Tooth Spring and Sweetgum Spring, and others that were just then being mapped, hidden away deep in the forest and swamp. Over the course of a very few days, Thompson discovered six new species of hydrobiid snails. All lived in the runs of tiny springs, and each was found no where else on earth.

In addition to this particular snail being endemic, Thompson told me about the vulnerability of all the species of his animal of choice—that if pollution generated upland or upstream from the snail clouds its waters, the snail will suffer badly. "These guys are the first to get whacked," Thompson said. They can't swim away quickly like fish, or walk away like some crustaceans. Indeed, the newly discovered snails are true homebodies—all live within a 100-yard-long stretch of flowing water just downstream from the headspring. When pollution arrives, they must simply sit there and bear it, slowly suffocating to death. (That's why a snail Thompson discovered years ago in Sanlando Spring in "The Springs" development can no longer be found there.)

Meanwhile, back in my aquarium at home, I watch my goldenhorn marissas closely. Every once in a while, the entire lot of them migrate up the glass to the top of the tank, as close to the water's surface as they can get. That's because there's been a problem with the dissolved oxygen down below—maybe an electrical outage cut off the pump that helps bring O_2 into the water. No matter, the little guys make a run for it—and, once I see it, I do what I can to bring some stability back into their tiny shelled lives.

Which brings me to a report issued by the Florida Department of Environmental Protection the other day. It identified over 120 "impaired waters" up and down the St. Johns River, including some not so very far from me in Lakes Harney and Monroe. Much of the impairment was due to the lack of dissolved oxygen, thanks to the thoughtless behavior that treats our rivers as giant sumps for our fertilizers, pesticides, and stormwater. In too many instances, there was mercury and iron in the water, and so much fecal bacteria you wouldn't much want to spend any time there. "Impairment," in this case, means harmful to fish, and anything that lives in the water besides fish, from snails and crayfish to manatees and alligators. Bringing stasis to this larger world condition requires more than readjusting an aquarium pump.

Sometimes this impairment comes as a byproduct of rainwater, which rolls in over the banks from pampered lawns or farm fields in the river basin. Sometimes it comes into the river from large drainpipes which channel either rainwater from the human-built landscape, or effluent from an industrial plant of some sort. Most of the impairment could simply be avoided, using modern technology and lots of old fashioned common sense. Progressive studies that consider the larger real world view of natural resources show that pollution is, more often than not, a result of inefficiency and waste. Long-term solutions cost more up front, but realize larger profits over the long haul. Short term approaches earn quick money, and pollute.

At the same time DEP was releasing its list of impaired waters, the river's Water Management District (WMD) was busy making plans to pump surface water from our flat, warm landscape. It was doing so because it has allowed real estate developers to squander our underground aquifer to the point that it's no longer sustainable. At least half of the residential use of this pure, clean, eminently drinkable water is used to irrigate our outrageously cosmetic lawns. Meaningful conservation could replace the exotic grasses and plants with natives that are drought tolerant—but this requires stewardship and caring and action. Old paradigms merely require repetition. Florida's growth management laws, which rely on local cities and counties to ethically balance new development with available resources, are routinely exempted.

So now, we're to trust the water managers who have degraded our aquifer to manage the harvest of water from our shallow Florida rivers—simply because they promise not to actually harm these rivers or wetlands or the habitats they create? There's some wonderful dissonance in all of that, a delusion of the sort usually found in old Road Runner cartoons where the hapless Wile E. Coyote blows himself up several times and falls off of high cliffs, but still lives. I wonder if at the heart of public water policy planning—somewhere deep inside the bowels of the offices of the politically appointed board of trustees of the water management district—a Road Runner cartoon isn't simply playing over and over again.

Nonetheless, many see no problem with this disconnect. And it's no surprise that in some way their livelihoods depend on the unsustainable sprawl that is sweeping across our land- and waterscape right now—a plague in which greed and not locusts ruins a natural legacy commonly shared by us all. A national magazine recently referred to this way of doing business as a giant "Ponzi scheme" wherein future Floridians will pay for the contemporary sins of our water-sucking developers and their political toadies. This tragedy of the commons will continue to accrue, like a really bad credit card bill. Except, in the sociopolitical Florida world of just-pretend, the guys running up the tab won't be held responsible for it.

I think if one of the pre-Columbian river gods could return from wherever gods go when their people are no longer alive to honor them, reality might take on new meaning. Maybe the playing field would be leveled, and responsibility would rain from the sky like the torrents in the old Chinese parable. Perhaps it would be those obsessed with short term profit who—magically shrunk down to match the size of their ethic—wear shells and dwell at the bottom of Florida springs and rivers. They would likely hoard great mounds of algae, just because they could. In this readjusted reality, it would be goldenhorn marissa and fish and other living things who periodically visit to point at the odd little shell people and their odd little lives down on the bottom, maybe make up a fable or two to illustrate how they came to be there.

And the gods, having readjusted this badly out-of-kilter equation, would sit back on their haunches and—satisfied that the natural world had regained its equilibrium—smile. It would be a smile of great aplomb.

23

The Sand Dollar

A Measure of Wealth

It was twenty years ago, during a particularly transient time of my life, that I found myself living on an island that was washing away. My wealth then was measured in sand dollars. The island was just off the coast of South Carolina and it was called—no kidding—Folly. It was an appropriate name, both for the rapidly eroding Folly, as well as the ambiance created by those who knew their experience on this slender spit of sea-washed sand would be as wondrously natural as it was brief.

Sand dollar.

My rented beach home, up on stilts, teetered just inside the lee slope of the dune. I would begin most mornings by walking out my front porch, over a narrow boardwalk that spanned the dune, and then down wooden steps to the flat, wide southern beach. In the winter, when visitors were scarce, I could hike a couple miles to the desolate northern tip of the island without seeing another set of footprints.

Life before Folly had seemed complex and I was ready to take Emerson's advice, to "simplify." I did so by tuning out the man-made world, and tuning in the natural one. I started every morning by counting what was really important—the brown pelicans soaring overhead, the bottlenose dolphins swimming in close to feed, and on the varnished beach, the fragile bleached-white skeletons of the echinoderms known as sand dollars. On my best sand dollar day, I counted seven. They were so common that after a while I only picked up the finest specimens to keep, stacking them in neat piles back on the ledges of my screened porch. Despite their abundance, each intact "dollar" was a new surprise. I found it remarkable anything that delicate could survive the powerful and capricious Atlantic at all.

Others were similarly affected: the city of Folly Beach, gloriously odd-ball as only a place that's washing away can be, used the sand dollar as its symbol on its city crest. In the one-block long "downtown" of Folly, there was a bar named the Sand Dollar, and in a little shop next door, someone painted the tops of the flat shells with pictures of pelicans and dolphins. Plastic bags of sand dollars hung from racks there, and packed inside were little sheets of paper inscribed with "The Legend of the Sand Dollar." The legend was a story of religious symbolism, one I would see retold again in little beach shops along the Atlantic coast; it relied on the configuration of the "keyhole sand dollar" to work. It went something like this:

The five-pointed "star" etched in the top represents the star that drew the shepherds to the manger where Jesus was born, the petals spreading out over the top and the bottom depict the Christmas poinsettia, and the five "keyholes" are the wounds Jesus suffered on the cross. When broken open, the allegorical Cracker Jack prize tumbles out—five tiny calcium "doves" of peace and goodwill.

Even after I left Folly, the sand dollar continued to intrigue me. By the time I stumbled across my second mother lode of sand dollars not so long ago, the biology behind those stars and holes and little doves had some meaning. My companion and I, in snorkeling gear, were finning out into a splendid little cove called Fernandez Bay on the southwest edge of a remote Bahamian island called Cat. The day was glorious, and the late tropical sun low enough in the sky to cast a golden light on the clear water.

We were headed for an offshore clutch of rock and coral, passing over a monotone of white sand, a bottom shaped by the Etch A Sketch of nature's geometry—gentle curvatures that mimic the surface waves. The ease of the Tropics and the endless white sand mellowed me so fully that it wasn't until we were several hundred yards offshore that the anomalies began taking shape in the bottom. They were round, topped with miniature stars, and bleached as ghostly white as the bottom itself. It was as if someone had seeded them there for us, scattering them like flat white Easter eggs. This was my old friend from Folly, the five-keyholed sand dollar. With some excitement, I held my breath and dove down for the first one, bringing it up to show my partner, and watching as her eyes grew big behind her mask. Before the afternoon was over, we picked up a half dozen, leaving several times that many behind for others to find.

Back at our cottage on the cove, we sat on the porch and examined our treasures. We shook them and heard the "doves" or ossicles rattling inside. If our dollars had still been alive, they would have been covered with fine purplish-brown spines. In fact, the live ones were likely just under the sand, for that is where they spend most of their time. But these were dead as doornails. The flat, gradual slope of the bottom helped keep them intact, just as it had off the Carolina coast.

Sand dollars are a bit like foreign currency—they may look alike from a distance, but up close they vary dramatically. There are many species of dollar similar to the five-keyhole, including a six-holed version, one with four notches around the edge of the disc, and one with no holes at all. All share the same class *Echinoidea* with sea biscuits and sea urchins. Indeed, you can think of a sand dollar as a sort of flattened urchin, for that is what it is. While the body of the dollar seems to be one piece, it is in fact a fine network of calcium carbonate plates tightly wedged together.

On the top between these skeletal plates are gills arranged into "petals" that allow the sand dollar to breathe. Movement is accomplished by the rowing action of spines. And as for the "keyholes"—called lunules—some scientists think they help keep the animal in place in strong currents. (In contrast, the bulky sea biscuit, which looks a bit like a dollar on steroids, sits supremely atop the sand, disguising itself with algae, grass and shell debris.)

In sex, dollars are like most echinoderms in that they are either male or female, although for us non-dollars, they are nearly impossible to tell apart. Look closely at the four tiny points at the tips of the star on top: this is where the eggs or sperm are released—usually late at night, on the dark floor of the sea.

If the sex act seems lonely and brief, it is blissfully simultaneous, triggered by rising temperatures in the spring. Like coral spawning (which happens during August and September), the eggs and sperm connect in the water, and the fertilized eggs spawn free-swimming larvae. Eventually, these zooplankton metamorphose and drop to the bottom, having magically turned into miniature sand dollars.

And there they live their lives, turning bone white after death. For those of us who marvel at the little miracles of the sea, the sand dollars then become available—for symbolism, or simplicity. Or just for the pure joy of natural discovery, lying unexpected and whole in the white sand. And there's no folly in that, after all.

24

The Gators Are Coming!
So Are the Angry Squirrels!

Large gator in the spadderdock not far from the edge of my kayak.

I walked down to Lake Monroe last night to watch the river continue to rise after our most recent tropical storm. It didn't disappoint me, as it's now washed over the southern bulkhead that usually isolates the flowing river from the human world that nudges up against it.

I couldn't get to the actual pavement that trails along the "RiverWalk" of Sanford between the fancy swings and the lake since it was underwater. So too was the road that winds along the shore. So, I zigzagged along the land side of the road, jumping now and then between the few dry clumps of earth to keep from getting too wet.

When I stopped for a bit, I noticed the river was actually flowing downstream atop the street. The yellow traffic control line in the middle looked a bit eerie under a foot or so of tea-colored river water. And then it got better: as if choreographed to do so, four mallards came along, swimming in single file atop the yellow center line. They were all handsome males, nicely colored, and were clearly scouting out some brand new territory. The flowing river-street was also transporting water lettuce and hyacinths, and with the ducks following the inundated yellow line it all became just downright peculiar.

I looked for gators, but guessed they were somewhere else, just fulfilling their gator destiny. I figured they were likely planning to terrorize our citizenry, since that is how the media usually portrays them. They are lower than us on the food chain—for now—and I'm thinking they are rightfully pissed about that. Whoever does the public relations for gators just doesn't seem up to the job.

A few homeless guys were sleeping nearby on some concrete picnic tables that were above water, and back in the road, two largemouth bass—one almost five pounds—floated, dead. There were a few dead stingrays here as well, and the presence of those marine animals always seems to puzzle folks who forget the prehistoric seawater upwellings along this river's bed allow it to have the only breeding population of stingrays in any freshwater North American river. Under normal conditions, the little stingrays do well here as they go about living their benthic lives in a river with more than its share of oceanic memories. But tropical storms are mighty to behold, and each brings a sudden surge of stormwater with it, saturating the river with pesticides, lawn chemicals, and a toxic array of human-devised chemicals. The dissolved oxygen level of the river plummets, and fish die, which in turn, sucks up more oxygen.

I slogged past a Fox News truck with one of those tall, skinny transmission towers unsheathed, and a video camera on a tripod facing the lake, no one there to operate it. The operator was safely inside the truck, just shooting some extended "B roll" of the flood, as if something might mysteriously rise up from it since the camera was on and running. This comes out of the same philosophy of leaving a camera trained on people: sooner or later, someone will utter a sound bite worth keeping, perhaps something profound, or since this was Fox, something profoundly inept. Nature, bless her heart, is thankfully more inscrutable and less predictable.

I looked at the *Orlando Sentinel*, our local daily paper—or what remains of it—online earlier this morning. The once-powerful newspaper has laid off much of its editorial staff, especially purging those more savvy veterans afflicted with larger salaries. Much of this is because of dynamic media trends that tend to decentralize old static paradigms; but a lot of it is simply from poor management and, at the corporate level, a brutal and desperate quest for money and power. The result is something that looks like a kid's giant coloring book—lots of dramatic blank spaces with outlines, but not enough experience to color them in. And so when I picked up the newspaper, I saw this nifty killer graph at the top of one of its flood-coming stories: "Now it's time to brace for roving alligators. And killer ants. And massive mosquito swarms. And angry, frazzled squirrels."

Okay, I understand the editors were trying to be ironic, in their own way. Nonetheless, it sounded as if George Romero had stopped making zombie films and was now writing for our daily newspaper. I briefly tried to picture an angry, frazzled squirrel, and wondered absently if it was now running with the roving band of alligators and killer ants, all edgy and ready to do some serious damage.

I've been hearing from lots of friends around Florida, all of whom respond to the flooding as if it is a giant Rorschach test on which they can imprint their emotions. A lot of men worry about property damage, economic loss, another blow to the Florida public "image," and so on. Four very smart women, three of whom actually live on the river or tributaries of it, approached the "flood" with far more composure. Two have had a tributary sweep through their yards for a few days now, while a third who lives on a larger tract of land has fifty-three of her fifty-four acres underwater. Only a high spot where the house is located remains dry. Her take on it was incredibly brave and refreshing: she enjoyed the peace and solitude of living on a newly formed island, and understood the energy the river had to remake itself, to become wild and unrestricted by the conceits of man once again.

A fourth woman who lives inland, a scientist with an appreciation for the spirit and art of our strange Florida wilderness, worries that folks regard a "flood" as a terrible and dangerous affair, rather than seeing it as another incarnation of a natural system. The river, she told me, surges rather than floods. I'm betting that's how the Native Americans, long here before we made them vanish, likely saw it as well.

The seasons of Florida were always wet and dry, and not the four marketable Hallmark events known back on the continent. We see "floods" because we build roads and houses in places where the Timucua would have only camped, and then, not for very long. We somehow have lost the language needed to more realistically describe our natural world. We've compromised the river's watershed with hard surfaces, and by doing so, have kept rainfall from soaking into the ground—or from being absorbed by natural wetlands. Then, when things go terribly wrong, we blame nature, since blaming ourselves for our lack of wisdom is simply not an option.

T.S. Eliot nailed it a while ago: "The river is a strong, brown god; sullen, untamed, intractable."

I'm trying to picture this as a headline in our paper, but the image of an angry, frazzled, half-mad squirrel keeps getting in the way.

25

Weathering the Tides, Just a Bit Upstream

It's an hour or so after dawn here on the slender spit of ground quartz and shell known as the Outer Banks of North Carolina. I am walking at a good clip with my daughter Beth, headed north on a beach that at this hour is almost deserted.

Beyond the breakers, the gray dorsal of a lone bottlenose dolphin rises from the sea and then sinks back down. A squadron of brown pelicans glides single file just above where the dorsal was, tips of their wings glazing the spindrift of the waves as they go, headed south. We

My daughter Beth Crawley during a morning beach walk.

are careful to walk right at the water's edge, where each incoming wave flattens out into froth before retreating, leaving the tiny bubbling holes of burrowing coquinas and tellins behind.

Later, swarms of tourists will descend from the McMansions that line the dunes here at Duck and hunch together in chairs, under umbrellas, their white skin turning as red as a steamed blue crab in the summer sun. By night, they'll crowd the local bars and restaurants, and sometimes, let their kids set off fireworks on the beach, jolting themselves with the rush of sound and flashing light, instead of sitting quietly to absorb the wonder of it all.

But, just for now, I can pretend this is the same beach I first visited as a young boy with my mom and dad and brother years ago—can imagine that the Outer Banks itself is still retro and insular and southern, flavored more by the raw brogue of fishermen and shrimpers than the flat dialect of suburban Washington, D.C.

Our family stayed in one of several "Gregory's Cottages" then, tromping barefoot through a low slot in the sandy ridge and sea oats with our surf rods when the tide was coming in. Some afternoons, we'd trek up to the massive 100-foot high sand dune known as "Jockey's Ridge," or climb the steps to the Hatteras Light House. Once, I went fishing out in the Gulf Stream for blue marlin, watching in awe as an animal four or five times my size rose up from the depths to chase our shiny teaser, the reflective sunlight drawing it up to us like some dark and forgotten dread. The mate set the hook and I fought it for a while, not really wanting to land it, grateful when on its third leap it finally threw the hook.

By evening, in our little cottage we'd cook up the spot and croakers we caught earlier in the day. Sometimes, we'd venture out on the night beach to watch the clumps of bioluminescence glowing on the sand. A few of the fishing piers that stretched out over the ocean had old southern beach amusements, nothing fancy by today's standards, some pinball and jukes. We didn't seem to know as much about how the world worked then, and it freed up a lot of space on the hard drive to immerse ourselves in the moment, to rejoice in the little shared joys of a place.

Today, Beth and I walk the few miles toward the research pier at Duck, where scientists study the drift of the littoral current, and how geography and climate and human-made contrivances encourage it to deposit sand—or to carry it away. The beach under us is dynamic, as alive as any person has ever been, and—like the giant dune to the west—prone to shift and change, as if constantly reexamining its own reason for being.

Beth and her husband, Chuck, and her grandsons Ray and Will live away from this beach, on the other side of Hwy. 12, the asphalt road that funnels tourists to and from this place. There, they are wisely nestled inside a maritime thicket of live oak, persimmon, cedar, myrtle, pines—all of it stunted and shaped by the wind and salt. Most of us have been conditioned to believe that an ocean view is superior to all else and insist on occupying a precarious wooden structure atop a dune, just yards from the sea. But those who live here year-round most often do so away from the ocean, preparing for that special moment when the sea stops being a smiley face postcard and, with a nor'easter gale behind it, turns into a raging force of nature.

This dynamic of the sea is repeated along most windward shores, such as where I live back in Florida. But it is particularly apparent here because the Outer Banks protrude into the Atlantic like the jaw of a punch drunk fighter, almost as if it is daring the ocean to smack it one. Indeed, the slender spit of quartz that holds Duck and Nags Head and Kitty Hawk transports us humans far beyond the barrier islands of the rest of the eastern coast. Out here, the Gulf Stream—even the continental shelf—is barely forty miles away. Everything is churned by its dynamic: broken shells are rounded as neat and smooth as guitar picks; jagged glass is tumbled relentlessly, its colors turned cloudy, its edges muted, safe. A broken soda bottle from years ago becomes desirable, reborn from the surf as "beach glass."

The world around me is ephemeral, here just for the now. It is like being with a striking woman who is simply not the right fit—her beauty is made even more so by the knowledge it will soon end, vanishing as surely as the sand ebbs away from the shore when the new and full moons squeeze the tides ever so tightly. For now, I watch, amused, as a large starling dances along the same foam line we walk, pecking quickly at the bubbling holes for a tasty bivalve. Blackbirds like this usually go for terrestrial insects and worms. But finding itself on an island far at sea, this one learned to make the best of it, figuring out how to tease the mollusks from their holes in the flat surf sand.

If there is any lesson in that, there's also one in the subtext of the place itself: these slender islands, bracketed by estuary and ocean, are an arena where natural forces collide, day after day. They do so out in the ocean where the south-flowing, cold Labrador Current meets the warmer, north-flowing Gulf Stream. On land, winds from the northeast and the southwest do the same, crashing into each other atop the string of islands and sound and marsh, keeping the big westerly dunes in place, torrents of air pushing waves of sand against the other.

And the collision of tradition happens, too; the old, isolated fishing culture not faring nearly as well when affluent tourists smack up against it, relic swales of authenticity here and there, but really, most of it displaced, caught in a rip of momentum.

And of course, the ideas of my own life collide here as well, ever shifting and dynamic as these monstrous dunes, every bit as shadowed as the cool and stunted maritime thickets of dwarf oaks and myrtles and bayberry. I look once over my shoulder at the line of whitecaps behind us, and follow Beth back up and over the dune. She has become a kind, caring, and insightful adult and I'm very proud of her. Above us in the sky, two frontal systems push toward each other as banks of clouds—just in case I'm too obtuse to know for sure that it's all about collision and loss, transformation and growth. The only barrier islands that won't wash away in our lifetimes are the ones ringed by bulkheads and steel. But then, they no longer have the magic of the natural pulsing that once made them so.

In the crease between the two cloud banks above, Beth sees a shard of a rainbow, glowing just for the now like beach glass on the sand. And then, I know for sure that the most bittersweet notions of all are the ones that are the most transient, the ones that you know will vanish because they must. Being in this moment is one of those notions, because soon I must travel back to my own home in Florida.

Then with a force of resolution and energy and light, I try to clear my mind and heart, and just let it go. And instead of pushing against some immovable force, I relax and begin to smile. It is subtle at first, and then more realized, because it is in great appreciation of the moment.

As Beth and I walk across the road and back to her home, a right whale skims just below the surface of the sea a mile offshore. She has decided, just for now, to keep moving northward. As she goes, she will discover great pods of plankton simmering like chowder before her in the dark and blue wonderment of the sea. Sometimes she will swim near others like her, great cetaceans who once lived on the land, now in solution together, back finally in their home. Sometimes the miracle of it all will become so great she will actually leap from the sea in joy and in thankfulness.

26

It's a Jungle Out There

The winds were blowing this weekend and between that and a nagging knee injury I stayed off the water and out of the woods. Instead, I spent some time puttering around outside, repairing the little white concrete bench that gravity and a dead live oak limb conspired to break in two a few weeks ago. Afterwards, I hung out in my back yard, now rescued from its monoculture of St. Augustine grass and converted into a place where anything sort of goes. The pond I built after I first moved in is cranking along pretty good, the submerged pump that recirculates water siphoning it up and back out through a large swatch of bamboo. I mortared the bamboo "pipe" into a pile of limestone rocks, some with veins of chert in it, and the water now shoots out of it into the pond, making that kinetic roiling sound that always comforts me.

A passion flower growing wild in my backyard.

Some months ago, I brought back a net full of gambusia from the river, and then added the oddly colored little comets the aquarium store sells as "feeder fish." The gambusia, although they will forever be minnows, are flourishing, and the comets are growing larger by the day, turning bright orange in the richness of the sun and oxygenation of the pond. Frogs and toads have now come, sneaking in under gaps in the wooden fence, and they help reshape the reality of any moment. One morning, I checked on the pond and saw the surface between the hyacinths and lotus lilies shimmering, as if electrified. Sometimes I feel that same thrill, that coursing of blood just under the surface, when I'm in a place or with people that invigorate my soul. Wild places in nature can do that for me, and if I am there with someone who also cares, it's even better. It is in those moments that the spirit seems to expand, as if making room for a small tender comet to soar through the heart. The shimmering in this pond was the surface tail-wagging of tadpoles, hundreds, maybe more, all joyful to be alive under the new Florida morning sun.

A few hours after sundown during the warmer months, the vocalizations of the adult herp males ring out across the rest of the neighborhood, filling the nights with the sound of happy ribbets. If they sing all at once, the sound is almost deafening and it's nearly impossible to separate one species from the other. But when they sing separately, I hear the distinct calls of the southern leopard frog, the southern toad, the bullfrog. Herpetologists describe this vocalization as "advertising," something the males do to show prospective female mates how dominant and cool they are. This all makes me feel pretty good, knowing I have created a little world where herpetological bliss is being broadcast far and wide, providing a natural vitality where previously there was only a green and silent lawn.

I've brought water hyacinths to the pond from the river since the exotic Amazonian floating plant is an excellent biological filter for nitrogen, and its tendril-like feathery roots bind particulates, helping to keep the water clear. Just inside the edges of the pond, I've submerged pots of the native pickerel weed, lotus lily, and the wild river iris known as the purple flag. Each blooms in its own time, just as they do out on the river. And I've added a native naiad grass as well as the exotic hydrilla to the mix, both submerged plants that help with the oxygen exchange, and in a pinch, serve as food. Managing the exotics is far easier than it would be out on a river or lake. If they become too abundant, I simply pull them out by hand and add them to my compost pile back in the corner, near the lone citrus tree.

Together, the yard has become a big ol' organic buffet of pollen and water and wildflowers. As I sat there this morning drinking my cappuccino and eating one of the last Valencias from the tree, I watched a small black racer snake move out of the weeds and wild morning glories and slip into the pond, hunting. Snakes are among the most elegant of animals, and watching one work can't help but make me want to write a haiku or two in honor of its Zen-like stealth. When snakes and other animals move through, I remain as still as I can so as not to scare them. Watching the racer, I noticed for the first time the way the sun illuminated the crosshatch of its scales. It reminded me of the pottery the Native Americans who lived along the St. Johns once made, imprinting the soft clay with a distinct check pattern from a carved wooden stamp before they fired it. Art imitated nature a lot then.

So the snake slips away, almost as if he is dissolving one molecule at a time, and a smattering of butterflies moves through. They are tiger swallowtails and some sulfur wings, and our state butterfly, the zebra longwing. They hung around a long while, twitting through the black-eyed susans and the hibiscus. The wind chimes hanging near the pond called out pleasantly several times, even though there was not a trace of a breeze. I figured one of the many brown or green anoles had jumped onto them from the top of the fence, living out some tiny lizard adventure.

I finished my cappuccino, puttered in the little herb garden a bit, and then watched as a red-shouldered hawk flew to an oak in the corner of the yard. He lives around here, doing a pretty good business with the squirrels and all. I figured he had work to do, so I went inside. A bit later, I looked out over the yard from the window in the Florida Room, and saw the hawk with a small native wood rat. The rat likely had sneaked under the cypress fence to root in my compost pile—bad move. It was deader than a doornail by now, and the hawk had itself a dandy lunch, rodent on the half shell.

My back yard has a palpable soul now, an energy that vibrates with life, natural and spontaneous. A good friend describes it as a refuge where, every time she visits, it gives her a certain peace. Certainly, each time I go there and open my senses just a little bit, I notice something new, something that wouldn't otherwise have been there if this were still a lockstep lawn with a buzz cut.

27

A River Parchment, Once Read

By 7:45 p.m. the waterfront of Lake Monroe is quiet, light breeze blowing upstream from the east, pushing small, low clouds in front of it like wisps of cigar smoke. I park near the city hall and walk a few hundred feet across the road and onto the peninsula that juts out into the water. No one yet on the benches, so I go the northern tip and find the one bench where I used to like to stop when I walked here with Shep. I sit and stretch my legs in front of me and breathe, just looking around.

Strange, while I have traveled all over the world, I have spent vital intervals of my life in this old neglected riverboat town. I think of the first time I walked out on this peninsula in the early 1970s, new to Florida and excited with the possibilities my young wife and I would make for

The marina in downtown Sanford, not far from where steamboats once docked. There's a nice walkway along the river here.

ourselves here. The place here along the river was pleasant, but unspectacular, just a cozy spot near the water where I could relax. It was non-threatening, a refuge in the very best way, even though I've never used those words before in describing it.

I can't say for sure what I've learned since first coming here. I only know for sure this river has taught me secrets, intimating how and why it flows, information beyond just the science. But sometimes even that seems like a single crisp revelation, a stereographic view seen perfectly once and then remembered, over and over again.

This evening, the broad, generous crop of water is distinguished only by a light chop from the wind. Too late now to even make out much of a color on its surface, other than a cobalt blue-gray. I think I see large fins or manatee snouts several times, but I look again for a while and see nothing, so I figure it was just a trick of the water and the late twilight. This lake is, of course, a flowing river, although at this point in its life it widens out enough to fool people, settling down like it does in a paleo-estuarine basin. A hundred thousand years ago, I would have been on the mainland side of a lagoon like the Indian River, and the far shore—across the wide swath of water to where Enterprise is today—would have been barrier islands.

But that's another story. For now, it's a quiet weekday evening in a little city that has never quite caught on like other trendy neighborhoods and towns in our region—Thornton Park in Orlando, Winter Park, Mt. Dora. And at least for now, that's saved it, rescued it from the ambitious designs the half-mad schemers once had for the village on this strange, north-flowing blackwater river.

Lights begin to appear, first from the power plant a few miles to the west, where the river passes under two large bridges and folds its way back into a channel. From here, the lights look celebratory, as if strung out for a party and not just utility. To my right, the neon bar signs at Wolfy's, the pub on the water by the marina, flicker to life, and the channel markers that trail through the lake gradually do the same. Sanford is the end of the dredged and marked channel on this river, and most of the bustle is downstream from here—although, admittedly, it's a stretch to describe Highbanks and Astor and Palatka as "bustle."

Two people individually jog past me, a white woman and a black man, maybe a couple hundred yards apart. Both are wearing MP3 players in their ears and moving with serious intent. Then a large black woman comes, walking fast, swaying her arms like she's skiing down a slope. Like most folks in the walk-run-exercise group, they are far more intent on marking time than absorbing much about the place. Finally, a young-ish white woman strolls past me with a dog on a leash, more casual now. The dog wags his tail and the woman says hi. All is quiet, and then from the dark street behind me, I hear a woman's voice belting out a quite good version of the "Star Spangled Banner." There is no activity or event to be inaugurated, just someone who likes to sing the National Anthem by herself in the dark.

Once, a few years ago, I had walked with Shep farther upstream on the waterfront, and stopped to look through one of the telescopes that are mounted every few hundred yards on the RiverWalk here. As I did, a woman stepped out of the wonderful old Spanish Mediterranean struc-ture that used to be the Forest Lake Hotel, and walked slowly down the street playing the bagpipes. I went home and, thusly inspired, wrote a poem about that—about the ghosts of the steamboats I had hoped to see, and the ghost of the woman I was waiting to meet.

It's more dark than light now, but the best I can tell, nothing moves in the water in front of me. I can see a flock of birds in the distance, fly-ing home, and an osprey overhead with empty talons. Although I live nearly a mile from this river, I have found dead fish dropped in my yard at least twice, and figured an osprey had simply lost its grip on a meal that was a bit heavier than she had figured it to be, natural mistake. And for now, there is just the gentle slosh of blackwater against the concrete bulkhead, not even a mullet jumping. I get up to leave my bench, and without thinking, I turn to get Shep, but of course, like a dream, he is gone. I had forgotten he was no longer here.

I have a sort of quirky, nostalgic circuitry that uses this peninsula and the nearby river shore as an emotional crossroad. People who have been deeply entwined in my life still exist, out here, as real in my mind as they've ever been. No matter that they have moved away, died, or vanished into those memory crevices where good friends sometimes go. At some time in the past, they were just a few minutes away from a telephone call or a tennis game or a fishing trip. But now they are inexplicably remote, as lost as they will ever be. The nature writer Barry Lopez says that places may take on the energy of people who have cared for them—not unlike the way that indigenous people imbue a meaningful geographic feature with a tribal sacredness. I'm figuring this is something that happens not because you force it to be, but because you simply allow your guard to drop, setting the glorious unconscious free to do its work of transcendence. The places themselves don't even have to be spectacular, like say, a tall waterfall in a tropical jungle or a freshwater spring hidden deep in the forest. They only require you to *be* fully there, relaxed and full of heart.

Maybe this peninsula and this small stretch of the river where I walk has become such a place. All I know for sure is when I least expect it, old animal buddies and human sweethearts, deeply loved kin and best of friends, live on here. They are all nearby, still on their way to meet me near the river by the bench, at the marina near the sea, or at home for dinner.

In a book I wrote once about this river, I tried to explain it as a palimpsest of history. In medieval times, a palimpsest was a parchment too valuable to be destroyed. Instead, those who were stewards of the parchment at any particular moment carefully erased what was written before, and then inscribed their own history atop it. If held to a light, all the incarnations of that parchment could be read, each engendered with the richness of memory, one atop the other, atop the other.

This place itself is likely a palimpsest as well, but it carries far more than the disembodied history of other men. In the lexicon of the spirit, it is the emotional corral for symbols that convey the passion and sway of one man's life—a small dog with a big heart; the intimacy of shared expectations and of joy with a young wife; the invigorating spindrift of the sea that splashes you and your buddy when you have each fought the greatest fish that ever lived. When first experienced, each was imbued with the sure knowledge that it was a moment buried so deeply in the heart that it would never, ever end.

And perhaps it never has.

28

A Yearning for Stories
to Lead the Way

A woman walks a small gator on a leash at the Wekiva Island Marina near Longwood, Florida. This is the living metaphor of John Sayles's ironic farce Sunshine State *in which Florida is described as "nature on a leash."*

The power of narrative has long played large in the imagination. We were telling each other stories around an open wood fire for thousands of years before we started writing them down. Some anthropologists say we're genetically inclined to need a narrative—that we insist on having a story to explain circumstances that can not otherwise be explained.

Recent books like *The Accidental Mind* suggest we follow deeply embedded behavioral signals, and then later, "confabulate" complex stories to explain our otherwise inexplicable behavior to ourselves and others.

Surely, if you're in the business of storytelling—that is, if you're a writer or a politician—then there's likely no better stage than Florida. After all, we're the home of mermaids and manatees and myths of salvation in the landscape. We've been making up stories here for thousands of years now, dating back to the paleo-memories of the first Floridians who followed herds of mastodons here because the spirits told them to.

Today, we yearn for stories more than most because our history has been so haphazard and uncertain, and our population just so darn new. We have grown so quickly that few have been here long enough to describe just what did happen fifty years ago. Three of every four people in Florida come from elsewhere. A few years ago, the *Orlando Sentinel* selected the "Floridian of the Century," the person who more than any other had shaped the character of modern Florida. The choice? It was the "Newcomer."

In a subtropical, water-driven state where natural realities are subtle and exotic anyway, it's always been easy for a flamboyant story to trump reality. Ponce De Leon first put ashore in 1513 seeking gold and glory, and not a mythological Fountain of Youth. Decades later in 1575, Hernando D'Escalante Fontaneda did report hearing of the curative powers of a river called "Jordan" in Florida. But even then, he explained it was highly unlikely Ponce had ever been in hot pursuit of it.

Nonetheless myth went to work, and today the intrepid explorer's name will forever be associated with a St. Augustine tourist attraction ("Drink from the World Famous Spring"), the "Ponce De Leon Mall," and a natural artesian vent west of DeLand that—before it was renamed "Ponce DeLeon Springs"—was known for centuries as "Spring Garden Spring."

But mythmaking wasn't limited to magical springs. Early Florida colonists routinely created stories with great flair: Jacques Le Moyne, the artist with the French Colony at Ft. Caroline in 1564, drew alligators forty feet long with large human-like ears and massive hands. His fellow colonists told of unicorns that came down to the river to drink, and of a supernatural animal that carried its young on its back. Hearing descriptions of the latter in 1575, Andre Thevet drew for us the "Succaranth," a fierce and grotesque animal that was half lion and half monkey. The supernatural animal turned out to be a possum.

When it became clear inventive stories could actually lure tourists and investors down and into the swampy, mosquito-infested Florida, fables took on a new twist. By the nineteenth century, tourist guides promised a Florida with "mineral springs" that were "salubrious"—able to cure everything from tuberculosis to dandruff. Even when they tried to stick to the facts, it was challenging. "There is malaria here," warned the *Handbook of Important and Reliable Information* in 1885, "but not to the degree commonly expected." But if that declaration seemed too realistic, the handbook writers added this consoling fact: "In Florida, the poor man becomes a lord, for Nature serves him. He knows no dread of long winters, frost and hunger." When not lazing around as a lord, the poor man could also search for the "lost" lake of Okeechobee, where other stories told of floating islands of wealthy Indians. By the early twentieth century, selling swampland to Yankees was the natural decedent of promising a salubrious experience in a sort of tropical neverland.

Modern writers have tried to take up the slack. Excellent storytellers like Marjorie Stoneman Douglas, Archie Carr, M.K. Rawlings, John D. McDonald, Thomas Barbour, Rachel Carson, and others gave us precise descriptions of people and place, which are particularly useful today in helping us discover the true identity of this reshaped and retooled landscape. Lola Haskins, the perceptive Florida nature poet, draws crisp images and metaphors that do some of this. But Haskins also understands that the role of the poet and writer who creates a "story" is to *gift* others with the heartbreakingly beautiful visions they see embedded in our rare landscape. In "Seven Turtles," Haskins writes what she sees on the Withlacoochee River during one Saturday paddle: turtles queued on a log, a gator with hooded eyes, the sabal palms that lean out low over the river, and the grand spectacle of hundreds of wood storks, our native ironheads, "hunched like priests in the trees." Visions like this, for those with heightened sensibilities, are so packed with rich color and form and eternal hope that it would be unconscionable not to share it with others. Or, as Haskins finally says—in remembering real life advice from a woman in a faraway land—*pass it along.*

While the very real task of a storyteller is to pass it along, we still remain faced with a Florida that has great patches of bizarre and unexplained history. In explaining these stories, there are those who take great glee in purposely defaulting to myth. Novelists of black humor, like Carl Hiaasen, benefit because their fiction is launched from Florida's unique landscape of implausibility. People do sometimes chase each other with weed eaters, although not grafted to their arms, and politicians sometimes act like they do in movie farces. Not so long ago, the mayor of a small central Florida town was accused variously of beating up a carnival barker, threatening the police chief, and stealing dirt. His response on local TV: "I ain't never stole no dirt in my life."

Obligations or dreams? Possums or Succaranths? Buggy swampland or paradise? Healing waters or natural springs? Or perhaps, the ineffably breathtaking moment when a dawn over a mist-filled river slips from reality to myth and then back again. Welcome to Florida, where the story is just about anything you want it to be.

☀ 29

Silver Springs

A Troglodytic Myth, Realized

At the mouth of Mammoth Springs—the main artesian gusher in the historic Florida tourist attraction of Silver Springs—I have only two choices.

The first choice is to go straight up, some thirty feet to the surface, where at this very moment a gaggle of tourists inside a World Famous Glass Bottom Boat is getting a classic theme park spiel. Within this reality, the spring beneath them is described as "a bottomless pit," a dark

Cave diving cartographer Eric Hutcheson makes a rough sketch of dimensions of a cavern inside Silver Springs. The soft karst limestone and sand is representative of what comprises much of our aquifer, and it holds the clean, transparent water that flows through it.

hole in the earth that mysteriously spouts up millions of gallons of crystal clear water from somewhere deep and unknown.

The second choice is the bottomless pit itself. It's accessed by a slender horizontal gash in the limestone bottom—a doorway to a water-filled labyrinth of caverns, caves, and tunnels. Like much of Florida geology, the deeper it goes down into the rock, the older the history of the rock will become. There are stories embedded here, some from long ago in geologic time, and some from long ago in my own life. One is told in millions of years, the other in decades.

Down here, I settle on the sand-covered limestone bottom next to the dark cave mouth, my legs and fins tucked under me. The entrance to Mammoth is about five feet high and over a hundred feet wide, creating the effect of one giant smile, Batman's Joker incised in the rock. There's well over a dozen springs between here and the first half mile of the Silver River that seep or gush up from the limestone and dolomite, together creating a flow of 550 million gallons a day. Mammoth accounts for 45 percent of that upwelling, so the force of the water flowing out of its giant smile is mighty indeed.

Although my two choices today seem as if they're exaggerations of reality, they frame the very real condition of Florida. Like so much else that is beneath the veneer here in this tourist-happy state, my choices are characterized by vast incongruities between what is promoted and what is actually going on. Melodramatic theme park spin often seems more real to visitors than the true nature of the place itself. And so, I hope to more fully realize—perhaps even to reconcile—the made-up caricatures and real life experiences that have conspired to bring me to the bottom of Silver Springs.

Here, I'll accompany a small team of cave divers exploring the underground plumbing of this famous, powerful spring system. Within this mission, our goals are to watch for unusual troglodytic life forms and rare fossils, to carefully monitor the air in our tanks, and—perhaps most important—to time our ascents so the Glass Bottom Boats and Lost River Voyages on their way to the giraffe and porcupine show don't run us down.

🐾

I have vivid memories of visiting this same Silver Springs as a bright-eyed eight-year-old on a family vacation years ago. We drove the "blue highways" in the pre-interstate days, back when Mom and Pop motels and Monkey Jungles were far more common than chain hotels and corporate theme parks.

At the springs, my dad, mom, younger brother Jack, and I climbed aboard a wooden glass bottom boat that floated over water as clear as our aquarium full of guppies back home. Beneath us, beach-white sand lay on the limestone walls of the spring basin like snow. We saw bass and bream and a small alligator swimming below us, as if we were watching a science show on television. We were introduced to individual spring vents variously named the "Bridal Chamber," "Spring of Fire," and the "Catfish Hotel." The set for the *Sea Hunt* TV series had been built in one cove, some of it constructed on the spring bottom, and we could still see it there. Rhesus monkeys yelled at us from the jungle-like shore. All that was missing was Tarzan and Boy swinging on the thick muscadine grape vines. And of course, that had happened too, back in the 1930s when several of those movies were filmed here.

When our guide gave us an earlier version of today's narrative, I was enthralled. Where does all this water come from, I wondered, and is the pit really bottomless? I yearned to find out where the darkness beneath the turquoise waters might lead me. At eight, everything unseen or forbidden was a fairyland of possibilities, a place where the imagination could gift you with stories that, otherwise, would go untold.

It was a seminal moment for me, one that would later draw me to scuba diving soon after I moved to Florida as a young adult to live. As a diver and journalist, I went on to travel to some of the most remote sites on earth to report on the local marine environment—the distant islands of Australia's Great Barrier Reef, the crater-like "blue holes" in the ocean bottom just north of Cuba, the isolated coastal reefs and cliffs off Panama, Nicaragua, and Venezuela, and the sinkhole-like cenotes of the Dominican Republic. All those explorations were revealing, rich with adventure and crammed with subsurface images I could barely imagine. My diving partners were marine biologists or archaeologists, all working on one project or another that would help the world learn more about their respective science. The places I visited were unknown to most tourists, sites where the unexpected became almost common-place for me.

But it wasn't until a friend who was a seasoned cave explorer invited me to join him in a mapping expedition to Silver Springs that I truly became giddy with anticipation. As we geared up for the dive, I realized I was no longer the veteran diver-writer with a portfolio of rare and offbeat experiences underwater, a guy who would try almost anything, at least once. Instead, I was an eight-year-old again. And I was finally getting to go inside the "bottomless pit."

Despite the fact that thousands of tourists still float in glass bot-tom boats every week atop Silver Springs, the caves that feed one of the world's most powerful upwellings are what divers call a "virgin sys-tem"—largely unexplored and unmapped. Sport divers have long been barred from the spring since they would interfere with the theatrical business of spin-making. And, over the years, various owners felt the danger of even a professional dive expedition created a liability that might outweigh any benefits. A dead or injured diver was problematic on so many levels—not the least of which was that it would be difficult for the World Famous Glass Bottom Boat guides to explain in an enter-taining sort of way.

And, there was this: "This is probably the largest cave-spring on land in the U.S.," a geologist who had studied the hydrology of the spring told me when I was researching the springs before the dive. "But it's incred-ibly difficult to explore since most of the original cave has collapsed, and there's a diversion maze right beyond the entrance." A "diversion maze" means limestone has crumbled over time, creating restrictions that are nearly impossible for most divers to pass beyond.

The point man in the push to explore Silver was Eric Hutcheson, an adventurer from nearby Ocala, Florida with a growing reputation as an artistic maker of underwater cave maps. With explorer and cinematog-rapher Wes Skiles from High Springs, Hutcheson had dived and mapped Nohoch Nah Chich, the extensive underwater system of caves linked by cenotes in Mexico's Yucatan, as well as a number of Florida spring-cave systems.

Earlier, I had accompanied Skiles and Hutcheson on a survey of Silver Glen Springs in northern Florida. With just Hutcheson, I dove into a chimney-like cave in the side of a remote limestone island in the Bahamas near Man o' War Cay. When Eric approached the managers of Silver Springs with the concept of exploring the main cave, they saw the marketing possibilities and agreed.

Eric would chart at least some of the conduits inside Mammoth for the very first time, and when possible, collect small cave-dwelling life forms for taxonomic study. Artifacts from the cave could be displayed at the attraction, and later, a more complete exhibit could be mounted at the state's Silver River Museum. Eric sometimes brought along specialists, like cave-diving biologist Tom Morris, to more carefully evaluate the science of the springs system. Whenever the dive team was entering or leaving the water, tour guides could also point them out to the passengers on the boats, weaving them into the myth of *Tarzan* and *Sea Hunt*, and the twenty-odd movies that had all been filmed there.

Silver Springs, after all, is the archetypical Florida theme park, one built around a spectacular natural geographic feature in a time when Florida had little else to sell. By the 1870s, steamboats traveled up the Ocklawaha River and then into the eight-mile-long spring run known as the Silver River to the headsprings here. A luxury four-story, two hundred-room hotel awaited them, making Silver Springs and its river a mandatory stop for anyone wanting to experience the exotic jungle mysteries of this off-the-grid peninsula. By the late 1870s, some enterprising soul figured out a way to put a slab of heavy glass in the bottom of a large dugout canoe; by the 1890s, the first commercial glass bottom boat was developed, and guests began to get their very first look at the magical subsurface world under them. The Florida that had been all green and entangled with terrestrial moss and vines would never be the same.

✿

Today, we assemble the gear, lights, and line that cave divers carry atop a temporary floating platform at the shore atop Mammoth. From nearby the amplified voice of a tour guide from a glass bottom boat drifts over to us. "What is under the water, you will be able to see clearly," he proclaims, as if he is a hypnotist putting his charges into a trance. And in a way, he is. As we gear up, other tourists gather along the railing above and pepper us with questions, as if we are audio-animatronic devices made to look like scuba divers. How deep is it in there, and what do you see, and, is it really bottomless? Eric fields most of the questions, good naturedly, and soon we enter the water—where it is thankfully quiet—and sink slowly under the clear surface of Mammoth Springs. At the edge of the natural spring pool above us, I see a seven-foot alligator slide down into the water from its log on the shore, and then—spooked by our exhaust bubbles—quickly swim away, swaying its giant prehistoric tail side-to-side as it goes. I notice the gator is far more graceful underwater than gators ever are on land.

I settle on the thirty-foot bottom outside the cave mouth and wait for the others. The water is clear, but not as transparent as I remember it as a boy, shards of stringy algae now swirling about us from problems with nutrients in the uplands that recharge these springs. I push against my mask to clear the pressure in my ears, and then ascend a few feet above the wide grin of a cave mouth—which seems to be blowing out water with the force of a very large fire hose. Hutcheson had earlier advised me of this, suggesting the best way to enter is from the top of the vent rather than the bottom. As I force my way in, I am against the cave ceiling, just above the concentrated force of the outflow. With my mask right next to it, I notice the ceiling seems to be made from thousands of fossilized sand dollars, left from when all of Florida was once covered by the sea.

Once inside, the narrow mouth-grin opens into an expansive cavern and the constricted, powerful flow has a chance to spread out. It's not unlike how the energy of a swift stream dissipates when it meets a wider river or bay in the lighted world above. From deeper in the cavern, I see flickers of Hutcheson's light in the darkness and move toward it. As I do, I fin over the boulder-strewn floor and see remnants of large prehistoric animal bones. They are mineralized black, gargantuan in size. Long before the Europeans ever arrived, the few springs that were then flowing were favorite sites for Paleo-Indians who stalked mastodons and giant sloth and bear over twelve thousand years ago. With the outsized bone yard below me, I am literally treading a fine line between myth and reality, part of me thinking this is an old stage set, part of me knowing it is real.

The cavern is massive, and boulders that have collapsed from its ceiling over time have created small cave-like alcoves amidst the rubble of bone and rock on the floor. I squeeze inside one of the dark openings. Down in here, I hold my light with one hand, and use the edge of the palm of the other to gently fan across the sand, as I have seen archaeologists do to find artifacts. When I stop fanning to allow the tiny vortex of sand to drift away, my light beam reveals a four-inch-long spear point carved from chert. Hidden here for centuries in the rock and sand, it looks as if it was carved just yesterday.

I gingerly turn and pull my way out of the little cave, and poke around some more on the bottom, exploring other large crevices. I see more paleo-artifacts, and finally, spot a tiny albino arthropod, a shrimp-like crustacean, flipping about in the crack of eternal darkness. I remove a small specimen collection bag from my dive vest and carefully coax the little animal into it. Many caves like this in Florida nurture endemic creatures, some of them not yet known to science. At the Smithsonian Institution, scientist Horton Hobbs specialized in classifying such animals for years; his last name appears at the tail end of many Latin taxonomic descriptions of cave-dwelling life forms. Later the little shrimp I captured will travel to that venerable institution, and will go through the complex naming process that separates the known animals from the unknown.

From the far side of the cavern, I watch as Hutcheson removes his tank and pushes it ahead of him into an even tighter "restriction" until he disappears in a cloud of silt and churning water. The conduit he has entered will take him farther back under the land above, following a route that—if he were the size of the tiny shrimp in my baggy—might lead him miles through soft limestone fissures below the distant uplands where fresh rainfall seeps down into the springshed itself.

I poke about some more on the bottom, following the edges of the cavern as far as I can. Under another boulder pile, I see large wooden timbers, charred black from a fire long ago. There is no way of telling for sure, but I know that the old hotel that once hugged the edge of

Mammoth Springs burned back around the turn of the last century. Earlier, Hutcheson had told me others have seen charred wooden beams down here. Famous people once stayed here, since that is what they did when they came to Florida over a century ago. I know the poet Sidney Lanier once rode the steamship *Marion* to Silver Springs, and wonder if any of this wood—as black as any fossilized tibia or femur—might once have sheltered him. If it did, would it have absorbed an unwritten lyric of the poet's sensibility, a fragment that drifted up from a forgotten dream?

Minutes later, when Hutcheson returns from the narrow tunnel, he carries a clam fossil the size of a breadbasket. I fin over to see it and marvel at its heft, at how clearly defined the striations of each rib still are on the surface of its shells, a bivalve forever welded shut by time. Later, after we finish the dive, he will tell me there are scores of such clams along the base of one wall, a bed of giant seabottom mollusks long extinct.

Mapping of the sort that is being done here helps scientists better understand the limitations of our Floridan Aquifer. The cave does stretch for miles into the limestone under the rolling north Florida landscape, veining out into tiny crevices and fissures, sometimes opening back up into gigantic cathedral-sized rooms. But it's not truly "bottomless," nor is its water supply endless. It's a hard lesson we are now learning throughout Florida as the magnitude of our major springs declines, and our potable water supply ebbs away. It is a lesson the extinct seabottom clams learned long ago.

It is time for the dive to end, and so I fin up and over to the cave mouth and let its energy literally blow me out onto the bottom of the spring basin. The force of the upwelling tumbles me, almost sideways, and just as I am regaining my composure, a load of tourist families in a glass bottom boat moves silently overhead. Despite the algae, the water is still transparent enough that I can look up through my mask and make eye contact with a little boy sitting in the boat, intently looking down at me. His eyes are big, and he seems entranced, pushing his face closer to the glass than the rest. It is a true Florida out-of-body moment, where the transect that connects us seems to shift there, for just a split second, and I am now the little boy in the boat, looking down at the bottomless pit and at the mysterious man in the mysterious suit who has emerged from it. And all the years in between disappear as if they've never been.

Can there be any difference between me, the bass and gators, the old *Sea Hunt* set, the imported monkeys, the bottomless spring? Another myth, a sacred story, in a little boy's imagination has been created. I don't know where it will lead him, long after I'm physically gone from this spring, this earth. But it gives me great joy to know that, in some way, I have entered the sacrosanct dreams of a child, an inviolable place. If he is careful, he might also store this moment away for a lifetime, just as the cave has stored its own relics from so long ago.

From behind my regulator, I smile broadly, watching the boat putter slowly away until all I can see now are the swirls in the water it has left behind. The other divers emerge and as they ascend, they motion me to join them. I shake my head as if waking from a long and heartfelt dream, and drift slowly upwards, toward the light.

✿ 30

What the House Remembers

I stopped by to see Zona yesterday. I had given her an orchid a couple weeks ago, and it was about bloomed out. I don't know much about orchids, but do know you can cut them back and fertilize them, and they'll send out more blossoms. Orchid or not, a visit with Zona is always full of deep and pleasant nostalgia for me.

Zona's father built the Cracker-style house where I lived for fifteen years before moving into downtown Sanford. It was outside of town, off one of those little dirt roads that used to define what the geography of the place was all about, back when celery was still big here. Her dad tenaciously assembled the house, piece by piece, with a hand saw and a hammer, no electricity, and certainly no power tools. It was 1928.

My former Cracker-style home on Sewell Road, right after I bought it.

Zona was a toddler when the house was completed, and she and her sister Evelyn lived in that finely constructed heart cypress home with the durable steel roof for about fourteen or fifteen years, until she was ready to start high school, and her parents wanted to be closer to town so she'd have more social advantages, without a long commute. Downtown was only four miles away, but then, that was a haul. Sanford had a real business district with pharmacies and grocery stores and little diners, whereas the farm homes of the celery "delta" were rural and isolated.

The house was built on what early photos show to be a pine flatwoods, a habitat underlain with nonporous clay. It's the sort of terrain that seasonally floods, so those few hardy souls who lived here took great pains to incise the perimeters of their homesteads with ditches. The ditches would drain the water away to the St. Johns River nearby. Although trees and scrubs eventually grew up and shrouded them, the ditches were still used for that purpose when I moved there in 1991. Sometimes they held so much water that small fish lived in them, migrating between here and the river or relics of natural creeks upstream.

After Zona's family moved, the Duraks lived there, and owned it right up to when I bought it. Afterwards, a mall was built near the home and the old Cracker communities nearby began to fall like dominoes. I wrote a book about that process, about what it was like when poorly planned growth washed over a landscape. There had been some very good books written about sprawl, accounting for the empirical impacts of it. But few fully measured the effects of sprawl on the community, and on the human heart.

After the book was published, I received a touching outpouring of letters and e-mails from readers around the country, many of whom shared stories of their own losses to out-of-control growth. True emotional loss can be painful, and the book clearly touched a chord. A few, however, didn't care for the book. Those criticisms came from two sources: those who championed unregulated growth in the countryside—which was still sprawl, even when it was dressed up with green spaces and mixed-use development. And, those who were uncomfortable with the personal nature of the story, figuring that emotion ought to be excised from arguments about planning, history, and growth. Overall, the response was not unlike what any writer should expect from any story that was as honestly told as he or she could tell it.

And so today, here are Zona and her husband Art, and myself, living randomly in two other homes beyond the original one, only four blocks away—a distance of pure chance. When I go over to visit, we talk about different things: how Zona's son is doing with his new restaurant in Tennessee; how Art and the boys used to fish out on the Wekiva River when it was really wild; how the sprawling 1920s-era hotel once known as the "Mayfair" used to kick off each "season" with a grand ball. Today, Art goes out and picks a bag of fine little sweet Key limes from a tree on their property and gives them to me. I tell Zona and Art of a recent hike I made through a thick hammock down to an old ghost town on the river; she wondered if I had seen any snakes (I didn't).

We usually mention the Sewell Road house at some point, because both of us had lived there at different times, and it is a connection that spans the decades, transcending family dynamics and geography and time. Art talked some about the artesian wells that used to be around Sanford, including one at Palmetto and Second Street, and how most of them had been paved over after they dried up. It was the abundance of artesian groundwater that allowed Sanford to prosper with its row crops, since pumps were not needed to bring the water up to the fields. But with poor crop rotation, the incorrect use of chemicals, and the decline of groundwater pressure, Sanford's reputation as the "Celery Capital of the World" waned by the early 1970s.

Zona is in her early eighties now, and I am a few generations younger. But I think that linear time is an illusion over the long haul. And all that really matters is that Zona was a little girl and then a pretty young woman when she lived in the house, and I was a grown man, still eager to learn new things. The nature writer Barry Lopez has written that we exude our energy so fully in a place that the place itself remembers us as having been there. And so, the house will always remember us as we once were. And somewhere in the cosmos where clocks keep a score that really matters, Zona will always be twelve and thirteen, happy and steadfast in her verve, joyous to be young and alive in the rural country of northeast Florida. And I will always be in my forties and early fifties, reasonably strong of body, and deep inside, still a kid who wants to learn why the world works as it does—always trying to record in some way how the delicate transect between art and nature left its mark on me, a mark that with the years, becomes more indelible.

Before I leave, the phone rings and Zona's granddaughter on the other end tells her a scan just showed her unborn baby to be a girl. And then she tells her that the baby will be named "Zona" in her honor. Zona is beside herself with happiness and pride. "I always liked having that name when I was growing up," Zona once told me. "It was different, no one could confuse me with someone else." She is still like that now, clear-eyed, spirit-rich, and I can understand why the house remembers her as a young woman, why it would never confuse her with anyone else.

I take the old bloomed-out orchid with me, and promise I'll trim it back and try to make it flower. Zona and Art walk with me just outside the back door. I admire the giant variegated pothos up on their oak tree, and we all express gratitude for the grand fall weather around us. And then I shake Art's hand and kiss Zona goodbye, and go on my way down the street under a canopy of oaks to my own home, just four blocks away, a distance of pure chance and righteous symmetry. It is the sort of distance that, despite all that has happened in my life, is still very manageable. Unlike a foreign land or a state on the other side of our own country, it is so close I can see from one end to the other, if I look carefully enough. It is a distance that can only be measured in beats of the heart.

✻ 31

What's Really in the White Space

The passion flower or passion vine as rendered by naturalist William Bartram during his visit to Florida. It was later published with other drawings of plants and animals in his book Travels *in 1791.*

It was warm this morning, even at 7:00 a.m., and when I go out in my yard, the anoles have already started scuttling about. They move in quick, time-stop jerks, navigating their world in a series of invisible leaps—almost like an old motion picture that doesn't have enough frames to communicate the art of uninterrupted, fluid motion.

I think on this some, watch the gambusia peck at the surface of the pond, listen as a cardinal begins her sweet call from somewhere low in the young magnolia with the bright green leaves. The passion flower has put so much energy into its vine that it's covered almost the entire reed-fence where I first planted it. It now blooms only at the very tips, as if the baroque flowers are trumpeters announcing the arrival of a tiny green army.

I sip on a cappuccino with a dash of chocolate and nibble on wedges of a sweet orange from the tree, thumbing through *The Book of Naturalists*, an anthology that the great marine scientist William Beebe assembled in 1941. I ran across Beebe's work several years ago when I was getting ready to go on an oceanographic expedition to the Galapagos Islands for a month. Beebe had been there in the 1920s, and did some of the early marine science there using a "hard hat" diving system. A female colleague of his produced some of the very first underwater art by actually painting what she saw "in situ" using oils that were not soluble in water. It was the underwater version of what "Plein Aire" painting has become today.

The anthology was one of the first to give me a real context for what this nature writing business is all about. Certainly, if you only read popular literature, you'll likely be left with the idea that "nature writing" is a modern invention that requires a great deal of hand wringing and flagellation. While I much admire those who are skilled in observing nature, I am less impressed with the exclusionary way in which this observation can sometimes be filtered.

Beebe sets us straight, reminding us that Aristotle started it all in 344 B.C. with "Fishing-Frogs, Cuckoos, and Other Things." The philosopher watched animals closely, reporting that fish sleep and many animals—including insects—may dream. It's the natural precedent to Billy Bartram who, in his own wonderful mysticism, figured humans are no higher or lower than any other member of the plant and animal kingdom. And, if animals dream, who are we to interrupt their dreams with our own overblown sense of ego? And isn't this what the nature ethicist Aldo Leopold also tells us—that humans exist as an essential weave of ecology, and not separate from it? To indulge in self-absorption requires a very large ego to set ourselves so completely apart from any other living thing. It's no wonder that otherwise gentle souls sometimes transform into authoritarian know-it-all's, delivering us not accounts of nature but advertisements of how all of nature swirls about them in an elliptical orbit, words and deeds simply satellites that exist only to glorify the ego.

Certainly, mysticism is deeply embedded into nature. Blake knew this, as did Thoreau. And, while he gets little attention from most modern nature writers, so did Marcel Proust, the early twentieth-century French novelist and essayist. Proust figured it was the artist's responsibility to confront nature, to figure out its essence, and to translate that to us in art.

Of them all, I most identify with Bartram, of course. Not just because he was an artist and writer with sensibilities informed by the sublime, but because he was so nonchalant about how strong his emotional stamina really was. Billy got some bad reviews of *Travels* early on, and of course, his entire life was widely misunderstood—thanks to a few historic footnotes that some scholars pass along with great glee. But in his era, few people went adventuring throughout the wild American southeast alone—especially to the forlorn, insect-and-Indian-infested swamp of Florida. To do so, a man needed more than emotional resolve, he needed substantial physical energy of the sort that let him sail and oar a small boat in storms or climb to the top of cypress trees. At the same time, Billy could then sit and write: "Birds are in general social and benevolent creatures; intelligent, ingenious, volatile, active beings . . ." And, there may be, in fact, no more "glorious display of the Almighty hand than the vegetable world." Egalitarian, almost to a fault, Bartram saw humans as no less or greater than the rest of "the boundless palace of the sovereign Creator." And within the "tribes" of humans, he saw the Native Americans as particularly wise, insightful, and informed—a perception that set him apart from most other whites who explored Florida.

But even those attributes don't fully explain my admiration for Bartram. He was not only devout about the power of nature, he was in great delight of it, and unapologetic in being so. At his core, he came not to exploit but to commune—and then to return with the results of his communion. It's simplistic to say Bartram was ahead of his time—indeed, he was ahead of *our* time. Strong, confident, scientific, artistic, poetic, adventurous—he was what most modern American men only hope to be, the kind of guy that women so often romanticize in popular feature films. Listen to Billy describe himself, as he and a temporary traveling companion prepare to go their separate ways:

> I sailed in the morning, with a fair wind. I was now again alone, for the young man, . . . though stouter and heartier than myself . . . chose rather to stay behind, amongst the settlements. . . . Our views were probably totally opposite; he, being a young mechanic on his adventures . . . (by) following his occupation he might be able to procure, without much toil and danger . . . the conveniences of life. Whilst I, continually impelled by a relentless spirit of curiosity, in pursuit of new productions of nature, my chief happiness consisted in tracing and admiring the infinite power, majesty, and perfection of the Almighty Creator. . . . (so) I might be instrumental in discovering and introducing into my native country (something) which might become useful to society.

Wow, what a riff. Are the anoles and cardinals, and now, the newly-arrived wood thrush, any better because I have pondered all of this? Or do they become more comfortable because I sit silently, not moving about in lizard-like jerks—absorbing not myself but the moment? No one can say for sure. And in fact, if another human were to observe me here at my patio table in my fenced yard that is quickly going feral, they might even wonder if I am doing very much at all.

And that, all by itself, is part of the writer's plight: if I were a plumber or physician, my work might be defined by how skillfully I use a wrench, or how well I use instruments and tests to interpret the human condition. Instead, it is more likely I appear like the anole that moves in time-warping spurts. No one even sees the actual movement; all they know for sure is where the lizard starts and stops. That blur of light in between may be a true dynamic. Or it may simply be white space on a historic map, territory that is too unimaginable to be known.

And, one second ago, I was sitting at my patio table with my cappuccino. And now, here I am, tapping little plastic keys on a strange machine. All the space in between is nothing more or less than a white blur.

32

Retracing Art through Memory

What can any of us really know about art? And why in the world am I trying to write about it here, when I ought to be outside playing under the sunshine and trees?

Well, I've been thinking a lot about art lately, and how it pushes buttons for so many folks. There's art intended to evoke a strong reaction—sometimes even a brutal one. There's art aimed at informing the senses. There's art that's a vehicle for the expression or communication of emotions and ideas, period—no judgment attached.

I've always liked the archaic definition of art as "to assemble." That would mean to pull together from the disparate parts. To make whole. Which Aristotle also defined as love: to make whole, or at least attempt to.

But I ramble. I thought that as a writer I would show, not tell. And so I have more closely examined the stuff hanging on my walls—stuff that some might call art. Individually, they each have merits; but taken wholly, they reveal more than their singular details. Not surprisingly, a lot of these pieces have to do with nature in some way.

Artwork by Jacksonville landscape artist Allison Watson entitled St. Johns River Edge.

Although I've taken thousands of photos during my life, very few of them were ever actually printed and mounted. I have framed and hung one, not because of the aesthetic but because of its straightforward nostalgia: it shows a good buddy, Dan Shaw, holding a handful of hard-shelled clams that one day long ago, we dug from the sandy shoals just inside Sebastian inlet. They are *mercenaria*, the common clam found along Atlantic sea coasts. Depending on size, they are known variously as "cherry stones" and "little necks;" if they grow larger, the flesh is tougher and usually needs to be chopped into smaller pieces for chowder. We had intended to use some of those smaller clams for bait while surf fishing. If we didn't catch fish, we at least had the clams to take home and steam up. Those clams and that moment are far gone, but by looking at the photo, I can remember that day and all the great times Dan and I had fishing and hanging out. We had a lot of laughs, and when we get together—geography has separated us—we still have fun. Dan's a courageous guy, a person who would stand up for you in a fight. Do you know how rare that is nowadays?

Another framed work is a mola as rendered by a Cuna (also Kuna) Indian woman in the San Blas Islands on the Caribbean coast of Panama. I was there once to write a story about water and diving and culture, and ended up riding in a cayuco with a kicker to a little coconut palm island where a small Cuna family lived. The matriarch sold me a couple of molas cheap, since there was no middleman or transport involved, just me and the mola, which also happened to be of fish. The photographer and the entire family, except for a young boy, maybe six or seven, seemed to vanish. He and I just sat there under the coconut palms, the great swash of the Caribbean Sea just a few yards away. He had not yet learned to speak Spanish, and I knew no Cuna. Using a sort of sign language, I asked him what his name was. He wrote it with a stick in the sand. I did the same and we each tried to pronounce the other's name; we mangled this so badly that we both ended up laughing good naturedly about it all. Then I snorkeled around their island— no one had tanks or a compressor—but it was okay, since the fringing reef was shallow. I saw a school of Caribbean reef squid, and they looked at me with human-like eyes before flying off through the water in elegant swoops. If only they had a backbone, I thought, they might be running things instead of us humans. Then again, maybe they are anyway.

The piece that is probably as close to traditional art as I'm going to get is a striking oil landscape by Allison Watson, a talented and brilliant artist who lives in Jacksonville. Once she and artist Jim Draper drove down with their kayaks, and I took them out to see the Blackwater Creek, part of the Wekiva system. It was in flood then, and we spent most of the day paddling in and out of the river and through the swamp. Later, she and Jim went back to their respective studios, and with photos taken of that day, created works of art from it all, a process I find transcendent. Do you know the energy of the soul that comes from being in the company of artists like that when they are contemplating their work from deep inside?

Allison's art did not come from that day, although it could have. It was a gift from her for spending my time guiding her and Jim. That's the thing about really good artists: they are whole enough, somewhere in their hearts, to communicate a truth beyond the ordinary. When sunlight hits this painting, the forest on the canvas mimics the one in real life, and the trees and water turn with the colors of the passing of the day.

A frame on another wall holds a hand-drawn map of the old pirate city of Port Royal off the coast of Kingston, Jamaica. I went there once for the Discovery Channel because Port Royal had once been the shining, opulent jewel of the New World, and it was mostly because of the plunder of seventeenth-century pirates. Then one day, an earthquake dumped the entire town into the sea. Archaeologists and even treasure salvers had been there since, and while the sunken city was off-limits to scuba divers, we got special permission to dive because of the Discovery connection. I stumbled into a striking young archaeologist working in a dilapidated building in Port Royal during that visit, and she drew the map in preparation for a dive she offered to lead there.

Visitors have asked if this is a "treasure map," and sometimes I tell them "yes," because the richness of my experiences were wealthy beyond imagination. After the dives, we went to a little pub and drank Ting, a wonderful Jamaican soft drink that I can't seem to ever find here. I learned a lot about the pirates, and came to appreciate how society has used outcasts like that to its advantage over the centuries. Underwater, I floated over brick streets that pirates had walked, moved over the thresholds of doorways that had opened to homes and bars. I felt as if I was in a dream much of the time. Compared to all the toadyness and spineless twaddle in our modern techno-world, there are far worse things a person can be than a pirate.

Near my bed is a small needlework of a little boy kneeling at the foot of his bed. He is in his pajamas, the kind that button up the back, and there's a little blond teddy bear resting on his pillow. The little boy's hair is also blond. The inscription of the needlework is: *Now I Lay Me Down To Sleep*. It is a prayer I said when I was a little boy with blond hair, when I carried a little stuffed animal, also blond, everywhere I went. My grandmother created that needlework, looking far and wide for yellow yarn to match the color of both the bear and me.

In my hallway, on an unframed canvas, there are four snowy egrets and they are all doing different avian things—feeding, flying, getting ready to fly. In the background is a green Florida hardwood swamp. The birds have exquisite details to their feathers, but most of all, they imply movement and the relentless dynamic of energy. I watched as an artist who was a quadriplegic painted this by holding a brush in his mouth. Carol Grimes, a very earnest and caring woman who helped facilitate an annual environmental award on behalf of her late husband up in Jacksonville, commissioned the painting for me as part of the award. It was a generous and heartfelt gesture, for me as well as the artist. When he was finished with the painting that day, he looked at me and said, "If I can do this, you can do anything. Don't forget it." I promised him I wouldn't, and in my darkest moments, I remember that promise, remember the way the egrets so gracefully flew out of the imagination of a man who couldn't.

Another one of my framed photos hangs in the bathroom. It is a shot I took once in Havana, and it looks at the front of a 1950s-era Plymouth, the kind that had those big chrome grills that always looked as if they were smiling or frowning. The license plate on the front bumper has a number, and below and above the number are the words: "Cuba" and "Particular." Behind the car in the background is a three-story building, likely of some shell-crushed lime rock, and the doors and windows are covered with detailed filigrees of black metal. Behind a door on the lowest floor, a man is standing facing me with a red shirt. Both of his hands are on the bars, as if he is in a cell, looking out. On the day I took that photograph, I met Fidel Castro later that night. He came aboard an oceanographic ship that had been exploring the wild southern coast of his country for over a month. One night, on a particularly deep oceanic pinnacle, I got lost and almost washed away in the strong currents, but I didn't tell Fidel this. He talked about drugs from the sea, and recipes for spiny lobster, and—in the midst of all else—hinted that humans may once have immigrated to the earth from another planet, maybe Venus, the planet of love. We Venusians needed to leave home because we had polluted it, not unlike we were now doing to our own planet. Not too long after that, Fidel collapsed during one of his day-long speeches; within just a few years of that encounter, he retired, trading his green fatigues for a jogging suit.

In my bedroom is an oil my mom painted when she was a beautiful young woman. Years ago, my dad framed it very nicely, and stained the frame a rich mahogany. I looked at it on our wall back home when I was growing up all the time, but I could never figure it out. It shows a large earthen wall, steep, jutting up from the water, and a lone faceless woman, added almost as an afterthought. It has a brooding quality about it, although my mom was never one who brooded long. I think about that painting today, think about growing up where I did, with the encouragement and love I once had. I asked my mom once what the painting represented, and she just sort of blew it off, said she had copied it from a magazine photo. Yet all my life, I thought that it was so much more, a time-stop moment of her own life when she was still a student in an art school down in Lakeland, back when her father was wealthy and the days and nights were gay and alive, and absolutely anything was possible in the world.

I want to tell my mom that I understand now, that the coming together of all the pieces makes it righteous for me, for those I care for. I can't do that, of course. But I can take great comfort in the knowledge that memory, as poet Marge Piercy has told us, is the simplest form of prayer. And so that is the story of some of the stuff on my walls that I call art.

33

An Afternoon Treasure Hunt

It's so hot by 2:00 p.m. today that out in my backyard, the leaves on the common nightshade—a hearty native with flowers like tiny white chandeliers—are beginning to curl. The vine of the miniature gourd, usually stout and robust, isn't doing too well, either. Elsewhere in the enfenced, half-feral jungle that once was a flat slab of St. Augustine, things seem okay, if a bit quiet. The only animals with enough ambition to move are the Cuban anoles, the darkish exotic bruisers from the Antilles beating up on the smaller green natives, Lilliputian lives waged and lost on the twig of a magnolia.

In the old historic downtown of Sanford on the river, here's my friend Yvette Comeau's bookstore, Maya Books and Music.

I've just finished a writing project, so I'm anxious to get out and stretch my legs despite the heat. I put on my shades and light out, by foot, for downtown. It's a nice stroll, 2.8 miles roundtrip, atop sidewalks and mostly under the canopies of large trees for most of the way. One of the reasons I moved to Sanford was so I could do stuff like this, because when I was a boy growing up, that's what I would also do—walk to town. There, I'd meet up with friends, maybe take in an afternoon matinee, especially if a good horror movie was playing. If not, we'd hang out at the drug store, drink cherry cokes, wait to see if any pretty girls might be around. Here in Sanford, the historic downtown bears an uncanny resemblance to the little downtown I knew as a boy. I make no bones about the fact that nostalgia still plays big in figuring out so much to do with my life.

The walk in today is a good one, and here in east central Florida in late spring, the air is full of the smell of blossoms and newly cut grass. After a few blocks I start to glisten, even with a light breeze blowing up Park Avenue from the river. I also begin to open my senses more fully to the experience, figuring the intellect had already done enough damage for the day. Unlike new developments where look-alike McMansions ostentatiously line the streets, homes here are all across the board, from Victorians and the Craftsman models of the 1930s, to a few cottages from the last half century or so, not unlike my own. Most are well kept, many with little gardens here and there bristling with a mix of natives and exotics, shampoo gingers hanging with lush rouge-faced blooms and the crepe-like flowers of the Turks cap—sometimes called "sleeping hibiscus" because it never quite opens—poking out in gay folds of red. Emerson, likely tired of enduring the grey New England climate, once described Florida as representing the "happiest of the latitudes" because its warmer weather births a vibrancy of plants and trees, and so it is for my little town.

On my saunter, I pass white picket fences with brick walkways and, next to one time-stuck Victorian, a vintage Texaco gas pump, the kind with the rounded glass light imprinted with the classic Texaco star logo. I walk beyond two "pocket" parks, one for kids with neat wooden boxes and stilts and ladders and labyrinthine stuff, a design architects once took from actual drawings children had made of what a playground would be, if they were in charge. And now, at least in this one park, they are.

I finally reach First Street, which is what the main street is called, and am struck, as always, by the quaint two-story brick buildings with the ornate cornices and trim, a vision right out of the 1890s. The businesses here are not as functional as they once were, back when there were stores selling hardware, groceries, and just about anything a local could need. Sprawl outside of town has taken that utility away, transforming it there with chain stores and the like. Nonetheless, there's still enough of a true downtown dynamic here to support a music store, an old fashioned country restaurant with chicken fried steak, a couple of lawyer's offices, a twice-weekly newspaper, and my friend Yvette's bookstore, where I am headed today. Nearby is Dave's Barbershop, where the peppermint pole still swirls; inside, the walls are lined with photos of old television cowboys. A block or so off First Street, there's even a grain and feed store where you can buy everything from crops and fencing to small farm animals. Sanford organically functions much like architect-planner Andre Duany's vision of the "Great American Neighborhood"—wherein newly created towns are built so their eclectic business district functions as the legitimate heart of the place.

Once on First, I walk a few blocks under awnings for the comfort of the shade. As I do, I can't help remember once walking down another sunny street with treasure hunter Mel Fisher in Key West on one hot summer afternoon. Mel was a pistol, a true American original, finally discovering the long-lost Spanish treasure galleon *Atocha*, long after everyone else had given up. "Let's walk on the shady side of the street," Mel suggested that day, and I agreed, even though it was only a few blocks to his favorite bar.

I had been diving earlier that week with some archaeologists off of Islamorada, and wanted to ask Mel about the way his treasure salvers might destroy the "providence" of a shipwreck, thereby ruining the historic integrity of it. Mel, always a good sport, a lover of good rum and pretty women, was up for the banter, and the afternoon would forever enrich my memory, taking my quest for a magazine story as far as I could take it, as usual. And why write about treasure and the grittiness of its maritime history if you hadn't experienced it, underwater, hadn't walked on the shady side of the street in Key West with Mel Fisher, hadn't seen the look of wistfulness in the eyes of the young women divers who had just found a handful of emeralds, buried all these centuries, embedded in the calcium of the coral. Mel's mantra was always "Today's the Day!," a slogan that, no matter how bleak and unyielding earlier salvaging had been, promised abundance. And one day, it came true.

And so, I leave the shady awnings of Sanford, cross over where the large clock on a pedestal marks the edge of Magnolia Square, and go into Maya Books and Music, the store owned by my friend Yvette, who at this moment is sitting barefoot on the floor, pricing a bunch of books a customer just brought in for trade. Yvette, astonishingly literate, is the antidote to every soul-sucking corporate bookstore ever invented. She diligently handles every book that comes in, reading the ones she likes the best, and then puts them into niches categorized by type—art, history, women's, nature, poetry, and so on. Some books, with nicks and bruises, go into a box by the front door marked "free." Others simply offer themselves to you, little treasures in the stacks. When a customer asks for a certain title, Yvette doesn't check the inventory on a computer; instead, she scrolls through her mind and provides an answer, just like real people used to do in real towns not so terribly long ago.

Yvette knows the book selling biz, knows the modern realities of the new McBook world that cuisinarts the integrity of knowledge and homogenizes culture. Still, she keeps on keeping on, every bit as courageous and optimistic and Quixotic as the treasure salvers of the Keys. I sit in a comfy chair covered with a Mexican shawl of some sort, gratefully inhaling the bottle of water I've been offered. Yvette, who sometimes uses a worldly edge to hide a warm heart, tells of growing up as a book worm—and when being made to play outside, taking her favorite books with her and reading them up in the protective crook of a tree.

I have learned from earlier chats that Yvette's dream is not just to sell books, but to help create a sense of community, a quality that is rapidly vanishing elsewhere as gentrification sweeps across the land. Sociologist Ray Oldenburg has looked at this disturbing trend and argues that we have compartmentalized our modern lives into two isolated and rarefied habitats—the private home, with its cocoon-enabling toys, and the sophisticated workplace, with its protocol and technology.

Oldenburg says there is a need for a viable "Third Place" where people can go and simply feel comfortable because that place captures the intimacy and congeniality humans instinctively need. I heard a country music song on the radio the other day that said the same thing, in far fewer words, as country music songs so often do. The lament of the refrain went: If the world had a front porch, like we did back then.

And so, at Maya, people come in to chat, to sit at a table and play chess, to wander about the racks of carefully chosen books, to just have a relaxing space to be. They do so in a place that is not unlike a very large front porch, of the sort I knew when growing up. Philosopher Thomas Moore says independent bookstores can particularly allow this, can exude a very real "enchantment." In this way, they feel less like a sterile government information office and more like a "haunted castle."

And of course, experiences like this are essential because, as Moore explains, "the soul needs a vernacular life," an existence defined not by a corporate and bloodless approach to money-making, but one which stresses the *local* aspect of place, and of belonging. This is what has been created here, and for those with discerning senses, there is no doubt as to how comforting that vernacular presence can be. Discovery still awaits around every corner, every aisle, inside every book cover. *Today's the day.*

Refreshed, I say goodbye and head back up the street for home, walking a carefully chosen path that takes me past old memories and new scents, always eager for the little moments which, unexpectedly, reveal more than I could have ever imagined. Kids ride by on their bikes, a dog barks in the distance, a woman pushing a stroller smiles and says hi.

It's later now, but still a scorcher of a day, and whenever I get a chance, I slip into the shade just like Mel would do, smiling now at the lavish splendor of the human senses, wondering what the next few steps will bring.

🐾 34

Doe Lake

A Movie of Nostalgia

Doe Lake is tucked away off a dirt road in the Ocala National Forest, surrounded by a hammock of live and water oaks. Its shore is green, crammed with native plants and soggy wet soils, and it sparkles in the late afternoon light, a sandy-bottom Florida lake as clear as they all once were in another time.

The old dining hall here was built by and for WPA workers who helped clear roads through the forest and build trails and kiosks back in the 1930s. It sits atop a bluff that slopes gradually down to the edge of the

Sea turtles, caught and turned upside down and kept alive until the butcher arrives. This is along the Miskito coast of Nicaragua.

lake. There were barely 1.5 million people living in Florida then, and the interior of the state was lonely and wild.

I park next to a row of big American pickup trucks and walk inside. There are already 150 people here, spread out under the rich hardwood interior or outside milling about at the edge of the lake itself. We're here for a celebration, one intended to bring attention to a little cabin once used by the family of the great naturalist Archie Carr for three generations. The cabin, built of cypress and pine in 1938, was a back-woods refuge for the Carr family, a place where they could learn about the wonderful strangeness that distinguished natural Florida from all else. The little cabin with its Cracker-style look and feel is symbolic of the ethics the Carrs embodied, ideals once learned and then shared with all who cared about the power of the natural world, and the animals that populated it.

Certainly, the notions vital to understanding ecology and the unique nature of Florida had simmered there. But like many righteous ideas that pass through our lives, they sometimes hide in the margins of ex-istence, not becoming evident until we really need them to be. All we know is that they urge us on when we walk an unknown, dark trail at night, or paddle a sliver of a tropical river that seeps through a rainfor-est, no real map and certainly no guide to show us the way. For me, life has often come down to that. And, while I am forever grateful to my family for raising me to have a quiet confidence in such things, I am also thankful for those mentors who helped me understand the difference between moving ahead with informed determination, and simply pre-tending to do so. A few times, these mentors were in the flesh, but more often than not, they spoke across the decades, like Carr, or centuries, like Bartram.

But there's more, and it's in that strange duality that a rare place like Florida—or any priceless natural place caught in the crosshairs of growth—must endure. I think once more about the poignant elegy Dr. David Ehrenfeld wrote after Archie died back in 1987: "Archie was one of the last great minstrels of wilderness, singing a song of joy mixed with an abiding melancholy—a song that both saddened his listeners even as it gave them the heart to fight. . . ." It is this duality I most appreciate, since it's one that most caring folks in this chronically put-upon state come to know on an intimate basis. Caring for Florida is a complicated business, and those who see it as a black and white exercise usually don't get it.

The dress for this evening is "Florida casual," and if we were at an upscale private club somewhere, that would mean the "swells" would be tricked out in their L.L. Bean outdoor garb. But here, folks are honestly relaxed, t-shirts and camo and jeans. We line up cafeteria-style for our dinners, and I heap piles of local flora and fauna on my plate, hearts-of-palms and venison and fried gator. When this fundraising dinner was being planned, all that was missing was wild hog. So Dr. Ray Willis, the archaeologist for the forest, went out and shot one, and the cooks roasted it. I grab a large glass of sweet iced tea, and sit at the table near the front, next to a good fellow from Umatilla who has fished and hunted most of his life. We talk about the St. Johns River, since he has loved fishing it, and I once wrote a book about it. We talk of gators, because, well, that's what Florida folks usually do—sooner or later, they trade gator stories about size and cunning and the forever inexplicable primal nature of the animal.

The idea behind all this is to raise money that will help restore the little Cracker cabin so that it becomes a functioning symbol of a true Florida-born conservation ethic, one embodied by Archie and his wife, Marjorie Harris Carr, his father, Pastor A. F. Carr, his wife, and their five children. Dr. Tom Carr, Archie's surviving brother, has donated the forty-six acres of land and the cabin to the United States Forest Service in the hope it might provide a sort of beacon in the come-and-go darkness of Florida's transient world. Eleanor Blair, an accomplished landscape artist from Gainesville, has rendered an oil painting of the cabin and donated it to the cause. Architects and restoration experts from the University of Florida have all pitched in. A "Friends of the Carr Cabin" has been formed, and is being shepherded by the Umatilla Historical Society. A nature trail will be blazed nearby to help interpret the natural history of the place.

After being approached by Ray some months ago, I've engaged Bob Giguere, my partner in a nonprofit dedicated to making nature films. Together, Bob and I have produced a short video about the cabin that recounts both the utility and the iconic value of the structure. Several of the Carr family appeared on camera to express their own feelings about it, including Tom Carr, who actually helped build the structure when he was a student in Umatilla High School so many years ago. When we finished the short film, I had asked Archie and Marjorie's daughter Mimi to narrate it. When the time is right, we will screen it for everyone here. Later it will be used to encourage like-minded souls to help with the restoration effort.

During the day of the filming, Tom drove up through the woods to the cabin, and the first thing he did after he arrived was to look for the last remaining vestiges of a wooden rowboat his father, Parson Carr, had once built. Left to decay near the edges of the lake, the boat first settled into the soft marsh. Later, when the lake grew smaller and the shores retreated, the top of the gunnels could still be seen in the earth. Finally, the rotting wood nourished the grasses and wildflowers that grew above it. When Tommy Carr finally returned on that day, the outline of the boat was defined by a few splinters of wood and the vibrancy of the plant growth—it was an elliptical halo of green in the white Florida sand. It is not unlike the legacy his brother left for us all.

There is a sort of protocol for presentations tonight, and we all file dutifully up to the lectern to add a few words when needed. We are not showmen, so the coming and going is often clunky, but in an endearing and genuine sort of way. Rick Lint, the ranger in charge for the forest, introduces the speakers, no fancy prelude, just a few meaningful words. Two former UF students of Archie's who have now earned worldwide reputations for their own work in conservation biology speak respectively, first Dr. Peter Pritchard and then Dr. Perrin Ross. Both are low-key, funny, informed, eloquent. A few years ago, Peter was named as one of the "Heroes of the Earth" by *Time* magazine, although no one mentions this. Both he and Perrin tell of the inspiration gifted to them, a quality they continue to pass along to all the rest of us students of the earth. Finally, Ray gets up and explains a bit about the plan to restore the cabin and why.

A woman next to me at the table leans over and whispers, "This is like a movie," and she is right because there is almost no pretense, no sign of acting, no individual promotion, just a bunch of guys who have all tried to do the right thing, and are doing it with their hearts. It is flesh-and-blood nostalgia, the sort of moment you know will never be again, even as it is happening. It is, if anything, a theater of altruism, and that sets it all decidedly apart from a mere just-pretend theater with music and narrative scripted and precisely managed. And do you know the old phrase, actions speak louder than words? Decisive action and caring is what the evening is really about, the very rich energy of an inner core infused by the light. It is not the sort of event where boasting and political grandstanding would play very well.

And I think again of philosopher Joseph Campbell and of his description of the "Hero's Journey." "All mythic heroes," says Campbell, "go to a place that is difficult to reach, and then return to their starting point with elixirs, food, or knowledge to share with the community." If, on return, they seem a bit ragged and humble, well, it matters little. Campbell reminds us that being courageous or strong is not the most vital quality of this archetypical "hero." Instead, it is *sacrifice*, which means "making holy."

And so, this evening from another century becomes one of hyperreality, a moment so rare that we can hardly find room for it in our imaginations, except to think that, just maybe, this might be a movie, one in which righteous and unselfish ideas really do prevail, after all. And outside a cloud bank drifts away in the night sky and the lake becomes luminous under the moonlight, just as if it has been perfectly cued to do so.

POSTSCRIPT: *Largely thanks to the intervention and tenacity of Ray Willis, many will sign on to help, and eventually, funds will be raised. The cabin will eventually be rebuilt and primed for the day when the public can visit it and also walk on a little nature trail not far from Lake Nicotoon and maybe look for the elliptical halo of green in the white Florida sand.*

🌣 35

The Wekiva

Between the Water & the Sky

A hardwood hammock with Spanish moss along a river shore.

On a weekday, the lower Wekiva seemed deserted, and the large pre-Columbian midden that used to hold Katie's Landing had a sense of abandonment about it. The state owns the property now, and the campers and little store and RV's are all gone, only big magnolias and cypresses with official tags on them, growing up from the crushed shell and pot shards. Even the waterfront bulkhead, the last true relic of the landing, was crumbling in on itself.

I fumbled with my kayak and got it in the water a bit before Steve unloaded his, and within moments, the strong rain-fed current was pushing me downstream, no paddle needed. The river had grown in size since last I saw it, becoming both deeper and wider because of our heavy rains over the last few weeks. The detritus from the swamp washes in and dilutes the clarity of the spring water at these times. And it also opens up old sloughs that were little more than troughs back in the swamp. In the days when the rainy season was guaranteed, you could count on following those sloughs until they became branches, and then splintered off into something else entirely. Old maps still show them, trailing away deeper into the swamp: Chub Creek Slough, Banana Creek, and so on.

With the new water, we figured we could navigate around the back of the first big island, and we each found openings in the tall grasses and willow that allowed us to try that. I came out closer to the edge of the island where an abandoned wooden dock had a biblical passage scrawled on the front of it, and a gator was growling from somewhere nearby. If given to Revelations, I would take meaning in that, but I was not, and did not. In fact, I was more interested in the blooming wildflowers, the marsh mallow bush, and the tight yellow bud of the spadderdock lily. Steve yelled to get my attention, pointing to what he thought was the white head of an eagle high above the tree line. Since we were still separated by the tall foliage, all I could see was his disembodied arm pointing upward from somewhere inside the green. I looked, and was even more surprised when the raptor turned out to be a swallow-tailed kite, looping and diving.

We finally reconnoitered, and then fought our way through the massive "bull hyacinths" where there was absolutely no cut except the ones our hulls each made. The first patch of floating weeds finally opened to a pool of dark, deep water. A black-crowned night heron was on a log at its edge, looking as surprised to see me as I was to see him. We floated easily through that open swatch of blackwater, and then the swamp closed in on us again. Next to come were some of the largest specimens of water lettuce I've ever seen, all huddled together in a sort of floating pasture. Bartram wrote about seeing great mats of this "pistia" on the St. Johns in the eighteenth century, so I'm going to regard it as native, even though the indigenous plant police will argue otherwise.

By the time we finally made it around the entire island, it was almost an hour later and I was covered in sweat. Years ago, when that back branch of the island was still wide open, you could have traveled it in five minutes. By now, a light breeze was picking up off the water from the confluence of the main branch, and it felt good. We paddled on northward, only a couple of old docks and a small fish camp left, a place where you could rent a small boat, maybe buy some Slim Jims and a cold drink. For the first time in years, the camp seemed to be closed, and the old guys who used to sit outside it on bar stools were gone. After that, it was all public land; the battered brown wooden sign that announced this as the "Lower Wekiva River State Preserve" looked as though something had been chewing on it. Just as we paddled past the sign, we saw a dead five-foot-long gator lying on its back with a black-headed vulture balanced on its stomach, happily pecking away at lunch.

We ducked back into another branch to the west, pushing over a newly fallen sweetgum log that submerged when we paddled onto it. More bull hyacinths and lettuce, and lots of deadfall. But back through the forest there was a shaft of light, likely shining onto yet another "lost" channel. It was here I stopped short. Something large moved back in there, crashing through the water and trees. Steve heard it and said, "Bear." I looked, but the movement was gone, the moment stilled to a quiet. In stopping to look, I did see a wild scarlet hibiscus shining as bright as a headlight on a dark country lane, a glory I would have otherwise missed.

The more we paddled, the more I was awestruck by the way the river had changed since the last time I was on it. The mosses on the cypress and baywood seemed thicker than ever, and muscadine grape vines trailed between it all like giant spider webs. The bald cypresses—the ones that were too small to be logged a century ago—endure with a sort of timeless resolve, obligate knees rising up from the water and mud like tiny nuns in a grand organic pew. I think that if a tree can be said to have wisdom, then the slow-growing cypress must be the greatest philosopher of all, reigning quietly here in this tropical river swamp, its knowledge locked into the flow of its cambium, forever linking the water and the sky.

Despite all we've done to it, the Wekiva has revitalized itself once again, becoming wild in its seasonal transformation, and I am immensely grateful for that. Steve had once studied for the priesthood, and I still think of him as one of the most spiritual people I know. I can't receive absolution from him, but our journey together, floating through the tropical forest of this Florida river, is redemption enough for any human. Natural sacraments surround us at every turn, reminders of the redemption a wild landscape still offers.

The breeze that was welcome and light now builds, and the clouds begin to push up against each other. Thunder rolls from somewhere deep inside the horizon, and Steve suggests we turn and begin the paddle back toward the midden. It is a responsible decision, one an adult would make.

Sure, I say, go on and I'll catch up. Then I turn to poke my bow down another little cut to get closer to a giant leather fern, a massive plant that fills a nook between two large hickories. Tiny fish, excited by the coming storm, are dimpling the water, and the sky is turning dark. A little blue heron, spooked, cries loudly and from back in the hyacinths, a gator groans. Steve looks at me, and without judgment, starts paddling back, taking slow, deliberate strokes.

36

Be Thankful for the Dragons

When I was a kid, maps were things that were stacked atop each other in great rolls on the classroom wall. The older the students, the more maps there were. Teachers pulled maps down for quick reference like pulling down a large window shade. Then, just as I was getting familiar with the lay of the land, zip, back up they went.

When our family took road trips, a map was that thing my dad kept in the glove compartment. All I knew then was the document had to be folded just right or it would bulge and look sloppy. Those maps seemed

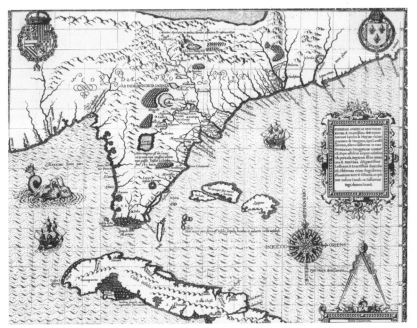

Jaques Le Moyne's map of how the Spanish saw Florida in the late sixteenth century.

to hold real world information, and my dad relied on them to get our family to where we needed to go.

Although I had used road maps for a while as a young adult, I didn't really trust my life to a map until I paddled through the Everglades. The trip took me and a photographer from Chokoloskee on the northwest tip of the Glades National Park down southeast to the tip of the Florida cape at the old fishing and pluming village of Flamingo. The paddle took us nine days, and zigzagged us across the Wilderness Waterway. It required three very detailed maps and, of course, a compass.

As most backcountry travelers know, a map isn't much good unless you know where you are on it. So having a map spread out on your lap while you paddle is only part of the required behavior. The other part is paying attention to each squiggle and point, matching your magnetic direction and what you see around you with how the topography is illustrated in the soggy document on your lap.

I've returned to the Glades a number of times since, and have marveled at how fast the mangrove islands there grow. They grow so fast, in fact, that they often don't appear on the maps that mark prominent backcountry features like the Chatham River, Lostman's, Graveyard, Lopez, etcetera. So reading maps also requires a healthy dose of common sense.

I went to Russia once, traveling to St. Petersburg by air, and then from there, three days northward through the Taiga on a Russian train to the remote, freezer-burnt city of Archanglesh. A stoic Russian physicist was with our little group of scientists and he marveled at a map I brought along because it actually showed us where we were as we traveled. Russia, in the draconian way of a totalitarian state, did not want an informed populace. Maps were information, and thus, not encouraged. My *National Geographic* map, finely detailed, was the rage of our train car as it click-clacked its way across the frozen landscape. When I left Russia, I gave the map to the physicist, and when I did, his facade of seriousness dropped away and he brightened up like a little kid at a surprise birthday party.

More recently, I rode an old riverboat upstream from Iquitos, Peru, searching for the pink freshwater river dolphin. I took another *National Geographic* map with me on this trip too, as it showed where a multitude of tributaries met upstream to create the Amazon: the Ucayali with the Maranon, the Picaya with the Samaria, and so on. One day, we stopped at a small village by late afternoon. We had already seen a few of the pink dolphins and were entering an isolated preserve where we were likely to see many more. The rainforest pressed in around us, lush, wild, and intimate, so alive it seemed to be breathing.

One modest wooden building held the "school," which had no electricity and shed-like windows with no glass. All of the pupils were in one classroom and covered a range we would know as elementary and middle school. Students older than that simply went to work, fishing the Amazon, hunting, trading for jungle products with merchants downstream in Iquitos.

I used my broken Spanish to communicate with the teacher, who also seemed to be the headmaster. I pulled the *National Geographic* map of Latin America out of my backpack and laid it out on a table. Florida jutted down into the top of the map, and I pointed to it, and showed the kids where I lived, tapping my finger on an empty place between Daytona and Orlando. Then I moved my finger to where I thought we were on the map, showing them where they lived. The headmaster spoke to them very excitedly in rapid Spanish, and all I could understand was something about the flow of the river, and how far it stretched away from them. The kids all gathered around the map like it was a holy grail, and I stepped back to watch as the headmaster interpreted different features for them. All were animated and smiling, curious about this unexpected gringo with an unexpected treasure.

As I prepared to leave, I went to give my map to the headmaster. He shook his head and said in Spanish that he had no money. I told him it was not required, that this was for the school and the students, a gift. He seemed dumbfounded I would leave a document of such value with them.

When I try to understand this peculiar place that is Florida, I often go to maps that show how others have chronicled the landscape over the centuries. In early Florida, maps drawn by the French cartographer Jacques Le Moyne (circa 1564) and others show a peninsula that's truncated, with the bottom half of the map falling away to nothingness. Below that southernmost edge of the peninsula is what we know today as the Glades. At the time, this "Lagoon of the Sacred Spirit" was unexplored, and so impenetrable that its sacredness would remain intact for a long time. It was not unusual in this era of discovery for mapmakers to write in Latin at the edge of known geography: *Hic Sunt Dracones*. Here Be Dragons.

There were dragons galore throughout Florida—some were in the form of real alligators, some were the mythic edge of nothingness, where unexplored territory commandeered great chunks of mystery. Even though waterways on this sponge-like peninsula were more sure than pathways on land, the rivers of La Florida were usually shallow and, with the constant accumulation of deadfall inside of them, often given to changing course. Nothing was certain, until the U.S. Army Corps of Engineers began to dredge old channels and to cut new ones between oxbows. Even our largest river, the St. Johns, was marked between Jacksonville and Sanford, but south of there—where the other half of the river existed—cartography seems to have gone haywire, even into the early twentieth century.

Yet, when browsing through this history of the landscape, it's difficult not to be struck by the difference between the maps that were offered to the tourist and potential landowner—and maps that were more realistically crafted by the drainage engineer. For instance in an otherwise detailed map of the state found inside *Florida: Land of Enchantment* (1918), the headwaters of the St. Johns is illustrated as "Lake Washington." But, in a series of excruciatingly accurate charts created by Isham Randolph and Company, the true landscape actually emerges. Randolph, an engineering company specializing in wetland drainage, was hired to produce a series of maps that helped show how the upper St. Johns River, as well as the Everglades, could be successfully dried out to make way for human indulgences. In its maps of the river, surveyors painstakingly described features such as "switch grass" and "saw grass," "cabbage" and "palmetto" in order to help direct those who would "reclaim" the land. Isobars, those lines that show a rise or fall in the topography, were even included. I'm figuring any tourist from the boom era of the 1920s who really had an encounter with a stand of sawgrass or the serrated fronds of saw palmettos would think twice before any excursion into the Land of Enchantment.

In its thoroughness, Isham Randolph also left behind a map of the upper river basin made in 1920 that shows dilations in the St. Johns—such as Lake Hell 'n Blazes—as being easily twice the size of today's lake, even spreading out to encompass the narrow marsh-shrouded bulge that today is known as "Little Helen." Considering that Florida has historically drained away at least half of its wetlands, it's not surprising that any surface water body was far greater in size 75 or 100 years ago.

In this way, rivers in Florida are less true bodies of water and more like mythological stories told by preindustrial people, organically weaving their way through time, embellished and illuminated with the verve and spin of each new storyteller. I much enjoy the St. Johns from Puzzle Lake south for this reason. When humans come here, they have to pay attention, whether they're driving an airboat, paddling a kayak, or more rarely, navigating a little kicker-powered craft. In fact, so few even make the journey through that it's not unusual to spend an entire day on this stretch of the St. Johns River without seeing another soul. It is the same when trying to follow any one of four rivers that splay out of the massive plateau of the Green Swamp in southwest Florida.

The notion of a "swamp"—a wetland with trees—still scares a lot of folks. But the truth is a marsh—a wetland with grasses and wild scrubs—is every bit as perplexing. Like a swamp, a wet prairie still has the capacity to confuse, to humble, and if you pay close attention, to inform. It is water seeping through grass, a shallow flood of a river taking its time to go where it needs to go, an enigma that resists modern persuasion. It's also a place that keeps wildness close to its soul, a place that could easily be today, or a thousand years before today. *Hic Sunt Dracones.*

So maybe maps can't do everything. Unless, of course, you internalize them and have the courage to allow the travels across the geography of your heart to settle in. As with blind reckoning, it's hard to tell where you're going until you know for sure where you've been.

37

My Favorite Florida Books

La Relación by Álvaro Núñez Cabeza de Vaca. 1555. De Vaca was the first European to explore Florida, Texas, and the Southwest. A remarkable account, made even more so because de Vaca was in Florida over two decades before the more celebrated de Soto. The author was part of a four hundred-man expedition that landed on the southwest coast of Florida, blundered badly, and then spent the next eight years hopelessly lost, eating saddle leather, nuts, and berries. The tenacity of the four survivors earned them a sort of mystical following among the Indians, like Forrest Gump running across the country, trailing along pilgrims in his wake.

Painting of naturalist William Bartram by Charles Willson Peale.

North and South by Elizabeth Bishop. 1946. The poet's poet, a woman who could clip off the end of a sea grape leaf and see the ocean in it. It's worth it if you only read the searingly lovely poems "The Bight" and "Florida" in this collection. And from the later, we learn: "The alligator, who has five distinct calls: /friendliness, love, mating, war, and a warning—/whimpers and speaks in the throat/of the Indian Princess."

Ecosystems of Florida. Edited by Ronald L. Myers and John J. Ewel (foreword by Marjorie Harris Carr). 1990. The first and most complete book to help us understand our wondrous oddball Florida habitats and the links between each. This is how Florida should be understood and managed—by ecology, and not by politics.

Floridays by Don Blanding. 1941. The "vagabond poet" spends some time in Florida and leaves behind some wonderfully eccentric poems—all of which are sharply accurate in their description of our landscape. The title poem was plucked by Jimmy Buffett for a song by the same name.

Key West Reader. Edited by George Murphy. 1990. Provocative compilation of short stories, essays, and poems about the Keys by writers who have lived or spent time there over the years. From John James Audubon ("The Death of a Pirate") to Jim Harrison, Wallace Stevens, and editor Murphy, whose "Rounding Ballast Key" is a deeply poignant poem (and not just because I know Murphy as well as Capt. Vicki Impallomeni, about whom the poem was written).

Roadside Geology of Florida by Jonathan Bryan, Guy Means, and Tom Scott. 2008. The single best contextual insight into the weird oceanic geology that makes Florida tick, from the limestone of the Suwannee River to the Florida Keys.

Tales of Old Florida. (various). An anthology of magazine articles and essays on Florida from the 1880s through the early turn of the last century. A time capsule look into how people have seen and experienced La Florida—usually from inside a filigree of baroque description of people and place, from "Sponges and Spongers of the Florida Reef" (1892) to "Mr. Wegg's Party on the Kissimmee" (1886). Most were written in a time when Florida was regarded as wild and untamed, a sort of mysterious Amazonia tacked onto the tip of the North American continent. Making stuff up has never been this much fun.

Travels Through North & South Carolina, Georgia, East & West Florida by William Bartram. 1791. The original eco guidebook to the southeast, but especially to Florida. Rich with the gentle naturalist's own drawings of plants and animals he collected and sketched along the way. For Bartram, our Florida springs were "vast fountains of ether" and the world itself was ". . . a glorious apartment of the boundless palace of the sovereign Creator . . ." The guy understood ecology long before it had a name. More importantly, he showed us you could live with nature without having to exploit or destroy it, a lesson most Florida developers and their shill politicians still need to learn today.

The Yearling by Marjorie Kinnan Rawlings. 1938. Rawlings won a Pulitzer for this touching, uplifting, sorrowful story of a young boy coming to manhood in the remote Florida scrub west of Lake George. The author borrowed from real places in the landscape, from Silver Glen Springs to the St. Johns River to the "islands" in the scrub (although she often renamed them). A gifted storyteller with a focused eye for people and place, Rawlings listened to the stories the Crackers told her and she got it right.

A Land Remembered by Patrick Smith. 1984. Smith spins a superb tale of three generations of a fictional Cracker family between 1858 and 1958. As the story unfolds, so too does the history of Florida with all its renegades, mosquitoes, cattle rustlers, hurricanes, and rare natural beauty. As the family gradually succeeds financially, it also becomes less connected with nature. Smith's research into Florida and the unique culture shaped by the land informs this book, as does his flesh-and-blood narrative. His characters are so real that some natives believed he had actually written about their own Cracker families.

A Naturalist in Florida by Archie Carr, edited by Marjorie Harris Carr. (foreword by E.O. Wilson). 1994. Archie's articles and essays written during his life and assembled by his wife after his passing. If Archie was a great southern storyteller, he was also a brilliant scientist who knew how stuff worked. What's the use of bemoaning loss, Archie once said, unless you also celebrate what still remains in our relic landscapes. Gentle and funny, literate and informed, Carr is the sort of guy you want to share a natural discovery with, because you know he would also get a kick out of it—whether it was a mamma bear and her cub crossing a trail, a Gulf sturgeon bursting from the surface of the Suwannee River, or an unmapped freshwater spring. It would be, as Archie was fond of saying, a fine sight.

Everglades: River of Grass by Marjorie Stoneman Douglas. 1947. I interviewed Ms. Douglas once in her Coconut Grove cottage when she was ninety-six for a story in *Newsweek* on the Glades. She was astute, stubborn, and sharp as a tack. Her book was the seminal one on this vastly misunderstood river system. Although loaded with sturdy polemics on how to restore the Glades, it was also gracefully written. Between this and Mike Grunwald's recent *The Swamp* and Peter Matthiessen's rich fictional trilogy about the Everglades *(Killing Mr. Watson* and others), you'll learn all you need to know about the massive wetland that once stretched up to southern Orlando and covered almost all of southern Florida. After this, you'll be ready to kayak/canoe through the western national park for seven or eight days, maybe even stop for a visit at the old Watson Place on the Chatham.

Mirage: Florida & the Vanishing Water of the Eastern U.S. by Cynthia Barnett. Why we're running out of water due to ignorance and bush league Florida politics. Cynthia did her homework and it shows. Our loss of groundwater, springs, and surface water quality isn't an act of nature or God—as some might have you believe. It's simple math. We're now taking more water out of the ground than nature can put back in. And we have an astonishing blind spot when it comes to electing politicians who, when the chips are down, will continue to shill for their growth-crazed cronies instead of listening to nature.

Up for Grabs: A Trip Through Time & Space in the Sunshine State by John Rothchild. 1985. First really honest modern history book to explain why Florida is just so darn strange (hint: it always has been). Laid the ground later tilled by *Some Kind of Paradise* and more recently *Land of Sunshine, State of Dreams* (both excellent reads in their own right). When first published, it so jarred the rigid Chamber smiley culture mind-think that a local columnist for a major daily actually wrote an essay to try to discredit it. It was not unlike an ant trying to outdo an ant lion.

38

Salvaging a Literary Memory

Naturalism Is Born off the Florida Coast

Writer Stephen Crane had to wait three months in the port city of Jacksonville, Florida to sign onto the S. S. *Commodore* as a working seaman at $20 a month. By the grace of good fortune—and good technology—it took me only a week to get on that same ship. But the conditions under which we both "boarded" the *Commodore* were striking in their differences—not the least of which is the fact he walked on the ship when it was still above water. Nonetheless, as I was to find, there were some commonalties.

Here I am in scuba gear at the surface of the water during a recent dive project. Photo by Bill Randolph.

Crane went aboard as a journalist for a New York newspaper syndicate to cover the civil war in Cuba that would soon lead to the Spanish-American War. The *Commodore*, a 123-foot long, seagoing "steam tug," was carrying guns and ammunition to the Cubans who were rebelling against the Spanish government and the sugar fiefdom run by its wealthy and repressive Dons. With limited travel expenses and strange politics, Crane had to be creative about how he got there. While his later reporting from Cuba was highlighted by the coverage of events like the charge on San Juan Hill, it was the accidental sinking of the *Commodore* on Jan. 2, 1897, and the subsequent night and day the young writer spent aboard a tiny wooden dinghy in the Atlantic, that left an indelible mark on American literature.

From that ordeal came "The Open Boat," a barely fictionalized version of his experience in the form of a short story. It marked the beginning of the literary genre of "naturalism"—the emergence of man-against-uncaring-nature themes at the turn of the new century. If there was any question about the raw validity of the experience, the subtitle for the story was: "A Tale Intended To Be After The Fact. Being The Experience Of Four Men Sunk From The Steamer Commodore." In the story, Crane described himself in the third person as "the correspondent."

I went "aboard" the *Commodore* as a correspondent for a national news magazine to report on the discovery of the shipwreck, and attempts to salvage artifacts from it. Instead of merely interviewing the divers when they came ashore, I thought it might be neat to replicate at least some of the adventurous spirit that first launched Crane on his own journey by diving on the wreck site. The waters of this part of east central Florida were well known for unpredictable underwater cross-currents, poor visibility, and a healthy population of sharks. The guys I would be diving with would be armed with bang sticks and spear guns. I was armed only with an obscure and highly impractical sense of romanticism, born in some dusty undergraduate classroom long ago and nurtured carefully ever since.

While waiting to book passage on the wood and steel steamship, Crane hung out with a fascinating young woman in the backwater port of Jacksonville. At twenty-five, he was already well-known for *The Red Badge of Courage* and *Maggie, a Girl of the Streets*. Both novels were acclaimed for their gutsy realism, a tone that set Crane decidedly apart from the Victorian moralists of his day. It was probably not surprising that Cora Taylor, the young woman with whom he spent most of his time, was a character out of one of his own works. Determinedly forthright and ambitious, Cora Taylor ran "Hotel de Dream," a popular brothel catering to rich folks like Florida railroad baron Henry Flagler. Perhaps she was the prototype for Maggie herself.

When Crane died just three years after his experience on the *Commodore*—from a lingering illness exacerbated by his time in the cold Florida winter waters—he left Taylor everything he had. Which wasn't much. For working writers, some things never seem to change. I identified easily with healthy chunks of Crane's predicament: bright, nontraditional, and striking women have always fascinated me, and writing has certainly kept me, if not poor, then of modest means.

If Crane was intrigued by Ms. Taylor's charms, he was less than appreciative of Jacksonville during his stay-over. "The town," wrote Crane in one of his letters, "looks like soiled pasteboard that some lunatic babies have been playing with." I felt those same babies had been charting the pell-mell sprawl that was fast-consuming much of Florida today. Chalk up another one for symmetry. So, it was with great anticipation that I approached the chance to visit the *Commodore*. In a state surging full-speed into the future, it was also an opportunity to journey backwards to an event where real life romance—passion, courage, chaos, and all—could still be found.

I would be diving with Don Serbousek, the dive shop owner who first stumbled across the wreck a few years earlier without knowing it was the *Commodore*. Serbousek's attraction to the wreck was easy to understand: like most shipwrecks, it was swarming with fish, and Serbousek and his buddies enjoyed spear fishing. Serbousek kept the wreck's location a secret, not because he knew of its historic value, but because he simply didn't want other divers to fish it out. Today, navigational coordinates will put them within hundreds of feet of the wreck. But what leads them directly to the site is the congregation of larger grouper, snapper, and other fish. Waters at this latitude are much cooler, and the Gulf Stream farther offshore than along the southern peninsula and the Keys. Much of the offshore sea bottom here is sand with the occasional low ridge of coral or rubble. Wrecks—whether accidentally sunk or set down purposely to serve as artificial reefs—perform much the same function as reef systems farther south. They act as habitat, offering a secure and durable place to alight for sponges, worms, shellfish, even a few hardy species of coral. Smaller fish follow the invertebrates, and larger predators follow them. Pretty soon, you have a self-contained food chain—a virtual oasis of life, if you will—on a vast subsurface desert floor.

But the fact that the wreck existed didn't identify it as the *Commodore* since nothing had been found with the ship's name on it. Indeed, it took some sleuthing by a professor of English at Jacksonville University, Elizabeth Friedmann, to put a name on it. Friedmann was writing a biography of Crane's sweetheart Cora, whom she also found to be a fascinating and accomplished woman. During her research, Friedmann reread archival accounts of the *Commodore*'s sinking, and then went back and studied "The Open Boat" more carefully. When first researching the story, I talked to Friedmann on the phone to better understand how she pieced the information together. She told me she was an avid sport diver herself, and was attuned to the fact that if the ship had sunk, it would likely still be there on the bottom somewhere. "Where else would it go?" she said.

As for its general location, Crane had written in "The Open Boat" of finally sighting a lighthouse from the small dinghy after the *Commodore* had sunk: " . . . this time his eyes chanced on a small still thing on the edge of the swaying horizon. It was precisely like the point of a pin. It took an anxious eye to find a lighthouse so tiny." The men knew the small thing on the edge of the swaying horizon was the lighthouse marking the Mosquito Inlet.

Like the *Commodore*, the "Mosquito Inlet" hadn't gone anywhere either. Indeed, it had been named so because it was once inside an entire northeastern Florida county that was also called "Mosquito." Modern public relations spinmeisters in Florida would recoil at the idea of naming places for real world constraints—especially unpleasant ones—but early explorers were far more honest: when the Spanish cruised this wild coast of sand and driftwood and mangrove in the sixteenth century, they mapped it as "Los Mosquitos." (It was not unlike what they had seen and experienced on the low Atlantic shore of Central America, a portion of which today remains the "Miskito Coast" of Nicaragua.) Although Mosquito County had been renamed "Orange" in 1845 for its citrus groves, no one got around to changing the name of the inlet until the Florida land boom of the 1920s. Dipping into its bag of worn but safe symbols, locals intent on luring Yankee tourists and land buyers to Florida renamed the cut and the light "Ponce de Leon." Despite its name change, the old brick light station remained—at 175 feet—the tallest lighthouse in all of Florida.

If the *Commodore* sank twelve miles offshore the Ponce light, as Crane reported, that at least gave Friedmann a place to start. Daytona and New Smyrna Beach are both near that inlet, so Friedmann began to chat up local dive shop owners to see if there was any knowledge of a century-old wreck at least ten or so miles offshore. Since she knew the *Commodore* was loaded with munitions, she also used that as a way of describing the wreck site.

The English professor was referred to Serbousek as the guy who would know, if anyone did. Serbousek was not only a veteran diver; he was a collector who had salvaged old wrecks for the fun of it. Even better, he had a decided fascination for unearthing the past: he once recovered much of the skeleton of an extinct giant ground sloth, *Megatherium*, which had its own room in a local natural history museum. Serbousek acknowledged he had been spear fishing a wreck of the era Friedmann described. In between spearing, he would poke about the site and, in doing so, found clump after clump of heavily corroded cartridges and what had once been boxes of rifles.

Friedmann wondered what other cargo ship of that age would be carrying munitions like that. She studied some of the ocean-worn ammunition and rifles Serbousek had brought back. Then she asked the diver if he could actually see the lighthouse from the wreck site. "Yea," he replied, "but from way out there it looks like a little pin on the horizon."

I track down Serbousek and drive over for a visit so we can plan a dive on the *Commodore*. Serbousek, tall, balding, soft-spoken, runs a combination dive shop and television repair service in Ormond Beach, not far from where Crane and his Open Boat mates washed ashore in 1897. The business, "Diving Don's TV and Dive Shop," looks more like something you used to routinely see in the Keys. A gigantic rusted anchor from some long-forgotten Spanish galleon is perpetually at rest in front of the shop. Inside, the place looks like a page out of *True* magazine, circa 1958. Fossils are everywhere, a bone of a mastodon, the giant tooth of an extinct shark, *Carcharodon*, even fossilized alligator scutes. Besides the fossils, there's also a bunch of transistors and TV repair things lying about, and in the middle of the store, a saltwater aquarium with a single occupant, a living spotted cowry as big around as my wrist.

Serbousek, who has a slightly absentminded air, seems more like somebody's high school math teacher than the adventurer he is. But I remember once meeting treasure hunter Mel Fisher in the Keys. Fisher had a similar lost-in-space composure, a curious disposition that represents only a fragment of the person inside. Later, when I dive with Serbousek, the math teacher façade fades and the confident explorer emerges.

Since the *Commodore* was carrying few valuables, the reward for its salvage today is in the satisfaction of making a rare find linked to an important event in literary history. I like to think the divers are helping to write the final page of Crane's brilliant short story, an act that Crane, the rogue adventurer, would have appreciated.

Since there is no mother lode expected, as with Fisher's *Atocha*, the small band of divers pay their own way, including sharing in gas expenses for the dive boat. Like Serbousek, they are all employed full time elsewhere and can dive only on their days off. During a half year's worth of salvage work, they have recovered a dozen rifles, hundreds of lead bullets, countless pieces of brass and copper hardware, and a human foot bone. But, since there were over fourteen tons of guns, munitions, and medicine aboard, they have barely scratched the surface. While much of the cargo has been lost to sea-driven decay, or simply washed away, a great deal is still expected to be found as the men dig farther into the sandy bottom under the hull of the ship.

There were originally twenty-seven men aboard the *Commodore* and most fled to full-sized lifeboats, except for seven who drowned during the sinking, and Crane, Capt. Edward Murphy, the ship's cook, and oiler Billie Higgins, who were left only with a tiny ten-foot-long dinghy. As the last men to leave the ship, the dinghy, used to ferry supplies to and from the ship when it was in port, was all that was left for them.

The ship floundered because it had been leaking badly, and its pumps were unable to handle all the water that began to pour in. After the sinking of the *Commodore*, newspapers—caught up in the spirited yellow journalism of the day—reported the ship was likely sabotaged by Cuban seamen loyal to Spain. On Jan. 4, 1897, Crane's own newspaper, the *New York Press*, claimed "A traitor in Spanish pay was the cause of the (ship's) leak." However, the *Commodore* had been jinxed from the start, accidently crashing into shoals in the St. Johns River as it left the port of Jacksonville and grounding twice before it ever entered the Atlantic. Poor navigation caused the collisions, opening the ship's hull to leaks. Normally, steam-powered bilge pumps would handle a certain amount of incoming seawater, but they were said to be disabled. Were they sabotaged, or simply the result of poor maintenance? One of the heavily corroded pumps has already been recovered, Serbousek told me, and the salvers hope to clean it by electrolysis and restore it, and in doing so, to be able to tell if it was intentionally damaged or not.

By now, I was anxious to get "aboard" the wreck. But this was late December and the waters along this part of Florida, normally rough in winter, were made even more so by a strong wind blowing in from the north. Serbousek tells me that if the wind shifts abruptly and comes from the other direction, we'll be afforded a brief lull that will allow us to dive. The water will still be churned with silt, but at least the seas will lay down for a few hours. After we talked, I was hopeful for a forecast that would give us a new southerly wind, and in two days, I got one.

Serbousek, who was also watching the weather, immediately called and told me to pack my dive gear and meet him at a coffee shop near the marina where they would launch their dive boat. It was New Year's Eve day. If we find the site right away, he said, we might have two or three hours before the winds pick back up again. We down our coffee, Serbousek asks the waitress to fill a thermos for the trip, and then we head across the street to the marina.

Here, I meet the other divers: Bob Wheeler, an old crony of Serbousek's, Wheeler's son Randy, a high school teacher, and Don Lucas, a building contractor. They're all amicable folks, although only Randy seems to fully appreciate how important the wreck really is. Bob Wheeler and Serbousek have been diving together for years, exploring uncharted shipwrecks off the central Florida coast back when diving gear was a lot less safe, and the outcome of any dive a lot less certain than it is today. In those days, Wheeler remembers, all they used were tanks and regulators—no gauges to tell them how much air was left, or buoyancy compensators to help them neutralize their trim underwater. Tanks then had "J" valves, with little wires attached. When you ran out of air, you simply pulled the wire and it released the reserve air, good for another few minutes that could be used for an ascent. Our dive boat today is Wheeler's twenty-three-foot sport fisherman, which is now in the water after he hauled it here by trailer earlier this morning.

Fully loaded, we cast off, Wheeler steering his boat expertly through a channel in the local estuary, and out through Ponce Inlet, passing the old brick "Mosquito Light" just to our left as we go. Today, the stormy weather has clouded the skies, and a light rain soon begins to fall. By the time we are only a mile offshore, it is so gray with drizzle and clouds that I can no longer see the land.

We bump along across a steady sheaf of building waves, Wheeler with one eye on the compass and the other on the navigational electronics. After an hour of this, we are near the wreck, identified by coordinates the divers routinely use to locate the site. But the data is not specific enough to put us precisely atop it. To do that, Wheeler turns on his fathometer, and its sonar gives us a rough bottom sketch made of thin green lines on a little screen. We slowly motor about the area, and at first, all seems flat. But in another five minutes, the screen shows sharp points dramatically rising up, peaks that represent the highest profile of the wreck itself. I notice the depth of the wreck is ninety feet.

Lucas tosses an anchor over the side. We climb into our wetsuits and gear, and then flop over the gunnels. The sea water is cold enough to momentarily take my breath away as it seeps into my wetsuit. Our strategy is to follow the anchor rope down, one by one, and from there, fin over to the wreck nearby.

This sounded good on the boat, but now that I am underwater I see there is far more sediment and plankton in the water than I had figured. I expected maybe twenty or thirty feet of visibility, but I can barely see beyond five or six feet. When I reach the bottom, I have no idea where the wreck is, so I simply sit there, waiting on the sandy bottom, ninety feet under the surface. Soon, Serbousek materializes from the murk, thumps me on the shoulder, motions a "let's go" with his arm, and turns and fins away, with me trailing very closely behind.

Suddenly, I am atop the wreck itself before I even realize what it is. Its presence is signaled by a large rusted metal boiler, by far the largest remaining chunk of the old steamer. I drop down to the base of it, where there is less current, and the visibility improves. The metal that is left has become enveloped with a century's worth of the sea—sponges, barnacles, corals. Spines of black and white sea urchins protrude from crevices. A school of Atlantic spadefish—which look like angelfish on steroids—undulate at the top of the boiler, riding the metronomic current swells back and forth in the water column.

I fin about twenty feet from the boiler, near where the gigantic prop is half buried. On earlier dives, the men have partially uncovered a six-by-eight foot section of the original planked wooden deck from under the sand, the largest piece yet found intact. I release all the air in my buoyancy vest so that I can kneel down on the deck, a place where Crane and his fellow shipmates scrambled about before abandoning ship. The lesson of Crane's literary naturalism was implicit: in man against nature conflicts, mere human muscle or intellect is a conceit, an arrogance that can't even begin to comprehend the power of nature. Most of all, the forces of nature were not evil, but simply uncaring, a view that also informs modern existentialism. As Crane wrote, "It represented in a degree, to the correspondent, the serenity of nature amid the struggles of the individual—nature in the wind, and nature in the vision of men. She did not seem cruel to him, nor beneficent, nor treacherous, nor wise. But she was indifferent, flatly indifferent . . ."

Most of the wooden hull has already been lost to the turbulence of the sea and the appetite of wood-boring torpedo worms. Cartoon images of intact ships under the ocean exist only in cartoons—or in theme parks. The only evidence of the size of the original ship is hinted by a small ridge several inches high of empty shells around the perimeter of what had once been the gunnels and hull. The shells, mostly snail-like gastropods of some sort, once attached themselves to the hull when it was still a hull. But when it disintegrated, their habitat disappeared, and so too did the animals that once lived inside the shells.

The longer I am on the bottom, the better I am able to see, as if focusing under the dim but sure light of a full moon back on land. Near what was the stern of the *Commodore*, one of the divers has uncovered a wooden crate from the sand. I fin over to take a look. There's scant wood left, and the supplies inside are heavily corroded and are now fused together in one large rectangular lump.

Serbousek is only a few feet away from the huge prop, and is exploring the bottom there by fanning the sand with rapid back and forth movements of his hand. Salvers who work such wrecks will use small rakes, larger hammers for chipping, and even, when needed, saws and crowbars. But most seem to rely on the more delicate "fanning" method as the best way to scrutinize the tiny, often fragile, bits and pieces of maritime detritus. Although I am close enough to touch Serbousek's tank, the storm of sediment created by his hand fanning has nearly fully consumed him in a brown cloud. When I try fanning the bottom myself, I create a similar predicament. Periodically, I stop and reach down into the small depression the fanning has created, and root around for something solid there. But when I find anything, I have to actually bring it up against my mask to see what it is.

The bottom seems to be covered with old bullets, their brass cartridge and gunpowder fused together by corrosion into hand-sized clumps. Every time I scoop my hand through the sand and bring it to my mask, I come up with more such bullets. As one reporter for the *Jacksonville Times-Union* noted after the sinking, "Old Neptune has been supplied with enough arms and ammunition to blow up the island of Cuba." Indeed, the manifest for the *Commodore* showed it was carrying 203,000 rifle cartridges, over 1,000 pounds of dynamite, and 40 "bundles" of Remington rolling block rifles.

As I move away from my underwater dust storm, I see the outline of the drive shaft, which runs from the bottom of the boiler to the stern. Looking up, I can make out a number of fish hovering over the artificial reef the wreck has created. Several dozen amberjacks, each the size of a small muscular torpedo, cruise by, and queen angelfish poke about in the wreck, their normally bright blues and gold muted to green by the plankton and the depth. Suddenly, the entire site is covered with thousands of tiny silversided anchovies. They undulate in unison, turning as one, and sometimes catching the scant surface light with their silvery bodies. When they do, they reflect it back, making them seem as if they are one great organic mirror, forming and reforming here atop this old literary icon on the bottom of the sea.

Near the edge of the school, at the limits of visibility, a large dark form with sharp and distinct fins appears, and—almost in the same instant—disappears back into the murk. I think of Crane sighting a large shark from their tiny boat by night: "There was a long, loud swishing astern of the boat, and a gleaming trail of phosphorescence, like blue flame, was furrowed on the black waters. It might have been made by a monstrous knife." And then: "The correspondent saw an enormous fin speed like a shadow through the water, hurling the crystalline stray and leaving the long glowing tail." Earlier, Serbousek had told me about the twelve-foot tiger shark that has been seen around the wreck site during earlier dives.

I grab the hose with my air pressure gauge on it and check my remaining supply: not much. I have just about enough time for a safety stop before I surface. In truth, I had hoped we might find the ship's whistle today, but it was a needle in a haystack possibility. Crane had written poignantly of it: "If there was ever a voice of despair and death, it was in the voice of the whistle . . . a song of man's end."

I head for the anchor line, using my hands to slowly pull myself across the bottom since the current is now too strong to fin against. The entire site has been churned into a dust storm by a new underwater surge, perhaps an advance warning of the impending southerly storm front back on the surface. Safely on the rope, I pull myself slowly up, hand over hand. I look back one last time and see the wreck of the *Commodore* fade back into a ghostly underwater haze. I make a safety stop at twenty feet to blow off nitrogen, and then break through the surface. Around me, the waves have begun to grow much larger, spitting white foam and crashing into each other, signaling the beginnings of the new weather front. Everywhere I look, it is all gray—the sea, the sky, even our own small boat. Crane, from his seat in the dinghy, experienced a similar reality, describing it as the "universal indifference . . . of the slate gray seas."

As the four men from the *Commodore* finally came ashore in the rolling January breakers at Daytona Beach and were flung from the small boat, oiler Higgins—by far the strongest man aboard—was the only one to drown in the surf. For Crane, it reinforced the notion that even the toughest humans are no match for natural forces.

The man who helped create literary naturalism would only live another three years after his ordeal, dying at the age of twenty-eight in Bedenweiler, Germany of a tubercular condition aggravated by the wintry day and night in the open boat. His sweetheart, Cora, was at his side.

While his short story emphasizes the indifference of the natural world toward man, it also taught that bonding between humans can be strengthened by confronting that same angst together. Crane wrote: "When it came night, the white waves paced to and fro in the moonlight, and the wind brought the sound of the great sea's voice to the men on shore, and they felt that they could then be interpreters."

Soon, all the divers are back on the surface and safely in the boat. The sky, once a solid gray of cloud and vapor, has become darker and it is raining now, a hard pelting rain. There is a good natured camaraderie among us, and a happy sharing of new artifacts recovered—including an encrusted Remington rifle. Weaver pulls anchor and we head ashore, crashing through the waves as we go. Because of the weather, there is no lighthouse to be seen sticking on the horizon like the point of a pin today, but there has been an immense thrill in the doing, in the confrontation of life by direct experience.

As we approach Ponce inlet I finally see the brick lighthouse and by now, it is far larger than a pin. One of the divers turns to me and asks what I will write of this day. I tell him it will be an account of diving the wreck, and maybe of relearning Crane's message of naturalism. He shakes his head and smiles, but I can't figure whether it's a smile of approval or one of bemused skepticism.

I think of how the ship's cook was quoted in a local newspaper after his rescue in the surf, and figure I could do worse: "These newspaper fellers have got spunk . . . even if they do tell such awful whoppers at times."

POSTSCRIPT: *After my story appeared in* Newsweek, *Serbousek, Fried-mann, and I were invited to travel to New York City to be on the national* Today Show. *I declined, but the other two went on, continuing to tell the story of the* Commodore *to the nation. In 1998, Serbousek and the Ponce Inlet Lighthouse Association were granted an "Admiralty Arrest" for the wreck which gave them the exclusive right to salvage the site. Technical divers from the Cambrian Foundation were contracted to help salvage the* Commodore *and to record a detailed site plan of it. By 2001, the Ponce de Leon Lighthouse Preservation Society created an exhibit devoted to the wreck and its history.*

39

A Morning on the Lake
of the Hololo

Lake Jesup by dawn seems primal. Jesup has one of the largest
populations of alligators in Florida.

I slide my kayak into the dark water just after dawn on the southwestern shore of the massive Lake Jesup and paddle north toward Bird Island. The shore here is mostly cattails, native bulrush, and the giant exotic reed called Phragmites. Two black guys with a small kicker-powered boat and fishing rods are getting ready to launch, but otherwise the ramp here is quiet.

Jesup is imitating a mirror just for now, and I take full advantage, skimming over it in my little boat. Gators are thick here—Jesup is said to have one of the densest populations in Florida—and on the flat glossy surface that is the lake, I count well over a dozen, both in front and behind my boat. The really big ones with tar black heads hang there much longer than their smaller brethren, much longer, really, than I would prefer them to hang.

Their heads are all that give them away, since the rest of the bodies are submerged, noggins looking like giant, gnarly gravy boats—only the nose tip and the eyes exposed with a bit of a slope in between. Jesup has a reputation for edgy gators, and I'm figuring it's because there are simply so many of them. Then again, the lake itself has been almost completely cut off from the rest of the St. Johns River for the last half century, thanks to the poorly planned construction of a mile-long cause-way and a state highway at its "mouth" over a half century ago. Pollutants that otherwise might have been flushed away simply accumulate. As they do, decaying vegetation absorbs them, so the result is that instead of a nice, sandy bottom the lake now has a layer of "muck" that is anywhere from nine to fifteen feet deep. Unlike the good muck of humus under healthy swamps and marshes, this is the stuff of your worst sci-fi-mutant-nature-gone-bad story, the sort of odoriferous muck that, if you were to fall into it, you'd likely sink down into a netherworld that Dante would have trouble imagining.

As per most melodramatic thrillers, the chemicals in the muck from fertilizers, sewage, and stormwater runoff have gone to work. No giant three-eyed catfish yet, but plenty of very annoyed alligators. Turns out the chemicals have disrupted the endocrine systems of the reptiles. That means that, generally, male gators that are so afflicted have less testosterone, and are becoming less virile and fertile as a result. I'm figuring this has got to piss them off. What's the point in being a bull gator if you can't swagger about the lake like a used car salesman in a singles bar?

Whatever the reason, at least one boat and one soft-skinned kayak have been attacked here, with the later being actually bitten into from the bottom up. I think of all the ways to go, and this is not one of my favorites. Despite the fact that, when kayaking, I never forget that I'm sharing the same waters with carnivores larger and much stronger than myself, I seldom fixate on it. Today, I'm fixating on it. In all of my years of paddling and trekking through swamps, it's the first time I've ever packed away a pistol with hollow-point bullets. It's not a weapon likely to do much damage to the thick pelt of a large gator, but it does have a bit of advantage over trying to reason with them.

I paddle into the rising sun and under the massive two-mile-long bridge that takes an expressway across the middle of the lake. Finally, I see Bird Island; with the low sun backlighting it, the island and all the water around it seem almost slate gray. It is as if someone had tinted one of those old black and white photos with silver and white, eliminating all the other colors. When Lt. R.H. Peyton, the man who first surveyed this lake for the U.S. Army, traveled here from Lake Monroe in 1837, he described the broad eight-square mile dilation in the St. Johns as "a noble sheet of water." In the lake was a round island, and "in the center of the island (I) observed a very picturesque clump of cabbage trees (sabal palms) which were fitted with nests of white heron . . . and a red bird with a spoon bill." Peyton, serving in the U.S. Army campaign against the Seminole Indians, ignored the Native American name for the island—"Hololo," for the roseate spoonbills—and named it for his commander, Maj. Gen. Thomas S. Jesup. The Seminoles were being "campaigned" against because they didn't have the politeness to leave their land when the pushy newcomers wanted to take it from them without recompense. Before the Seminoles lived and fished around this noble water, pre-Columbians inhabited much of the shore and even the island, leaving behind middens full of pots and artifacts, a culture severed from its people.

As I near the island, I see that a higher rise in its middle holds a hammock of old sabal palms. The hammock itself is surrounded by a field of scrub-like plants and reeds which cascade down to the water. To the east, I see what seems to be dozens of old pilings from a dock. When I look through my binoculars, I realize they are all wading birds, standing just offshore the islands in inches of water. A few years ago, a local Audubon chapter led a field trip to this island and came away proclaiming it as the largest wading bird rookery in this county.

Once Jesup was made safe for white settlers, steamboats regularly visited here from the St. Johns, stopping at "landings" along the southern shore of the lake, wharfs named "Solary's," "Tuskawilla," and "White's." Freight delivered here by boat was transported to Orlando on wagon, for this was the closest "port" to that land-locked settlement. Later, in the middle of the twentieth century, the lake was still clear and healthy and known widely for its great sport fishing. *Field and Stream* magazine wrote of it, and fish camps around the lake did a brisk business. Today, the lake is one of the most polluted in Florida. In addition to the toxins, algae blooms and a related decline in dissolved oxygen routinely kill what few sport fish are left.

The sun rises higher in the sky and to the north of the lake I can still see thick mist in coves and sloughs along that shore. Within a hundred feet of the edge of the island, I slow and paddle cautiously so as not to scare the hundreds of birds who are still living and nesting here. There are white ibis, and glossies, tricolored herons, and great blues. There are snowies and wood storks and cattle egrets. There are little gallinules with their bright red beaks. Ospreys circle overhead, watching for a movable breakfast. A fat mullet jumps next to my kayak. In the distance, a very large animal with a fish-like tail splashes in the water, and I have no idea what it could be. The chattering of the birds is raucous, the sort of pure avian joy usually found in rookeries.

I circle the island and then on the eastern shore, see a wide flat opening in the willows and paddle my kayak into it, until the bow scrapes atop the hard shore. In the center is the palm hammock and I walk to it. Both John and William Bartram visited here when exploring the St. Johns in 1765. When the Indian-fighting army arrived, it proclaimed the territory upstream of Monroe as "unknown," thereby ignoring the earlier visit by the naturalists, and of course, the long habitation by the indigenous peoples here. Lt. Peyton also wanted to name this "Circle

Island," since it was symmetrical. But the presence of all the wading birds trumped that notion, and it was mapped as Bird.

As I get closer to the stand of palms in the middle, the topography of the island becomes ever so slightly higher as it rises up from its surrounding shores. The hammock here is thick with the smooth and weathered trunks of very old palms. There's no guaranteed way to measure the life of these palms since they are really classified as grasses, and have no growth rings like trees. Comparing archival descriptions with contemporary landscapes, historians have found some palms to be more than four hundred years old. I think of Peyton's description of the "cabbage trees," and figure these are likely older versions of the same ones.

I wonder how the landscape can communicate secrets to us. I figure this one has plenty to tell, but nothing's firing at the moment. I'm guessing that's life—relationships fire when the time is right, and not on command. Why wouldn't a sacred place in the landscape function the same way? If it had wanted me to understand something new by now, I'm figuring I would have gotten a whiff of it. Today, most of what I know is what I have read or what I see, little communicated from the deeper senses, and less from the great collective unconscious. Some days are like that.

The slightly higher relief here is made even more so by millions of shells, collected by the Timucua and Mayacan who once camped and lived on the island. Like most middens along Florida rivers, the primary shell is the banded mystery snail. Back at water's edge, I had picked up a few of those snails newly shucked by the birds, and had noticed the distinct and colorful bands around the tawny knobby shell, a feature that older, bleached shells lose in the middens.

Around me on the little island, frilly elderberry bushes are coming into blooms of white, and the wildflower known as the marsh mallow is showing off its hibiscus-like pink flowers. At the shore, water locust, gator, and camphor weeds and smaller, white wildflowers I can't identify are thriving. No Hololo's today, but otherwise I can't complain.

Back in the kayak, I head around the windward side of the island, where most of the hard-packed brown sand distinguishes the bottom from the muck that characterizes so much of the rest of the lake. Bird

Island, geology tells us, was born of subsidence—not of the island, but of all the land around it. History still has secrets here: large fossils of giant ground sloths and ancient whales have turned up in muck around the lake shore, and an endemic species of killifish and an endemic snail were found at Clifton Springs, south of here. The fish is *Fundulus bartrami*. When the Bartrams and later, the soldiers came through, the St. Johns only nicked off a corner of Jesup. But it was enough to allow the ever-flowing river to circulate through the great splay of water, and then to exit, just as any good river would want to do.

Now, with berms and bridges at SR 46 having interrupted that flow for so long now, the lake is not tannic like most of the St. Johns system, but a light green, as if it is one giant vat of pea soup. A sign back at the ramp had warned of both amoebas (which tend to swim up your ear canal and dissolve your brain), and algae, which has its own toxic properties. Lake Jesup, despite all of its glorious history, is what happens when linear-thinking engineers are allowed to function as the grown-ups in charge, and the wonders of biology are afforded the respect reserved for children's make-believe games.

A restoration that has removed the old roadbed across the lake's mouth has finally started, but there's still an enormous amount of bad muck here and it's not going away any time soon. As with most restoration stories in Florida, this one emerged not from government agency employees wanting to do the right thing, but from a well-informed and very stubborn group of local citizens who just wouldn't give up. Like most eco-fixes, it could have been avoided long ago if the folks with money had listened to the folks with good common sense.

For now, there is the lake, the island, the archival memories of Bartram and Peyton, and the grand commotion of the nesting birds. Like always, there is hope, although it is that rarefied, convoluted hope that is special to Florida. The wind is now picking up, and the water from the west creates a great fetch. And the waves on my return journey back to the ramp roll toward me with great determination. And I do what I know, I do all that I can, literally and otherwise: I keep paddling.

40

On Visiting Jody in the Big Scrub

Not so long ago, I traveled up into the Ocala National Forest to ferret out some very real places in the landscape that Pulitzer-winning novelist Marjorie Kinnan Rawlings once wrote about. Relics have always fascinated me, whether they're artifacts and structures or an actual part of the breathing geography that others have once recorded.

My specific reason for the trip up into the "Big Scrub" was to research and shoot some footage for a PBS documentary we were making at the time. It was entitled *In Marjorie's Wake* and it retraced a 1933 journey

The Cross Creek home of Pulitzer-winning author Marjorie Kinnan Rawlings, with a vintage Oldsmobile like the one she used to drive sitting under the carport. Photo by Michelle Thatcher.

that Rawlings once made on the St. Johns, and later wrote about in the "Hyacinth Drift" chapter of *Cross Creek*. Our film was more than just the re-creation of Rawlings's literary river journey, of course. There were many "characters" in this documentary, and they include Rawlings and her intrepid neighbor and river companion Dessie Smith, and the two modern river sojourners who followed the historic journey on camera, Leslie Poole and Jennifer Chase.

Threads of this story also have to do with wildlife and where it lives, the way nature—and our rivers in particular—influence art, and of course, how Marjorie Kinnan Rawlings herself learned to pay attention to it all. Her skills as a narrator and her ability to listen and record the world around her were profound. As a human, she was imperfect, as we all are. But as a writer she transcended her mortal life, and taught us something about ourselves along the way. For now, Bob Giguere, the coproducer on the film, and I drive up into the Ocala National Forest to hike and to shoot some footage along what is now being called the "Yearling Trail," west of Lake George.

I have always found a singular beauty in the rolling pine landscape of the "Big Scrub" of the forest, and have always cherished the springs here. For fun, I've scuba dived into Alexander and, during research projects, into the chasms of Salt and Silver Glen. With friends, I have paddled the runs of those springs along with that serpentine sliver of ether that flows out of Juniper. While I know the scrub and sandhills on public land not far from my home in Sanford, I am less conversant with that of Ocala. The visit today gives me the chance to better understand the intimacy Rawlings once knew here with both the landscape and its people.

As part of the film research, Bob and I earlier traveled to the Smathers Library's special collection at the University of Florida in Gainesville. There, archivist Flo Turcotte graciously arranged for us to have a look at the Rawlings memorabilia willed to the school. We both put on white gloves, Bob to shoot and myself to sort through files of photos, letters, old home movie footage, and original manuscripts. When the cardboard boxes were brought to me, it was a bit like being gifted, just for a few hours, with the Holy Grail. There were photos of the Fiddia family, with whom Marj stayed when researching *South Moon Under*, and of Barney

Dilliard, who was preparing to skin a large Florida black bear he had shot. Dilliard's story of a giant, marauding bear made it into *The Yearling* where the bear was immortalized as "Old Slewfoot." Another faded photo showed Calvin Long with a hunting dog, holding a shotgun in front of his homestead on Pat's Island.

In another box, I found an astonishing 1938 map of the Ocala National Forest on which Rawlings had scribbled handwritten notes to identify the real places she had fictionalized in *The Yearling*. On the map, Pat's Island in the scrub became "Baxter's Island." Other notes marked where the "first tangle with Old Slewfoot" took place on Juniper Creek run, and identified the fictional "Forrester's Island" as "Hughes Island." I also sifted through a chronology of old family photos, from Marjorie at age two to just before her death at age fifty-seven. She grew into a pretty, vivacious young woman before my eyes and then, prematurely, grew heavier and jowly, her smiles less frequent. Toward the end, her face was puffy and her eyes were tired and she looked as if she were in pain.

I held the original typewritten pages of *The Yearling* and *Cross Creek*, let my fingers retrace the Courier type and penciled-in edit changes Rawlings herself once made. The moment moved me, to be sure. It was as if the yellowed page in my hand was more than processed wood fragments, was in fact an image capturing the split second when information passes between the human heart and the human mind, and is thrust out from the spirit onto the tangible worlds that flash when a spring bursts forth from the lime rock, or when a lightning bolt leaps from the heavens to the earth. The creative gust is no less than that; it is simply much better at pretending to be invisible.

I thought a lot about all of that during our drive up into the Ocala National Forest, earnestly hoping that deconstructing any author's work is not an intellectual charade. I remember what the poet Robert Browning once said, "When I wrote that, only God and I knew what it meant . . . and now, only God knows."

Finally, we reach the entrance to Silver Glen Springs on U.S. 19. Just to the left, the palmetto scrub rises up, following the landscape under it. A sign with a fawn on it identifies this as "The Yearling Trail." I am grateful that someone in the national forest service had the good sense to match literary fiction with reality. It is a sunny midmorning during the week and the road we have taken is straight and quiet. The forest itself is bordered by both the St. Johns and the Ocklawaha rivers where hardwood swamps rim the water's edge. But here, in its heart, its geography is vastly different. It is this rise in the topography, these many square miles of sandy terrain, that serve as the geological sponge where the great springs of the forest are recharged by rainfall.

We pull over and walk to the trailhead kiosk where we find some shorthand description of the literary heritage of the landscape. We learn that "Pat's Island" is one of the most popular historic attractions in the entire Ocala National Forest. Here, of course, an "island" is not surrounded by water, but instead is a fertile, cooler hammock of longleaf, wiregrass, and turkey oak in a virtual sea of rolling, arid scrub.

I shoulder the tripod and Bob the camera satchels, and we hike a trail, past the low saw palmettos and the gullberry and the little wild blueberry bushes, tiny leaves reddish and shiny. It is November but after a mile or so we are both covered with sweat. We find the old cemetery where the extended Long clan is buried, a tiny plot of weathered gravestones surrounded by a dilapidated picket fence, its gray slates peppered with lichens. The air is heavy, no sound but that of our own breathing. I open the little gate in the fence, and we walk in.

From earlier research, I know that a Rueben Long first settled here in 1872 with his family. Others followed, and by the turn of the century the population of the 1,400-acre "island" peaked when about a dozen families worked the land, making a meager living with small crops, cattle, hogs, fishing, and moonshining. By the time the national forest was created here in 1908, many of the original settlers had sold or leased their homesteads. When Rawlings visited descendent Calvin and his wife, Mary Long, in 1933, they were the only ones left. Calvin told Marj colorful yarns of the scrub, narratives made real because storytelling was still an art then. Rawlings heard the tale of a fawn being nursed to a yearling by one of the Longs when they were young boys.

My time here in the Long cemetery under the hot Florida sun is difficult to fully process. It means fiction and history have met and that the poignant, heartbreaking stories that Rawlings told so well were once lived by men and women and children, and that many of them—the prototypes for Penny, Ma, and Jody Baxter—are still here, beneath the sandy graves at my feet.

The irony is that there were plenty of people throughout Florida living hardscrabble lives, scrapping together a subsistence existence from the land and its rivers. Some were courageous and some were not, but they were all human, with deeply abiding human qualities and human frailties; they laughed, loved, lived, died. A writer brought some of them back to life, and then with the grace of a god, animated them so that the eternal amalgam between her heart and theirs became one. And now they are all gone, the evidence that they lived at all found here in this place, in the oral histories their surviving kin tell to each other, and in the literature of the books one human once wrote.

We pack up and leave the little cemetery, hoping to find our way to the sinkhole, the one the fictional Baxters used to draw water for drinking and washing. We walk from the open, hot scrub into the hammock where it is cooler and more pleasant. A hammock is not unlike a river, because you can no longer see straight ahead across the horizon; your vision is blocked by oaks and pines, and the trail inside of them seems to meander, almost without purpose. A hammock begs a story to tell what is behind the next tree, the next thicket of muscadine vines.

Jody's little friend Fodderwing in *The Yearling* told of seeing "Spaniards" in the hammock, willing mythic images from the mystery of the dark woods. And Rawlings herself wrote of the enchantment found in the dim light of the hammocks and groves, and how comforting it was for her. "I do not know," she wrote, "how a person can live without some small place of enchantment to turn to."

Suddenly, the edge of the earth falls away and the entire terrain descends into a giant earthen hole, steep sides thickly colonized with foliage. This was the Baxter's sinkhole, where limestone catchments held tricklings of cool, clean water flowing through lateral cavities in the limestone under the scrub. The prehistoric collapse of the sink breached those cavities, allowing access to the water where normally there would be none. With no well, it was the only fresh water for miles around for the Longs and the Baxters. I stumble cautiously down the edges to the bottom and look carefully for water, but see none. The terrain of Florida is much drier now than when Rawlings lived here: we have drained over half of our wetlands away, and our springs are now declining in magnitude because of overuse and the loss of places where rain once replenished them. It's likely the "pure filtered water" that seeped into the sink from limestone veins in the earth has been compromised by all of this.

At the lip of the sink almost a hundred feet above, I see Bob with his camera, and he is dwarfed by the scale of it all, a stick figure in the midst of all the shadowy green. With a child's eye, he could easily be a Spaniard moving in and out of the narrow shafts of sunlight.

The day is growing long and I am still anxious to visit the little spring where Jody Baxter built his flutter mill and made it work. It is the sort of place I would also have loved as a child, the sort of place I still love now, really. Most of my own wonder for nature as an adult comes from that nascent awe I first experienced as a little boy, walking in the woods with my dad, fishing, and hiking for miles through the countryside.

I know "Jody's Spring" is across the road beyond the main spring at Silver Glen, so we pack up and head over there. We walk beyond the two large vents of the main spring along a quiet trail into the hammock, following a clear rill that arises from somewhere deeper in the woods. Jody came here to be alone as a child, to build his little "flutter mill" out of sticks and palmetto fronds, and to watch it turn in the flow of the current. Rawlings wrote of it: "A spring as clear as well water bubbled up from nowhere in the sand. It was as though the banks cupped green leafy hands to hold it . . . Beyond the bank, the parent spring bubbled up at a higher level, cut itself a channel through white limestone and began to run rapidly downhill to make a creek." This Silver Glen creek joined the St. Johns at Lake George and then flowed north to the sea. Although the headwaters of the larger river system is a couple hundred miles south of here, Jody saw the little spring as its genesis. "There were other beginnings, true, but this one was his own."

When Ma Baxter complained Jody's play took away from his chores, Pa Baxter said, "A boy ain't a boy too long . . . Let him kick up his heels, let him build his flutter mills. The day'll come when he'll not even want to."

The sand boils still roil today, small gambusia and killifish skirting about the edges of each, and the roils flatten out into mirrors of light, and just as in Jody's time, they flow out to the run of the larger spring, to the great river and then to the sea. Bob fiddles with the camera, shooting some footage of the sand boils. I tell him I will try to build a flutter mill so we can capture it spinning on tape. On one level this is true; but the deeper truth is I simply want to build a flutter mill. And so I do, using my pen knife to construct a crude version with green strips of a frond and sweetgum twigs. For a few precious moments, I watch it spin about in its own beginnings, poetry and science and a boy's dream captured in this moment, in this place, just for now. The peace it gives me is immeasurable.

And then we pack up and leave the timelessness of the hammock and return to the harsh glare of the sunlit world with its roads and traffic and all its grown-up chores. And I think with great nostalgia of the stories Rawlings told, and of the life I have known as a man growing up in Florida, traipsing about in nature. And I have a great longing for it all, both for my own past as well as the one Marj saw and imagined, a mythical place cobbled together from spring water and dreams and old timely yarns. Maybe a boy ain't a boy too long. But if he works at it, he can carry a sense of wonder with him that lasts a lifetime.

41

Riding the Karst

From Shoal to Swamp and Then Some

A newly "discovered" freshwater spring tucked away in the hardwood swamp at the bottom of a heavily forested slope. This is Helene Spring; it flows into Sulphur Run, and from there into Blackwater Creek, the Wekiva River, the St. Johns, and then, the Atlantic Ocean. Hiking partner Yvette Comeau is kneeling at the edge.

The long black strip known as SR 46 is an asphalt blur as it rolls across two northeast Florida counties, only dipping conspicuously when it approaches the river valley. I have entertained myself by reading bumper stickers on the vehicles that appear and disappear in front of me. From a battered pickup: "Barrel Racer, Cowboy Chaser." And from a large American sedan: "Beer: Helping White Men Dance Since 1942."

I thankfully exit the volley of traffic at the entrance to the Seminole State Forest, driving in past the self-pay kiosk and picking up Steve, who is ready to unlock the combo on the cattle gate across the dirt road as soon as I give him the number. I have recently finished writing a new book, and Steve has finished teaching a grad course on Bartram. It has been months since we have hiked together, and when Steve walks to the lock, he claps his hands, as if in gracious applause of an impending performance.

We drive in beyond the open gate, no hunting season for a couple weeks, but some trees are still hung with the bright plastic flagging nearsighted hunters use to find their way in and out of the thick subtropical forest. The road takes us through the uplands—dry scrub and even sandhills, a stunted forest of saw palmetto and myrtle and oak, just tall enough so the rare scrub jays can flit low, calling to each other in their ancient songs.

The terrain drops gradually near the blackwater, taller oak and even cypress back along the shore, and then up again to the valley slope on the other side of the creek. We park near Shark's Tooth Spring, and shouldering our packs, walk a narrow trail up into the sandy scrub. The slope rises dramatically, and muscles on the back of my calves I hardly ever use on the Florida flatlands begin to come awake.

Ahead, we see a pair of scrub jays, the blue on their backs and wings far more vivid than other jays, not unlike the color of deeper springs I have seen before. A third joins them, and instead of fleeing, they prance about in the low trees, spooking a few other birds, including a yellow-bellied thrasher and a catbird. They always seem gregarious and friendly, but I realize that's my own human-mammal precept. The low altitude of the stunted forest here keeps them from flying to higher altitudes—but, more to the point, they evolved in the low-slung safety of the scrub without the sort of avian predators that might threaten other birds.

The dry scrub, sand as white and fine as that of a Gulf beach, is not unlike a desert with a patina of green. The diversity of plants and animals is far less than in the swamp down at the base of the slope. But what's here is special, sometimes even endemic, like the jays. The northern edge of the Lake Wales Ridge trails through this forest, allowing us a look at one of the most endangered natural systems in our country. Author John McPhee, who has taught me so much about the joys of detailed observation, was one of the first non-Floridians to celebrate the values of the scrub in his book *Oranges*. Thirty and forty years earlier, author Marjorie Kinnan Rawlings described this as harsh and unforgiving to settlers who homesteaded it, more a man-against-uncaring-forces-of-nature reality.

We are walking across what is mapped as "Sulphur Island," an ancient shoal from a distant prehistoric sea, a relic of a couple of square miles that first pushed up from the liquid blue and then, with other islands, coalesced into the ridge as the sea retreated. A study once characterized Sulphur Island as "sandhill karst" hiding the uplifted limestone of the Floridan Aquifer below.

Our upward jaunt is just a warm-up, a prelude to our plan to follow the sloping terrain downward, all the way to the bottom of the hardwood swamp below. There, with the wetlands nearly dry from drought, we hope to trace the more defined creeks, maybe find some new springs that otherwise would be drowned by the swamp. It is the "sandhill karst" that makes this so: while some water seeping out of the springs has been in the limestone for decades—longer, even—the porous scrubland is excellent recharge that allows new rains to more quickly revitalize the springs of the swamp.

A couple more miles take Steve and me across the last of the white sand, and down a steep slope to the edge of the soggy landscape. It is fall now, and wildflowers like the Glades lobelia with its orchid-like blossoms are open, tiny violet lights that seem to almost glow from the edge of the slope. There is a spring down here we have been visiting now for several years. It's not on a trail, but it can be found by carefully watching the landmarks, all of which change over time: a tall gray snag; a large, tortoise-shaped berm of white sand; a blue blaze on a pine raked by the strong claw of a black bear until it bleeds golden sap. I take a quiet sort of satisfaction in identifying and then remembering these clues since they seem to bind me more fully to the landscape. Linguists speak of a vernacular language, a sort of "mother tongue." For me, this is best realized by feeling the sensory touches of a specific place—touches that set it apart from all other places. Maybe in this way, we can at least learn a few words—even whole phrases—in the dialect of a particular geography.

Isobars, the lines on the topo map that mark the rise and fall in the land, squeeze up tightly here. This means the next forty to fifty feet below us falls away in a steep angle remarkable for this region of Florida. It's a sharp gradient that will send you in a good foot-first tumble if you try to rush it, as I once did.

The perspective from the top of this slope is always one I cherish, though; standing at the edge of the rim, I look out across the swamp below, watch as the shafts of sunlight dance on the fine silica in the run of the spring, prisms of silver and white refracted inside the wondrous jungle of green, geology as alive as the organic walls that surround it. We carefully make our way down to the swamp, moving slowly in switch-back-style patterns rather than taking it straight on.

At the bottom, we circle the large natural limestone boulder that—to me—has always looked like a small bear dipping his head to drink of the clear water that swirls around his "paws." In honor of this, we call it variously "Stone Cub" or "Rock Cub" spring. The state of Florida, which only recently charted this spring, reached deep into its prosaic imagination and named it "Boulder."

From Rock Cub, we move through the swamp bottom, scrambling up to an old trail that's tiered mid-slope to give us an easier go. We joke, as usual, about Steve's reliance on maps and gadgetry, and my Neolithic insistence on paying attention to the way the landscape unfolds around us for clues. Either way, we've really only been lost a couple of times, and never for more than a few hours.

We talk about what we see and have seen, the scrub jays, the flow of the little spring, the new pile of bluish nuts that is fresh bear scat, the way we are so fortunate to have such a place like this, ever so close to bumper-to-bumper traffic and deadening sprawl. We speak of natural-ist Bartram, as we usually do, and wonder—as one of Steve's students recently asked—why he never mentions the very-prevalent sweetgum tree, and only once lists it in an inventory of plants. We don't dwell too long on any one idea, like the sweetgum mystery, because that would jeopardize the broader ecology of the moment.

Steve's getting ready to teach a new grad course, "The Song of Creation from Walt Whitman to Ernesto Cardenal"; it relies on the energy of "Song of Myself," Whitman's keystone epic, to help explain how others have woven their own stories into a mystic celebration of nature, of transcendence of geography and time. We talk some about this. I have only started reading Cardenal, a Nicaraguan priest and poet who once studied under Thomas Merton. I have been heartened to learn Cardenal had moved more fully into activism when his country was being trundled by bullies.

Whitman, our own true democratic poet of nature and spirit, can also be considered a revolutionary in thought and in spirit. He once wrote: "I too am not a bit tamed, I too am untranslatable." A century later, Cardenal and others said the same, men and women with enough true courage to jostle the political stasis of their time. And, what is the point of deep feeling if you can't take it beyond the elitism of poetry, music, art? All this resonates deeply with me, especially now that we're inside a prehistoric terrain, a moist bottomland that—having resisted burns over the centuries—reasserts itself to us, to anyone who cares to fully absorb it. Steve, not content to rely on his academic credentials or his classroom performances, knows the value of feeling the wildness of a place, and has also become more of an activist through the local grassroots group that lobbies for protection of this larger river basin.

As for me, I have come to realize why lyrics like Whitman's have moved me so. It is partly the universal art the poet summons—the art that reminds us we all swim in the same stream. But it is also because I too am not a bit tamed—nor always easily "translatable." And I take solace in that because the landscape now surrounding me is likewise situated: to fully know the worth of the complex scrub, the karst, the swamp is to appreciate what can not always be translated—but which certainly can be deeply felt. It is the senses that can do that.

We pick our way up and back over the slope, and continue on along the edge of Sulphur Island, heading for another spring, one marked by the upland plateau of an open field rimmed by piney woods. This one is not on a trail, either. It is one that—because of the crooked sweetgum trunk that arches out from one edge—we once named "Sweetgum." Unlike Rock Cub, Sweetgum is a flat pool of clear water in the floor of the swamp, rather than at the base of the slope. The approach is far gentler than the one to Rock Cub, and takes us down a gradual slope that flattens out into the swamp. Sweetgum is actually a pool of water maybe twenty feet in diameter, and at least one small vent—perhaps two—are under the surface, gently pushing spring water up from the soft bottom. Near the larger sweetgum tree, I notice a fresh pile of bear scat, dark black and richly packed with the indigestible shards of nuts and berries.

A whitish, sulfur-rendering bacteria is growing in the pool and in the narrow run. It is not unlike the bacteria that flourishes deeper inside the limestone caves of the Floridan Aquifer, conduits that channel water to the portals where our springs meet the light of the terrestrial world. It is a good bacteria, the kind that endemic albino crayfish will feed on deep inside the rock, and that tiny fish will eat out here in the daylight. Scads of minnows are flitting just under the surface of the pool, many of them gambusia scored with dark melanistic pigments. Oddly, they seemed colored like little aquatic Dalmatians. A few years ago, a study showed that male mosquitofish in Florida were more often colored in this way, and that—who knew?—the females of the species prefer a melanistic mate when given a choice. I have seen these markings on small fish before, and it is almost always in a spring or in its creek. There is a whole world within a world here, and we could ponder it for the rest of the day. Instead, we will take advantage of the dry swamp and the remaining daylight to search the area for any "new" springs that might otherwise be inundated in the wet season.

And so, from Sweetgum we move carefully along the northern shore, stepping on fallen branches and stumps to keep from sinking into the green and soggy morass that was, until just recently, covered with water. I'm heartened to see so many of the rare needle palms growing in great clutches, to see the many ways mosses and lichens colonize the snags and trunks. I reach down and bend back a frond of one of the palms. There, pushing up from the stem base is a quiver of sharp brown spines, organic darning needles hidden away in the Florida swamp.

There is a creek running through here that transports the outflows from several small springs, and it is called Sulphur Run. Reports have hinted that Sulphur Run—which can, during high water, be formidable—simply flows out of a swamp. Given the karst limestone that holds sway over this landscape, though, I have always believed it arises from a spring, or series of springs. And so, we stumble along in the half light of the swamp following this run downstream. When sunshine does penetrate, it filters through the canopy. The light here ranges narrowly along the spectrum from bronze to dark bronze. When Whitman considered the southern swamps of our new country, he gifted them with lyrics particular to the feeling of these places: "O the strange fascination of these half-known half-impassable / swamps, infested by reptiles, resounding with the bellow of the / alligator, the sad noises of the night-owl and the wild-cat, and / the whirr of the rattlesnake." I have seen or heard all of those animals in these places, even though the rattlers are most often the smaller dusky pygmies. Indeed, if the upland scrub—bright and airy—is a natural atrium, then this is the monastery, cool and sacred, cypress knees a choir that seems ready to burst into a Gregorian chant at any moment.

Although dry, the swamp bottom is still soggy enough to suck in a hiking boot. And the vines and briars are every bit as thick as I've ever seen in the Amazon. Movement here is like a film slowed down to a frame-by-frame synchronicity. If the swamp is timeless, our relationship with a higher mammal time also becomes transformed. Soon, we realize we have been in here for three hours, pushing almost constantly against an organic gridlock not used to being pushed. Suddenly, the creek we follow unexpectedly changes course and flows upstream instead of down! It seems a branch has sluiced away, and that the two-pronged juncture of its leaving may lead to a new spring. Steve and I agree to split up, with each of us following one of the prongs of the run, promising to meet back here in ten minutes. And off we go, the soft organic animal that is the swamp swallowing up any sound of movement before we are barely fifty feet apart.

And then finally, when I am back in so far that I have lost track of which direction will lead me home with any certainty, I see it. It is small but deep, and water is magically rising up to it, surging from under a toppled sabal palm trunk. It is a spring, one not yet mapped. I shout out to Steve with excitement, but am not sure if he hears me or not. There is yet another flowing rill nearby, and I'm compelled to follow it. I do, and within minutes, I find a second new spring—this one emerging from a dark hole in the floor of the swamp, augmented with a nearby seep flavored with the pungent scent of my old spring friend, the white, sulfur-rendering bacteria.

Steve and I soon regroup, and we more closely examine the new "vents." Steve takes a GPS reading, and we then name each: "Sabal Trunk Spring," and, for the very last upstream spring with the sulfur smell, "Sulphur Run Head Spring." They are modest vats of transparent water upwelling from the rock and humus, runs alive with gambusia and killifish, flowing ever onward, toward an eventual rendezvous with the sea itself. It is the same sea that once accrued the limestone, porous rock that enfolds the hydrology piping each cryptic vein of water to the surface, guiding it from the darkness to the light.

It is understandable that others have figured the swamp itself was the headwaters of this run. Its inundation—except for just now—has hidden its secrets very well, indeed. It is a day before the Thanksgiving holiday, and I smile broadly at the primeval greenscape of lianas and palms and ferns around me, smile in great appreciation and real thanks-giving for the companionship of a true friend, for the never-ending de-sire to go beyond the safe and ordinary, for the gift of never having sought comfort in being tamed or translatable, simply because we are told to be so.

42

Riverkeeping with Tree

The upper river of the St. Johns is altogether a separate place, wide marshes and big skies, airboats and gators, and so many braided, shallow channels that I usually spent as much time getting lost there as not. Most maps of a century ago don't even show much of the river at all below Lakes Monroe, Harney, and Jesup, even though it extends southward beyond there for another hundred miles or so.

A friend is on a quest to paddle and chronicle all of the hundreds of miles of this complex river system for a documentary film she's shooting. I sometimes come along, sherping kayaks from car top to water, and once in a while, I paddle. Today is one of those rare times. The channel isn't dredged or marked down here, so paying attention to navigation is essential. We're low tech and sort of snobbish about it, preferring a compass and map over a GPS. Besides, even when electronically charted, the channel can transform, reinventing itself overnight. So we've brought along a good topo map, camping gear, some food, and drinking water. You realize how little you actually need to sustain yourself when you have to physically paddle all of it in and out of any place.

The Vietnam vet known by his CB handle of "Tree Trimmer" with one of the bones from his collection at his camp on Puzzle Lake. Photo by Michelle Thatcher.

Earlier in her trip, my friend navigated Puzzle Lake in a kayak by herself. But in doing so, she ran across a Vietnam vet who was getting ready to set up camp out in the marsh that is Puzzle. The vet, who likes to go by his old CB handle of "Tree Trimmer," had just finished an extended twenty-year camping excursion on the nearby Econlockhatchee River, a tributary of the St. Johns. But much of the Econ is in a state forest, and officials there finally decided that twenty years was long enough for any single person to be camped out in their forest. When she first spotted Tree from her kayak, he had broken down his entire camp and was floating it on a jumble of wooden pallets and buckets and canoes out toward Puzzle Lake, pushing it along with a small aluminum skiff powered by a gasoline kicker. Atop the moving flotsam flew a small black "POW-MIA" flag.

To her, Tree looked like a guy who'd been camping out for twenty years—deeply tanned with a wild, sun-bleached beard and hair frizzed out as if he had just been struck by lightning. Sure, he was raw—neither practiced nor socialized—but there was also something intriguing about him that begged for a closer look. "He just seemed like a guy who would know a lot about the river," she had told me. "I really want to go back out and see if I can find him on Puzzle Lake, and shoot some footage of him."

Having a guy living off the land in modern Florida had great appeal to me, for all the obvious reasons. Still, there was that great unknown factor—after all, this wasn't a movie character from central casting, but a flesh and blood ménage of a half wild man who took more comfort surviving in the marsh and swamp than in a condo. And there were all those Vietnam memories that had been simmering in a hot Florida wilderness for the last two decades. A single gal in a single kayak spending any time in a remote place with a war-torn Grizzly Adams was ripe for possibilities, and not all of them artistic. And so I came along—part paddling buddy, part chaperone. As a guy who doesn't put a lot of value on mainstream socialization, I had to admit I was looking forward to learning a bit about the inimitable river world of a man who called himself "Tree."

Tree's biggest compromise with civilization seemed to be the use of a cell phone. It's an image that's hard for me to shake, like trying to imagine the crazed and reclusive Col. Kurtz from *Apocalypse Now* surfing the internet. But the phone comes in handy for us today: this stretch of the river is, after all, named "Puzzle" and without help, Tree's new camp will be nearly impossible to find. So my friend calls en route to let him know we're headed his way. Tree suggests we meet him at the county launch ramp called Hatbill Park, on a slice of water and land about eight miles south of SR 46, the east-west road that bisects the St. Johns valley here. He also suggested we bring along a 12-pack of Old Milwaukee and bags of ice. In turn, he would cook us a dinner of fresh-caught softshell turtle and catfish, maybe some young and tender gator if he could land one in time.

Hatbill is one of those parks where mostly country folks come to launch motor or airboats, or just hang out and fish from the marshy shores. There are no fancy playgrounds or pavilions, just one lone Port-o-Let. To the east of us are a straggle of "lakes" connected to the St. Johns by a series of obscure creeks and cuts—Loughman and Clark, Ruth and Salt Lakes. Like the rest of the Puzzle Lake complex, they are less true lakes than wide and shallow depressions where the river simply puddles up in the landscape. Down here, ancient connate seawater trapped in the aquifer when the basement of Florida was being formed by the sedimentation of the sea seeps up through sandy river bottoms, sometimes changing the equation of the rain-fed marsh water so that it is more brackish than not. While it does this via a few springs to the north of here—such as Salt Springs, Croaker Hole in Little Lake George, and Island Spring in the Wekiva River—those point sources deliver the very old seawater through definable "vents" in the limestone. The dynamic of the prehistoric salt upwelling is far more subtle here.

We arrive at Hatbill by midmorning. By the time we have our kayaks off the car and loaded with our gear, Tree comes puttering around a narrow slice of river in his battered aluminum V-hull boat. His black lab, "Gator," has its forelegs up in the bow seat like an organic figurehead. Tree drives his bow up on the sandy shore and my friend introduces us. We offload the brew and ice to his boat, and tie her kayak to Tree's V-hull for most of the three miles to his camp. I decide to settle into my own kayak and paddle for most of the distance, because it will make me feel good to do so. The aluminum boat is so loaded down that Tree's top speed is close to my own—about four to five miles an hour.

There are no other paddlers on the river today. It is sunny and clear and very invigorating to be here. The air is clean and feels good when I breathe it in deeply. As I do, I imagine there is the slightest scent of the ocean in it, a memory from the prehistoric sea water. But this notion may be more in my mind than in my senses. Over the next hour or so, five or six airboats zoom past us, frothing up the water and making it tremble beneath my hull. We round a sandy point with the sun-bleached bones of an alligator, and another with a newly dead cow, legs up in the air, running forever. Right off another tiny cape, four baby gators hang in the water, just their heads out, watching us with that timeless reptilian gaze.

Since the journey is mostly tight oxbows interspersed with an occasional wide bend, it's hard to get too much momentum going. Finally, we see the black "POW-MIA" flag flying over the high marsh grass, and after one more oxbow round of marsh, come on the camp itself. Tree has a small generator, a propane camp stove, and a large cooler stocked with chunks of bacon. Several blue plastic tarps cover three separate tents that, together, make up the camp: one to sleep, one for storage, and a large open one for cooking and hanging out. Feathers and bones are scattered everywhere, including a pelican skull sticking out of a hollow tent post and several large cow femurs. "I collect 'em," explains Tree. There is a fire ring and piles of hard wood, already cut. The ice is already starting to melt, so the first thing we do is to transfer it and the beer to the large white cooler.

A few small cedars and spindly willows grow here and there in the flat prairie around us, but nothing large enough to count on for firewood. Tree brings supplies like wood in from Hatbill or he trades with airboaters for what he needs. On the trades, cigarettes, beer, quarts of coleslaw and potato salad, and ice come in; gator, turtle, and catfish meat go out. Except for the cooler and generator, Tree found most of the other components of his camp along the river bank, or floating in the water.

I notice Gator is wearing two collars and ask about this. Tree tells me this is actually Gator II. His predecessor, Gator I, had been eaten alive by a real gator. After tracking down the culprit, Tree shot it, carved it up for meat, and—out of its stomach—retrieved the collar. Gator II wears it as a sort of memorial, reminding Tree of the goodness of his former animal companion. We settle in, my friend and I setting up our tents a hundred yards away atop a slightly higher bluff at the water's edge. As we do, Tree goes about the business of checking various trotlines baited for whatever bites. I notice someone has given him a small white sign that looks professionally painted. Nailed to a post, it reads: "Tree's Catfish House."

Tree knocks back a few brews and then, after sharpening his ax, begins to clean a live softshell turtle. Music from a CD player powered by batteries is blaring, great old rock-n-roll from the Vietnam days: Jefferson Airplane, Jimi Hendrix, the Grateful Dead. Tree is now wearing only a pair of ragged cutoff shorts and flip-flops. He "arrggs" a lot, not unlike a movie pirate, and throws back the cold beer as if it were water. The sight of him, half-buzzed, blood-splattered, and bare-chested, swinging sharp hatchets and knives about to strains of "Stairway to Heaven" is a sight to behold. It's not one that Florida tourist promoters would likely use as a lure on any of their manic, come-and-visit-us brochures.

We wash up with cool tannin river water and gather at Tree's camp, sitting on lumps of wood or camp stools, and settle in for the late afternoon transformation of the wet prairie around us. Roseate spoonbills and white pelicans glide over, and glossy ibises feed at the edge of the marsh in the golden afternoon light. An ancient grassy midden mound rises from the flat terrain to the west, as distinct as any Mayan temple against the pancake-flat terrain. I ask Tree about it, and he tells me the airboaters come there late at night and, with the strong aircraft props, blow their way up to the top. There, they stand and jowl, drinking beer. They call the venerable old midden "Bullshit Hill." A smaller mound is just behind Tree's camp, an assemblage of bone and snail shells, braided by the thatch of wild prairie grasses. I walk back there, finding small shards of pottery embedded throughout the surface.

Archaeologist Jefferies Wyman made it all the way through Puzzle Lake in a series of expeditions here in 1860, mapping out the most distinctive middens he found. I know he made it a bit farther south to "Bear" and "Orange" mounds, where the composition of shell was so massive that great hardwood and palm hammocks grew atop it. But I'm unsure if he saw or bothered to explore these two smaller ones.

Tree, ever the complete host, asks if we're hungry and when we reply we are, he starts to roll slabs of reddish meat in corn meal, and then drops them to sizzle in a deep fryer. My friend follows him closely with her camera, until, feigning anger, Tree begins to shoo her away with his cooking fork, saying she is interfering with his art. Soon the air is pungent with the scent of the simmering food. I let the gestalt of Tree fully settle in, and as I do, his generous, ragged spirit comforts me. There are no cheap shots here, none of the clever backstabbing that can punctuate our so-called civilized world. A smart man who had spent most of his life in academia once explained away that atmosphere as "The smaller the stakes, the larger the politics." Out here on the wild Florida savannah, all of the stakes are big, as expansive as the prairie itself, and the man who lives in the midst of it all seems to have benefited from it. If insanity is being detached from the true nature of reality, then Tree is likely as sane as it gets. Back in the world, the charade of "manners" has played enormous tricks on folks, fooling so many into believing that the artificial landscape and its holographic culture are real.

In a few more minutes, Tree uses the large fork to stab the chunks of catfish and softshelled turtle from the hot oil and puts them out to drain on paper plates. I thought of the wonderful drawing Bartram once made of the "great softshell tortoise (turtle)" over 240 years ago when he visited Florida and lived off the land himself. On his first journey into La Florida with his father John, Billy actually made it all the way here to Puzzle Lake. Seeing the massive and confusing sheet flow across the marsh, the naturalists decided this was the headwaters of the "grand and noble San Juan," and after a night or two here, turned around. Helen Cruickshank, author of *Bartram in Florida*, examined John's diary closely and figured the mound to the east where he reported spending the night was "Baxter's Mound," back near Hatbill. Today, a "Baxter's Point" there has a few homes on it, most up on stilts for the inevitable rise of the river. Baxter's is just south of Puzzle Lake, although still inside a maze of creeks, ponds, and marsh. Since we've lost at least half our historic wetlands, I figure there was simply more water in Florida then, too.

Had the Bartrams muddled south for a few miles, they might have found the upstream channel that led to the southernmost river, dilations mapped today as Lakes Washington, Poinsett, Winder, Saw Grass, and Hell 'n Blazes. It is this upper river that is the most isolated of the entire system, veins of north-flowing rainwater surrounded by the natural sponge of the marsh. It is no wonder this is the only drinkable "Class One" quality water of the St. Johns, while most of the river north of here is suitable only for "Class Three" activities such as boating. Puzzle Lake, which author Marjorie Kinnan Rawlings called "a blue smear in the marsh" when she got lost here in 1933, is the perfect habitat for the man I know as Tree Trimmer.

By now, the cooking oil has drained from our turtle and catfish onto the paper, and we each pile brown chunks of cooked meat onto our own plates, garnished with some French bread. I take a couple of bites—it's wild and fresh and succulent—and sit back on my log. It's quiet out here, and the low growl of a gator from somewhere near the next river bend is easy to hear.

The sun is now sinking into the horizon across the savannah, backlighting great pillars of clouds with shades of golden red. The columns of clouds appear like a nomadic army pushing its way across the vast prairie, shoving every civilized thought and deed aside, leaving only the scent of sun-baked grasses and mild brine and the low rumble of alligators in its wake. Twilight out here is at once breathtaking, and—with dusky hints of the black, untamed night to come—full of ancient premonitions. I understand better why the Bartrams turned around.

In the few moments left between twilight and full dark, we hear the roar of an airboat from the south, and soon the craft itself approaches, skipping from cut to cut, sliding its sled-like hull over the slabs of low land in between. Tree knows who the airboaters are from this distance, some local twenty-something kids who have visited him before. Their airboat pushes in closer, blowing its way up on the low bank where we've beached the kayaks. The guys come over, bringing Tree more beer and ice, which seems to be the *lingua franca* of this place and this moment. He is glad to see them, but as soon as one stands between him and the last dim light of the departed sun, Tree pretends anger, shooing him away like he shooed my friend earlier with the fork. "You're ruining my M-F-ing sunset," he yells, and the kid moves without saying a word.

Soon it is full dark and the stars appear, covering the sky from end to end. I shine my flashlight beam along the edge of the river and spot four sets of gator eyes, glowing red like the embers of our fire. The old Vietnam War field music comes back on, and we talk some more. I ask Tree about why he's been living outside so long, and I get an answer that I expected. "I felt closed in after I came back from Vietnam," he said. Living in a tent in the jungle for four years prepares a person to come to the edge of the wildest river he can find, and once there, to settle in.

It's only 10:00 p.m. or so, but it seems much later, so we head for our sleeping bags. It's warm tonight, and I simply sleep atop mine, leaving my rain fly off the tent so I can watch the stars through the mesh until I drift off. The dreams come quick, and seem to last most of the night.

By the morning, we pack up, chat a bit, say goodbye. Tree offers to ferry us back to Hatbill, with both of our kayaks tied to his boat. This time, I don't turn down the offer, and we're off, zigzagging our way back through the blue smear of a marsh, until finally, we reach Hatbill. Along the way, Tree has stopped a few times to collect cans and trash he has found floating in the river, or tossed out from an airboat. When we pass the gator skeleton again, he stops to get the skull for his collection of feathers and bones.

Tree exists for now in a little time warp, insulated by the remoteness of place. I try to review all I have seen and heard over the last twenty-four hours. Finally, I end up thinking of Tree as a true American river character, maybe what happens when Huck Finn goes to war and then comes home as a mad-sane drunken shaman. If Tree didn't exist, author Tom Robbins would have to make him up.

Before we leave, I give Tree my new ball cap with the logo of the St. Johns Riverkeeper and a graphic of a belted kingfisher on it. He grins widely and thanks me. Goodbye for now, Tree.

43

Spring Comes to Florida

Not in a Bang but in a Tiny Indolent Blossom

The seasons are now changing in Florida—although that's a reality many fail to acknowledge. Unless they really work at it, migrants and visitors to our odd, elongated state often cling to paradigms of a temperate "back home" where the four Hallmark seasons are more clearly defined. I'm convinced at least some of the inability to enlist new residents into a true community has to do with this. It's akin to perceiving the world from the outside-in, instead of trying to burrow fully into it.

Wild river iris, also known as purple flag, blooms in the springtime in the fish pond I built in my backyard. This is part of the wildlife habitat context that gives animals a place to forage for food, have access to water, hide, and even raise their young.

But Florida's subtleties go beyond seasonal changes. With over 50,000 miles of river, some 7,700 lakes, and a complex system of marsh-swamp wetlands that cover at least 30 percent of our landscape, our geography's driven by the stories of water. And those stories are most often explained by biology, a science that very quietly informs our knowledge of all living things. Geology, like that found back on the valleys and mountains and foothills, has an in-your-face majesty to it. It's a natural phenomenon that's nearly impossible to miss. Florida certainly has geology, too, but like its seasonal changes, it's cryptic, tucked away in the sedimentary rock under us. Florida's geology is more a murmur of the sea than an ancient explosion of tectonics.

Rocks transform, of course, even towering northern ones. They are weathered, cracked, shaped, and sometimes even crystallized. But the process takes thousands if not millions of years. The natural system of a plant or animal is at once far more dynamic, and often far more hidden. A wetland, despite the bacchanal of growth going on inside of it, is a place that keeps its secrets to itself. Our Florida Chamber of Commerce, tooting shrill horns to over-hype almost everything to do with growth and prosperity, must have a tough time with the mysterious energy that brings our springtime to life here. Photosynthesis isn't a snow-capped mountain peak or raging whitewater rushing down to the sea.

There are other perceptual dilemmas, too. In *The Great South*, Edward King wrote in 1875 of one of our major rivers, "It is not grandeur that one finds on the banks of that great stream, it is nature run riot. The very irregularity is delightful, the decay is charming, the solitude is picturesque." King was speaking of the St. Johns, but he could have been referring to the banks of any slow-moving Florida river—the Suwannee, the Withlacoochee, the Wacissa. For those northern intellectuals who dreamed up theories of aesthetics, this must have seemed like heresy then. Although our senses give us direct access to nature, history shows we often filter those senses with prejudice at any given time. Immediately after the Civil War, the rivers and wetlands of the moist, soggy South were regarded as unkempt and frightening places by those critics who arbitrated the appreciation of beauty. In that case, the aesthetics of the moment directly reflected the Northern perception of indolence and moral uncertainty of its conquered enemy. King was at least going halfway with it—admitting to a sloppy sort of terrain, while also praising its natural enchantment.

And so, my own Darwinian backyard is thusly situated. It is also a microcosm of nature run riot, a place where the arrival of spring is in biological Florida time and not Northern geological time. It's a level playing field where nothing gets chemically sprayed or enhanced, and exotics have to buck up with the natives if they're going to make it. I'm figuring my neighbors, still addicted to their manicured, chemically enhanced lawns, likely see this as a sort of horticultural chaos. Nonetheless, it's a chaos that never fails to refresh me: soft green needles begin to burst from the trunks and branches of the two bald cypress trees next to the pond. They will be full of this vibrant green soon, and by doing so, will become symbolic of a more ancient time. Indeed, a newly refoliaged cypress looks for all the world like a giant fern on a very large and elegant stick. It endures, a retro vision of how all the world used to be. In my pond, the skinny blades of the river iris (purple flag) are beginning to bulge with their own spring growth, wrinkles in the green growing larger almost every day. Soon, the spectacular iris blossom will burst to life, and the bright blue rods of the native pickerel weed won't be far behind. By then, the male leopard frogs and southern toads that live down in the benthic mud under the water will emerge by night and sing their heroic songs of courtship, creating a rill of boasts that will consume the night. Throughout the yard, wildflowers will burst to life: the dainty white innocence, the colorful nub of a blossom known as cupid's paintbrush, the radiant yellow of tickseed—a plant so vibrant and showy it has become our official "state wildflower." It will surely be at once indolent and uncertain, picturesque and charming.

In my little garden, the tropical habanero pepper plants, knocked back by the freeze, will again sprout until they are large enough to adorn themselves with white flowers, and soon enough, will produce bright orange peppers, the source for my home-built salsa. I will later pick, chop, and mix them with other spices and vinegar, and decant the potent sauce into small bottles which I label with my made-up brand, "Mi Salsa es Su Salsa." The two small black racers that live inside this enfenced sanctuary somewhere will move around more, breeding, making more little snakes, icons with a bad rep, sweet-minded herps that just want to live their lives. The fat bumblebees, scored with a racing stripe of yellow atop their furry black bodies, will bury themselves as far as they can inside the grand red and white flowers of the azalea bushes, hunting for nectar. When I rustle one of the bushes, the buzzing sound will be that of low static, as if someone has turned on a radio to somewhere between two channels.

The citrus tree is already full of its own tightly woven white blossoms, and in another week, they will begin to open and effuse the yard with their own scent-driven allure. The mockingbirds and the cardinals will soon build their nests here in the branches of the live oak and magnolia, as they have always done, and the little Carolina wrens will fly into the screened porch whenever the door is left open, gregarious and adventurous, looking to assemble a nest or two as close to the human space as they can. New tiger swallowtails and zebra longwings, incubated by the warmth, will arise again from their chrysalides.

High overhead, the swallow-tailed kites will return from Brazil, ranging out from the Wekiva wilderness as they do, riding the updrafts, swooping with their V-tails, reminding us of the genetic destiny of every migrating bird, reminding us—just in case we forgot—of the way the art and determination of such flights evoke the very best kind of poetry. Despite all I have seen and done in the world, I marvel at how much joy all of these visions still bring.

The Greek philosopher Heraclitus once described the natural world—and all of life—with one very succinct phrase, *Panta Rhei*. "Everything flows." In this way, the world is forever in flux because it is alive. Nothing can ever remain as it is, for all is destined to change, to flow, to grow.

And that is at the very crux of our seasonal changes, at the crux of our water-driven peninsula, at the heart of the never-ending dynamic in our souls for growth. To keep it from flowing—to keep it safe, constricted, dormant—would stagnate it, just as it does to those forlorn souls who steadfastly protect themselves from having the courage to fully face each new day in their allegorical Florida springtime. It is not unlike building a concrete bulkhead around a lake to make it look neat, controlled, safe. Those indolent, chaotic wetlands, which the lake needs to stay healthy, are severed from the equation.

Wisdom, Emerson once wrote, requires that the soul always remain liquid. Like a river, it must always be in movement. And that flow is not only downstream; it is outward, embracing every artist, every poet, every child who ever gave themselves over to its divine and everlasting promise.

And so, in this new Florida season, we again have the blessed opportunity to celebrate our singularity, to immerse ourselves in the flowing river that is our life. For a few magical months, we are gifted with the scent of the orange blossoms, the rise and fall of the soaring kites, and the knowledge that, somewhere in the wetlands and rivers and ponds, the frogs are rehearsing for the very best song of their lives.

44

A Memory Shard

Under the Sea

Hiking through the water on a trail, I'm trying to figure out where I am. Photo by Michelle Thatcher.

Except for a few wayward souls with an obscure interest in literature, Rachel Carson is known only as the author of *Silent Spring*, the well-informed scientific riff against the gluttonous pesticide industry and all it was doing to our earth.

But Carson, an aquatic biologist, was also one of those rare writers who could eloquently translate science into the wider ecology of feeling and perception—one who could alert us to the thousand tiny eyelets hidden in a coral reef in the Florida Keys, and then explain what they were and why it touched her so. In this way, she was like other scientists who have artistically reveled in the profound and mysterious spirit of the natural world: E. O. Wilson, Archie Carr, Loren Eisley, and of course, William Bartram.

In the posthumous *Lost Woods*, Carson wrote, "I can remember no time when I wasn't interested in the out-of-doors and the whole world of nature." Explaining her affinity for discovery, she tells of spending time at sea on a converted fishing trawler being used to seine not for seafood but for scientific specimens. When the trawls dragging the sea bottom were retrieved and their harvest dumped on the stern of the boat, Carson was as excited as a little girl. "I think that first glimpse of the net, a shapeless form, ghostly white, gave me a sense of sea depths I never had before. As the net rises, there is a stir of excitement. What has it brought up?"

I think of that question when I go under the water, in a spring, onto a coral reef, far from land. Once, when I was on an oceanographic expedition to the Galapagos Islands, Dr. Bruce Robison of the Monterey Bay Aquarium's Research Institute explained to me that—for centuries—seining and fishing the sea were the best humans could do to experience that Other World. It was not unlike a spaceship dragging a seine atop skyscrapers in New York, Robison said. What would be revealed would be only the tiniest sliver of the earth and the people who lived on it below. While Robison was particularly describing the more extreme depths where only submersibles could go, he also meant anywhere under the surface that scuba might take a person.

In the Galapagos, we had the chance to immerse ourselves in that world, to become in solution with it. We spent a month there, in that strange archipelago six hundred miles off the coast of Ecuador, and I can't think of one morning when I didn't wake from my bunk without a great sense of anticipation for what the adventure of the day would reveal. One crisp, sunny November morning, I became separated from the scientists during a descent near an oceanic islet and found myself alone, hovering at ninety feet, the rays of the bright equatorial sun flashing around me like a giant strobe. Large Galapagos sharks circled just at the edge of my vision in the clear water. Perhaps they were curious, perhaps predatory.

I was either too ignorant or too buzzed with nitrogen to feel fear—or maybe, my idea of a real and whole experience is so vastly different from most that it simply doesn't translate well. The sharks around me moved through the water with a primal elegance, more graceful and essential than any ballet I have ever seen. I thought that this is how a large wild cat, a panther or a jaguar, might dissolve and then reform itself as it slowly undulated its way through the understory of a tropical jungle.

I stabilized my buoyancy, and then moved my fins just enough to allow me to rotate in a very slow 360-degree turn in the water so I could take it all in. After that, I hung there for God knows how long, breathing very slowly and gently so my exhaust wouldn't frighten the animals around me. I could see a rocky bottom another hundred or so feet below me, but I had no interest in it. I was suspended in another dimension, just for now, and I felt almost transcendent.

Finally, a large school of tiny butterfly fish swayed through the water, surrounding me in a ménage of blue and gold, odd little heads pinched into an image that looked more like a small bird than a fish. I was already smiling inside my regulator, and when the little butterflies surrounded me, I actually laughed, blowing my regulator out of my mouth. The fish scattered, and even the sharks widened their range, spooked by the bubbling from this strange alien cobbled together from neoprene and metal and rubber.

I recovered fairly nicely, and after checking my air pressure gauge, realized that—while time had almost stood still for me, the air in my tank had not, and I began the slow ascent back to the surface. Once there, I inflated my buoyancy compensator and hung in the water with my mask off and my head back, letting the sun warm my face.

Through the troughs of the waves, I could see the small Zodiac we were diving from, could see the others either in it, or heaving themselves over the gunnels and back into it, clumsy as sea lions would be on land. Robison and others on the expedition were all there. Those guys were all courageous and bright souls, living their lives with passion, and I miss their company. In the distance, a wisp of smoke from the caldera on Isla Fernandina rose into the deep blue tropical sky. I put my mask back down over my eyes and finned on the surface toward the boat, making slow, deliberate strokes against the strong current.

I had gone beyond the seines, beyond the tips of the skyscrapers, down to a deep place where the only real shard of the experience was the one that I would forever keep in my memory. It seems as if the times I most cherish are the ones that are also fleeting, ephemeral. They are made more heartbreakingly beautiful and full because of it.

Excited with anticipation for the trawl's harvest, Carson wrote, "What has it brought up?" And of course, now I understand: it has brought up dreams.

45

Coontie Magic

Reading the Message in the Relic

I've always been fond of relics. Maybe that's because I'm a nostalgic sort of guy to begin with. Or maybe it's because each vestige of the past has a different story hidden in it somewhere, and I'm also a lover of great stories.

Once I lived in an old Cracker farmhouse on a dead-end country road outside of Sanford. The house, built from heart cypress in 1928, was a

The cone of a coontie, which can contain both seeds and spores. It is a classic Florida native plant and as such is symbolic of the native landscape and culture.

relic itself. As was the acre or so of land that surrounded it. Both the home and its place in the landscape seemed encased in a sort of time bubble.

Outside, the anxiety of a region made giddy by the fast bucks of eye-blink-quick sprawl roared on. But inside, for a long time, all seemed safe, stable. You could almost believe it might never change.

Near the east ditch that marked the boundary line in the backyard, there was a little coontie growing under a blood orange tree. It was barely higher than a cinnamon fern—indeed, it seemed as if it might have wanted to be a fern at some time in its own prehistory. But unlike a fern, it had narrow shiny leaves that looked more like a palm. At least once a year, ocher-colored cones that hid bright orange-red seeds spiked up from its base.

Although this coontie was a native plant, it was seldom found in the wild anymore. I knew that for thousands of years, the Native Americans here used the tuber of the plant as a starch, shaping it into cakes and breads. In the Antilles, their counterparts, the Taino, did the same, cooking it on clay griddles over fire, making cassava. Today, the most likely place to find a living coontie in Florida is in a state or county park where it is used for landscaping. In such places, it also serves as a symbolic reminder of the truly special nature of our peninsular landscape.

The fact that it still carries part of the name given it by the early Creeks, *conti hateka*, is a blessing all by itself. In this way, the coontie's a relic that still allows us to say words out loud that others used here long before us. Like the names of some of our rivers—Econlockhatchee, Wekiva, Loxahatchee—the simple act of pronouncing the word itself can be, in the best of moments, evocative of our departed "earth people" who named them and of their deeply spiritual natural world.

Beyond its iconic status, the coontie is pretty special all by itself. Neither a palm nor a fern, it's a cycad—one of those dinosaurs of the plant world that thrived in a distant time when plants were just coming to grips with this post-smoldering planet and its primeval canvas. It was a time when nature still had the freedom to experiment. No population explosion, no nuclear bombs, no global warming, and certainly no shifty-eyed little mammals coming down from the trees to screw it all up. Just the pure tabula rasa of the new earth and all of its possibilities.

A good time to try out the coontie. If that works, maybe give the turtle and then the alligator a go. For a nice chuckle, toss in a bowfin or two.

Funny thing is, these guys never really evolved with the rest of their counterparts from the Jurassic. Nor did they become extinct. Turned out, they did just fine by remaining faithfully prehistoric (which I'm sure is a quality many of the old Florida Crackers would appreciate).

When I moved from my old country home to the edge of the historic district in Sanford, I took along a lot of that coontie with me. And I brought a clay pot with another I had grown from a seed, a plant that was now becoming bonsai-like from its years in the pot.

Ray Willis, a good, solid fellow who is the archaeologist for the Ocala National Forest, brought me by a pickup truck bed full of coonties the other day. Ray, who grew up on the Panhandle before going to UF to get his doctorate, lives in Umatilla with his family and works in the national forest nearby. The bed of Ray's pickup was full of cooties he had culled from his patch back home—little ones with whole tubers, and larger ones with the tubers sliced in half.

Coonties take a long time to germinate, and it takes a patient, patient man to grow a coontie—one who appreciates the way the thinnest of lines from the past still hook onto the present. Ray unloaded the coonties in my side yard, and then covered them with sabal palm fronds to protect them from the light and heat. He did it so gently and with such great care that it seemed as if he were tucking his children into bed.

I was both thankful for and excited by the little prehistoric native plants, figuring all the ways I could spread them around my own landscape. They fit easily into the fenced backyard, where everything was going natural anyway. In the front, it gave me great pleasure to rip up two narrow avenues of St. Augustine grass around my sidewalk and to plant the coonties there instead. I also gave two plants to a neighbor, one to a friend, and a pot of fat coontie seeds to a very with-it lady who wants to start a nursery on her land.

As I did, I thought of all the Native Americans—the Taino and the Timucua, the Creek and Seminole—who had relied on this fern-palm for sustenance for so long, a gift that was so vital to them that they named gods after it. I wondered vaguely if the *conti hatekas* that surrounded me now were more than icons, wondered if they might approach totemic level, like the great spirits that once were carved from pine and posted on middens along the mighty St. Johns River, homages to owls, otters, and other protective scouts from the netherworlds.

If, like physical energy, this spiritual dynamic isn't created or destroyed, perhaps it can still be found in the coontie's tubers and inside the seeds of its cones. Maybe it's encoded within the genetic memory that rests inside the heart of the plant itself.

And if this code could be cracked, what would it tell us about the people who lived here before us for thousands of years? What stories would it reveal that help us understand how they saw the earth and the universe unfolding around them?

I'm guessing this wisdom would be far more than a historic souvenir, and its use far more than that of an organic heirloom. If we're lucky, we might even figure out how to let those old native gods know that modern engineering and cold-hearted manipulation of our landscape hasn't worked for us. And that, just maybe, some of us are ready again to trust in their everlasting natural power to sustain us.

46

Mothers Arms

Sinking into Gator Time

It's 8:00 a.m. on a clear and bright summer morning, and Mothers Arms awaits.

Yvette and I drive to the edge of the man-made peninsula called Marina Island near the heart of the historic downtown of the old riverboat landing of Sanford. Here, I coast the SUV down a new concrete ramp on the northeastern edge just outside the harbor and park a few feet from the water. No one's around, except for a large black woman who is sitting under a pavilion nearby, reading. We quickly unload the kayaks from the rooftop racks, and I drive back up the ramp and park my car.

Paddling partner Yvette Comeau headed out toward Mother's Arms to the east on the large dilation of the river known as Lake Monroe.

The waters are calm, flat as glass almost, and the tiniest notion of a breeze is lifting up from somewhere far away.

Yvette's at once vivacious and cool, ready for most anything. She owns one of the most lively and eclectic independent book stores in the region; instead of trying to make it sound pretentious, she has named it Maya, for one of her cats.

We wedge ourselves down into the cockpits of our individual boats and push away with our paddles. Within a couple minutes we're a hundred yards from shore, out on the vast blackwater lake. The map shows a peninsula charted as "Mothers Arms" jutting out from the eastern edge of the lake. I'm figuring the "arms" are the bayous of water that surround it on both sides. Whatever the origins of the name, I'm excited to be paddling toward it, happy as always to be able to have a chance for discovery in a place I've never been.

Yvette's every bit as thrilled as I, perhaps even more so. The last time she paddled was on the Russian River in California almost fifteen years ago. Despite the fact that she's lived in Ormond Beach over on the coast and here in Sanford, she's never paddled this unassuming section of the river. We've brought along bottles of water and a few granola bars.

We move easily across the lake surface, feeling the cipher of gentle swells at the edges of the experience. Although this is a broad splay in the St. Johns and not really a self-enclosed lake, it's as big as one— nearly fifteen square miles. There's close to six miles worth of big water behind us right now, a sleeping liquid god with enough potential fetch to bat us around like one of Yvette's cats would bat a tiny anole. I had been closely watching the forecast, waiting for a day when the winds were expected to lay down, barely a knot or two an hour. But this is Florida, of course, and anything can change within a couple of hours, the cotton-white cumulus behind us turning black with vapor and coastal breezes sweeping inland, simply because they can.

For now, we paddle directly into the morning sun, bright now and halfway up in the sky, high enough so that a jet trail passes evenly between it and the horizon. As it goes, it underlines the sun with its white thread of smoke, almost as if the sky wants us to remember something. I figure we can reach the tip of the peninsula, mapped as "Grassy Point," within fifteen or twenty minutes as it's barely a mile, and we do. Since the river flows north, we're actually paddling upstream, but the current today is slight, particularly so where it broadens out and is absorbed by the giant expanse that is Lake Monroe. There's not much for me in paddling across open waterways. I've done it before down in the Glades, the Mosquito Lagoon, and elsewhere. But skimming across broad bays and lakes is only a way to get somewhere else, to a place more intimate, maybe even a bit cryptic.

Funny, while I've paddled and hiked for days at a stretch, I don't consider myself a marathoner; each day, each corner and oxbow simply offers the chance to see something new in the landscape.

As we approach Grassy Point, I realize it is less grass and more of the tall exotic water weed, Phragmites. The reed-like grass has consumed this tip of land, and it continues to do so as we paddle around its northerly shore. I have seen the tops of hardwood trees from the kayak, so I know there is likely dry land deeper inside the peninsula somewhere, and I look forward to what it will reveal. Now that we're squarely inside the aquatic embrace of Mothers Arms, we slow our paddling to allow more time to examine the shore. We push in and out of stands of reeds, spooking some mullet that jump and a little blue heron who was feeding in shallow water. We are headed toward the northernmost "arm," a splotch of blue mapped as "Big Smokehouse Cove." From the cove are two upstream cuts, and we will take the closer one, planning to follow it eastward as it shadows the peninsula.

Soon the shore turns into hard-packed sand, like a little beach, and I see wading birds have left behind the empty shells of *Viviparous*, the small snails expertly plucked from their homes by the sharp beak tips of the long-legged predators. The shells are russet colored, lightly striped and shiny from the varnish of the water. Not long after the first beach of shells, I see two very old cypresses side by side just a few yards out from the peninsula. One is a dead gray snag; the other is very much alive, its crown of soft green needles sitting atop the old trunk, at once haphazard and neat, as only a cypress can be. The live tree is a dwarf, like those I have seen up in Lake Norris and down in Blue Cypress Lake, no more than seven or so feet high, but with a trunk base that is almost five feet in diameter. I guess it's also hollow, like other bonsai-style cypresses I've seen, and when I paddle next to it, I gently thump it with my paddle blade. The big trunk resonates as it would if I hit a drum made of heavy wood. The outer cambium of the trunk keeps the tree alive, allowing water and nutrients to flow upwards from the roots below. In this way, the "heart" of the tree isn't its core at all, but rather the vital skin of its exterior.

I turn to see Yvette paddling just ahead, close to shore. She has exclaimed several times at the wildness and singularity of the place. We are both astounded this old peninsula is so close to where we live. Yet, like those too-familiar parts of our lives, we have never bothered to examine it because we figured it would always be here. Nearby, great blooms of the wetland flower known as the salt marsh mallow shine in the early sun, crimson throats giving way to lighter pink petals, not as red as the scarlet hibiscus but every bit as grandiose.

To the north is Stone Island, where the Bartrams camped when they journeyed through here in 1763. Later, archaeologist Jefferies Wyman scouted the same waters in 1860, reporting one of the largest shell middens on the entire St. Johns on the shore here at Old Enterprise. Native Americas lived and camped around this lake for six thousand years, tribes of the Mayaca and Jororo fishing and hunting here when the Europeans first arrived, the Seminoles migrating down later. We know that Monroe was named Wepolokse (round lake) by the Seminoles, and John Bartram referred to it as "the middle lake" when he mapped it in 1766. It was called Laguna Valdez by the Spanish, and finally mapped as "Monroe's Lake" in 1823 for the U.S. president. But its very earliest inhabitants were dispatched before we could learn what they called it.

The deeper we get into the cove, the more trees we see on the peninsula, some sweetgum, a few nut trees of some kind, and of course, the occasional sabal palm. We push onto a low flat beach and go ashore to explore. The exotic known as the Chinese tallow is growing here, its trunk thick and gnarly, its leaves shaped like delicate green hearts. A few feet more and we see little yellow fruits on the ground and then find several wild guava trees nearby. I use my pocket knife to slice one of the fruits open, and when I taste it I find it has an overly sweet flavor, not unlike that of a mango a few days beyond ripe. Luxuriant, and then some. Caught back in the underbrush are the flotsam that washed in here when the river was high, old grayish cans, and tattered strands of nylon rope. Water marks from the last tropical storm inundation are three and four feet high on the tree trunks.

We push off and continue our circumnavigation of the shore. The low, growl-like calls of gators, scarce at first, become more frequent, and we begin to see a few of the reptiles hanging at the surface looking like charred logs, an ancient animal with all the patience in the world. I have taken to calling back lately, groaning way down in my throat to try to capture the primeval grumble of it all. No matter how deeply I reach back to mimic that sound, I'm still too high on the scale, off by a few million years worth of octaves. Sometimes I wonder what it would be like to sink completely into gator time.

I sound the bottom with my paddle and learn it is hard here, not muddy as it can be in the downstream reaches of the lake. To the north, we see a lone angler in a small boat several hundred yards away, fishing in the bulrush there. Out of the cove now, we nose up the narrow stream and pass another boat, this one with three men fishing. A creek that will allow us to round the peninsula opens up just ahead, and I realize this is not a peninsula at all but an island. Just ashore, I see a patch of midden shells, about the area of a large cottage, rising several feet high. I imagine hunters or fishers from a Mayacan tribe camping here for several generations, long before presumptuous white men claimed this as their own.

Nearby, spats of apple snail eggs begin to appear regularly on the stems of plants; the presence of the eggs is a good sign ecologically, for the large snail that lays them insists on healthy water. I wonder if this eastern portion of the "lake" isn't cleaner since it's upstream from the stormwater drains that regularly pipe street and lawn toxins into the water. It's also upstream from where the concrete bulkheads of Sanford rob the lake of its historic wetlands and the biological filter they provide. Whatever the reason, both Yvette and I take great pleasure in knowing that at least this portion of the lake—native and wild—still carries with it a legacy that others have known here for thousands of years.

The creek is narrow and deep, and as we enter it, I hear a motor boat coming up behind us. I slow as I hear him throttle down to idle speed. It is a FWC patrol boat, and for the fun of it, the officer has checked our speed with a radar gun. He shouts to me over the motor: "You're clocking 6.5 miles an hour." Happy with this information, I give him the thumbs up, and he waves and speeds off. It is nearly twice as fast as I thought I was paddling.

As we approach the eastern shore of Mothers Arms, the land becomes higher, more hardwoods and even some old pasture land with a rusty and broken cattle fence. Another creek, Woodruff, nearly splices this pasture in two; when we round the corner to the wide old canal that will take us back to our launch, I see a few cows grazing on the island. Ahead, taller trees rise from the shore, and I'm elated to see they are cypresses, relative giants at 100 or more feet, at least one crowned with a nest of both an osprey and a great blue. I explain to Yvette that these guys are big and old enough to have been here when the Bartrams sailed through, and she smiles at that idea.

We paddle strong now, headed out beyond the natural shore to where the bulkhead begins, passing the old Hotel Forrest Lake as we go, a gilded time-stuck vision from the tourist boom of the 1920s, back when a few paddlewheelers still steamed here to this "Gateway to South Florida." In the distance, it seems like a giant colorized postcard, except painted onto a canvas of water and air. As we get closer to our launch, the large rivership *Romance* with its twin faux smokestacks churns its way out of the harbor for a lunch cruise, exhaling its deep bass hoonnnk as it goes, a boatful of visitors learning about how things used to be on a lake that is really a river. From a distance, I can imagine it to be an old steamship, its decks stacked atop the other, narrow and boxy. Like the stunted cypress we saw earlier, it is a bonsai of a ship, its nautical business sized down to match the needs of where it is. While the sight of it is odd enough, I am just happy that it introduces other humans to this great primal arena of a river.

Yvette moves ahead, closer to the ship, and I wonder if the presence of our plastic dugouts carries any symmetry with it, tiny boats of voyagers juxtaposed against so many poignant images of a rich river past, moving with careful stealth now toward our inevitable return to the present. I glance once over my shoulder at Mothers Arms, silently thanking her for the morning's revelations, and just for now, I paddle away, trailing a soft V of sepia across the canvas as I go.

47

Epilogue

A Young Boy and Why He Walks

I grew up in a home on a dirt street. One day, the street would be paved and the few houses would turn into a neighborhood. But this was still the country, and things happened slowly.

There was a large corn field behind our home, and behind that, a state farmers' market and several large packing houses. In the summertime, in my early teens, I would make a few extra bucks loading watermelons onto tractor trailers from the smaller flatbed and pickup trucks the local farmers used to bring their crops to market.

I found this hand-tinted card in my grandfather's trunk. He first moved to Florida seasonally in the 1930s.

With my neighbor Rick, I walked miles out into the countryside, zig-zagging across farm fields, through isolated tracks of woods with little streams running through them, and down long winding roads under thick canopies of hardwoods. Sometimes we would see old farm homes hidden back away in the forest; sometimes we would pass open pastures with horses, maybe a few cows. We seldom carried water or a backpack and had no stated intent except to explore.

I was intrigued by bugs then and had even bought a book about them. Sometimes I would find strange ornate bugs like a rhino beetle, and if they were dead, I'd bring them home to put in little dioramas I made for them out of shoe boxes. I knew the most common birds: they were sparrows and robins, and sometimes cardinals and starlings. Rarely, I saw a great blue heron hidden down in a little thickly wooded creek that spilled out of a lake. In early fall, Canada and snow geese would migrate, flying over in great V formations. Their cries were haunting even then, since they meant for me the end of warmer, boy-friendly summer weather, and the beginning of the cold season. But they were harbingers, too, marking time visually.

I knew the names of some of the fish, since we had an intimate relationship with them from the other end of a fishing line. There were striped bass, which we knew as rockfish, and spot and catfish. If we were in tidal creeks, there were blue crabs swimming through; sometimes there were "doublers" in which the larger "Jimmy" male held onto the molted, soft-shelled female as they mated. Instinct for that was so strong they held fast even when we scooped them up with long-handled nets and dumped them into bushel baskets. We ate the crabs, steamed with Old Bay seasoning and dry mustard sprinkled on them, and Mom cooked the rock fish, usually with strips of bacon and butter. For most who grew up in the country, wildlife could also mean food; it was no different for our family.

We roamed the countryside, Rick and I, because we felt a need to do so. There was nothing we were ever sure we would find, but we always looked for new ways of seeing, for new things to see. Following creeks upstream was full of discovery since they always led to lakes and the lakes to more streams, each with its own wooded furrows cut into the earth. Sometimes I carried a knife in a sheath, but I never had anything to use it for.

We lived on a peninsula, the flat slab of land that held the Eastern Shore of Maryland, a spit of Virginia, and all of the state of Delaware. We had strong territorial country prejudices and thought of Delaware and Virginia as states not hardly worth knowing about. But that peninsula isolated them as it isolated us, almost as fully as an island. As a very young boy, I remember riding a long ferry across the choppy Chesapeake to get to Baltimore to the west, since there was yet no bridge across the bay. We did the same to the south, where a much longer bay-bridge tunnel system eventually spanned the great mouth of the Chesapeake.

The ferries had kept us safe in so many ways, had kept anyone from driving over a bridge just because they wanted to. Taking a ferry required time and money, and it was a wondrous deterrent to expediency. Later, when the bridges came—except for a few old timers—we welcomed them. We had absolutely no idea of the cultural and environmental impacts this new accessibility would eventually have on the integrity of our long-ignored "Shore," a place *Harper's Magazine* a hundred years earlier had called "the last peninsula of the Lost and the Vague." We would become diluted, our accents washed out, our behaviors less certain, more influenced by the outside world beyond the bay. And then the great new mass of people living in the watershed of the bay began to transform it.

Even as the tidewater nature of Shore living infused nearly every moment of my life, I took it for granted, expecting it to always be there. But now, with all the decades in between for perspective, I miss it terribly, and I miss the speciated and passionate people the Shore had once created. Accessibility spelled an end to most of them, just as it did to the wide open countryside. Now when I think of my life as a young boy approaching manhood, I can imagine no place finer to have lived than under the broad skies and atop the flat terrain carved by the tidal rivers and creeks on the lower Eastern Shore.

I think now of those geese flying south for the winter, and instead of having an image, I hear those soulful, primal sounds they left in their wake as they soared across the broad winter Shore sky. As a boy, I was wistful for all that the flight of those birds took with them when they left, and I am wistful now.

And so, I keep walking through the woods. Now, I walk with like-minded souls, or I walk by myself.

The landscape I walk across is no longer temperate. I walk now for miles in the hammocks and flatwoods, the marshes and swamps of Florida. I walk to discover new things, and to remember in my heart the ones I once found. I walk in celebration of discovery, and in the evocation of people and place. I walk to remember.

Acknowledgments

Many thanks to all who have accompanied me on my journeys through the woods, swamp and marsh, and on the water. My companions have been gracious sports who most often come along because they appreciate the joy of discovery. Thanks especially to Yvette Comeau of Sanford, Fla. and Ormond Beach; Dr. Steve Phelan, Dr. Bruce Stephenson, and Dr. Leslie Poole of Rollins College, Winter Park, Fla.; Capt. Vicki Impallomeni of Key West; Capt. Steve Harris of Key Largo; Dr. Terry Anderson of Villa Park, Calif.; Julie Fisher of Longwood, Fla.; Margaret Tolbert of Gainesville, Fla.; Colin Freeman, M.D. of Maitland, Fla.; Bob Boswell, M.D., of Winter Park; Lisa Roberts of Maitland, Fla.; Annette L. Miller of DeLand; David Strickland of Jacksonville; Ginny Maxwell of Apopka; Bob Giguere of Orlando; Michelle Thatcher of Altamonte Springs, Fla.; my daughter Beth and grandsons Will and Ray Crawley of Kitty Hawk, N.C.; and Capt. Dan Shaw of Cape Coral, Fla.

Of those special folks who made appearances in my two time-warp stories, I thank Don Serbousek of Ormond Beach, Fla., and intrepid underwater cave cartographer Eric Hutcheson of Ocala, Fla. The late explorer and photographer Wes Skiles of High Springs, Fla., was also one of the first to help me understand how the hidden dark magic of our Florida springs works and why we should pay much closer attention to it all. Wes's intrepid, down-home spirit still moves me today. I'm also appreciative of the careful readings of the manuscript by outdoor writer and photographer Doug Alderson, and Clay Henderson, who seems to practice law in order to continue his real "jobs" of birding and fly-fishing. Thanks also to those good folks at USF who are bringing the eclectic disciplines of the humanities to bear on the ever-shifting mosaic that is Florida Studies: Drs. Gary Mormino, Ray Arsenault, Tom Hallock, and Chris Meindl.

I'll always be grateful to my brother Jack of Parsonsburg, Md., and to my late mom and dad (Kathleen and Bill, Sr.), originally of Salisbury, Md., and later of Lake Wales and Frostproof, Fla. They were there with me from the very first, and they cared deeply. In one essay ("A Young Boy and Why He Walks"), I try to show how essential that caring can be and how a childhood that allows us to roam the woods in search of adventure is one of the greatest gifts a family can give. A long overdue thanks goes out to my late grandfather J. H. Dulaney who first blazed a new trail down to the interior of Florida earlier in the twentieth century—even though he didn't know he was doing so—and to my grandmother, Mom Mom (Margaret R. Dulaney), who made all the story books come alive for a little boy growing up in a small country town. Finally, a deeply felt thanks to Bonnie Martin Church who selflessly and graciously supported the light of my own dream back when it was barely more than a glimmer a long time ago.

My sincere appreciation goes out to all those readers from Florida and around the country who have taken the time to write and e-mail me over the years with kind words of praise. Earlier books that celebrate nature—and express my heartfelt lament for its loss—clearly resonate with far more people than most politicians might ever imagine. There truly is a great extended family out there bound together by their connection to nature and their yearning for a functional sense of place. I'm proud to be part of it in any way.

Several of these essays have been published (*Forum*; *Elsewhere: A Journal of Place*; *Salon*; *Travel Channel's Worldhum*; *Sierra Magazine*; and *Islands Publications*), but the great majority have not.

Bill Belleville is an award-winning author, specializing in nature and conservation. *Salvaging the Real Florida* is his sixth nonfiction book. He has also scripted and produced films for PBS and radio documentaries for NPR and written over 1,000 articles and essays with bylines in *Outside, Audubon, Sierra, Islands, Los Angeles Times*, and the *Washington Post*. He lives in Sanford, Florida.